Foundations of Marketing Thought

The study and teaching of marketing as a university subject is generally understood to have originated in America during the early 20th century emerging as an applied branch of economics. This book tells a different story describing the influence of the German Historical School on institutional economists and economic historians who pioneered the study of marketing in America and Britain during the late 19th and early 20th centuries.

Drawing from archival materials at the University of Wisconsin, Harvard Business School, and the University of Birmingham, this book documents the early intellectual genealogy of marketing science and traces the ideas that early American and British economists borrowed from German scholars to study and teach marketing. Early marketing scholars both in America and Britain openly credited the German School, and its ideology based on social welfare and distributive justice was a strong motivation for many institutional economists who studied marketing in America, predating the modern macro-marketing school by many decades.

Challenging many traditional beliefs, this book provides an authoritative new narrative of the origins of marketing thought. It will be of great interest to educators, scholars and advanced students with an interest in marketing theory and history, and in the history of economic thought.

D.G. Brian Jones is the founding Editor of the *Journal of Historical Research in Marketing* and co-editor of the Routledge Studies in the History of Marketing. His research focuses on the history of marketing thought and has been published widely.

Mark Tadajewski is the Editor of the *Journal of Marketing Management*, an Associate Editor of the *Journal of Historical Research in Marketing*, the co-editor of the Routledge Studies in Critical Marketing and the Routledge Studies in the History of Marketing series.

Routledge Studies in the History of Marketing
Edited by Mark Tadajewski and D. G. Brian Jones

It is increasingly acknowledged that an awareness of marketing history and the history of marketing thought is relevant for all levels of marketing teaching and scholarship. Marketing history includes, but is not limited to, the histories of advertising, retailing, channels of distribution, product design and branding, pricing strategies, and consumption behaviour – all studied from the perspective of companies, industries, or even whole economies. The history of marketing thought examines marketing ideas, concepts, theories, and schools of marketing thought including the lives and times of marketing thinkers.

This series aims to be the central location for the publication of historical studies of marketing theory, thought and practice, and welcomes contributions from scholars from all disciplines that seek to explore some facet of marketing and consumer practice in a rigorous and scholarly fashion. It will also consider historical contributions that are conceptually and theoretically well-conceived, that engage with marketing theory and practice, in any time period, in any country.

1 **On The Origins of Self-Service**
Franck Cochoy

2 **The Foundations of Marketing Practice**
A history of book marketing in Germany
Ronald A. Fullerton

3 **Pioneering African-American Women in the Advertising Business**
Biographies of MAD Black WOMEN
Judy Foster Davis

4 **A History of American Consumption**
Threads of Meaning, Gender, and Resistance
Terrence H. Witkowski

5 **Foundations of Marketing Thought**
The Influence of the German Historical School
D. G. Brian Jones and Mark Tadajewski

Foundations of Marketing Thought

The Influence of the German Historical School

D. G. Brian Jones and Mark Tadajewski

Routledge
Taylor & Francis Group
LONDON AND NEW YORK

First published 2018
by Routledge
2 Park Square, Milton Park, Abingdon, Oxon OX14 4RN

and by Routledge
711 Third Avenue, New York, NY 10017

Routledge is an imprint of the Taylor & Francis Group, an informa business

British Library Cataloguing-in-Publication Data
A catalogue record for this book is available from the British Library

Library of Congress Cataloging-in-Publication Data
A catalog record for this book has been requested

ISBN: 978-1-138-18180-9 (hbk)
ISBN: 978-1-315-64675-6 (ebk)

Typeset in Times New Roman
by Apex CoVantage, LLC

MIX
Paper from responsible sources
FSC® C013604
FSC www.fsc.org

Printed and bound by CPI Group (UK) Ltd, Croydon, CR0 4YY

to Paula and Ruth

Contents

Figures

Tables

Preface

We hope that this book will appeal to, and be read by, all students of marketing and economics. It will be valuable to scholars with an interest in the history of marketing theory, thought, and practice. This book pursues questions about the legacy of the German Historical School. But it does much more than this. Some of the narratives we unravel will shake the foundations and knowledge of our discipline and will doubtless be revelatory for those working in economics as well. As is made clear, both political economy and marketing have developed in tension with the world that surrounds and enables them. At formative periods in the development of both subjects, there have been serious questions raised about alternative political-economic methods of organization. Put very simply, and very succinctly, some of the major turning points in the account that we present here are conjoined with debates about ethics, distributive justice, and the viability and possibility that socialism might replace capitalism as the political-economic structure of choice. This tension feeds throughout the development of marketing theory and practice. We illuminate these connections, highlight a tapestry of links that have not been articulated in relation to marketing theory previously, and, in short, provide a novel and frequently surprising account of the conditions of possibility for the marketing discipline.

Acknowledgements

Archivists and librarians are a special breed. They offer support and often insights to researchers and in so doing become an indispensable part of the research team. We are grateful for the assistance of Harry Miller (on two separate visits, twenty-five years apart), Senior Reference Archivist at the Wisconsin Historical Society; David Null, Director of the University of Wisconsin–Madison Archives; Robert Chapel, Reference Assistant at the University of Illinois (Urbana-Champaign) Archives; Emily Haddaway, Curator of the Ohio Wesleyan University Historical Collection; Karen Jania at the Bentley Historical Library of the University of Michigan; Harriet McLoone at the Huntington Library; Florence Lathrop at the Baker Library Archives; and Anne Clarke at the Cadbury Research Library, University of Birmingham.

At Queen's University (Canada), David D. Monieson's doctoral seminar on the history of marketing thought ignited my passion for learning about the history of our discipline. It was Monieson's 'theory' that the German Historical School of Economics had profoundly influenced the pioneers of academic marketing. For my doctoral dissertation, I began a study of Monieson's ideas about the connection between the GHSE and marketing thought, a project that expanded beyond graduate work and has followed me throughout my career. I would be remiss for not mentioning Stanley Shapiro in that connection since it was he who convinced Monieson to supervise my doctoral dissertation on the history of marketing thought, and who served as the external examiner on that dissertation. Portions of the material in this book were previously published in the *Journal of Marketing*, the *European Journal of Marketing*, and *Pioneers in Marketing*. Funding for various parts of this research was provided by the Social Sciences and Humanities Research Council of Canada and by the Quinnipiac University School of Business Dean's Office.

Brian Jones

A huge number of people have been a significant influence on my intellectual and personal development; way too many to mention. As such, I limit my attention to five: Ruth, Brian, Paula, Kate, and Ziggy. They have enabled what I've done in relation to this book and my contributions simply would not exist without them. It's as simple as that. Thanks all.

Mark Tadajewski

1 Introduction

This book is about the intellectual foundations on which the academic discipline of marketing was constructed. Ever since the 1930s, when our predecessors began to reflect on the history of the subject, it has been widely accepted that it emerged as a specialized field of applied economics. This interpretation lacks considerable nuance and is a function of the influence of Robert Bartels. He wrote the major work on the history of marketing thought (Bartels, 1962) which is now a seminal reference point. Its comprehensiveness has ensured that it has rarely been challenged. However, what we get with Bartels is a limited interpretation of the development of marketing. He leaves us with the unmistakable impression that early marketing academics were trained in, and influenced by, classical, and to some extent, neoclassical economics. Bartels was wrong.

We now know that many of them were heavily influenced by the German Historical School of Economics (GHSE). They were fluent in the philosophy, concepts, and language that underwrote this school of thought – areas that are now discussed more formally using the terms of axiology (core values), epistemology (theory of knowledge), and methodology (general approach to the study of the topic and phenomena of interest). We track the influence of this school of thought in America and Britain.

During the 1980s there was a renaissance of sorts in historical research. Much more work was being done, more seriously, more rigorously, and more critically than before. Historians were starting to be openly critical of Bartels' work. Dixon (2002) described his claims that marketing thought originated in the United States in the twentieth century as "a myth" (p. 737) and ridiculed Bartels for suggesting that the term "marketing" emerged between 1906 and 1911 (p. 738). He urged scholars to "stop ignoring, or at least stop denying, the existence of a rich heritage of marketing literature" prior to that articulated by its most prominent historian (1981, p. 26). The actual nature of the content being explored and claimed as the foundations of the discipline was also questioned.

Much of the discussion centered around twentieth century textbooks. This material was often descriptive. It told us what had been said and by whom and buttressed this with extensive descriptive statistics. Put otherwise, we gained a great deal of description about the world of marketing theory and practice without any substantive insight into the background factors, the environmental influences, and the intellectual motivations that generated the discipline and the practices that were being chronicled. Ron Savitt (1980) put this nicely when he wrote that much marketing history was not analytical – it did not analyze the enabling factors that contributed to the emergence of the discipline. Since Savitt's fairly damning critique, productive marketing scholars have continued to shake Bartels' pantheon. Shaw and Tamilia (2001) do an excellent job of summarizing the critiques of his work.

> [It overlooked] the influences on the early marketing pioneers, misstating the time and place of the origin of marketing thought, using fixed time periods to characterize marketing history, [there were] inconsistencies in [his] bibliography, including too much chronology and description and not enough analysis and evaluation . . . [and it was limited] . . . almost exclusively to marketing authors of American textbooks.
>
> (p. 162)

Yet, there was no other work that offered us such a panoramic sweep of marketing thought in the twentieth century. It deserved kudos for the broad-brush perspective it provided. And this leaves us with a rich tapestry whose threads need tightening, reworking, and unpacking in varying proportions. This is something we undertake in this book.

To go beyond Bartels, we have to move beyond pure description – although description has its place in marketing history and the history of marketing thought – towards greater analysis. Focusing largely on the twentieth century, moreover, was overly limiting. Scrutinizing the end result – the published work – means we bypass the enabling conditions, the factors that helped intellectually form the people writing the work – whether these were personal influences or important ideas gleaned from lectures, reading, and general discussion with colleagues. In this book we want to foreground these factors.

We will make the axiological, ontological, epistemological, and methodological discussions and the view of human nature that appear in this work as clear as possible. In order to do that, we will examine the heritage of academic writing about marketing. We move beyond Bartels by journeying into the late nineteenth century, to investigate the origins of modern academic marketing ideas and describe the intellectual foundations of those ideas.

Historical research in marketing

Historical research in marketing can be segmented into roughly two separate but related fields: marketing history and the history of marketing thought. The former examines the history of marketing practice. What we mean by this is what practitioners have done or how they have articulated their practice, putting their tacit knowledge into a form for wider dissemination. This can include – but is not limited to – histories of advertising, retailing, branding, distribution, consumption behavior, and so on. The history of marketing thought involves the study of ideas, concepts, theories, schools of thought, and the lives and times of great thinkers. That the two fields are, of course, related will be evident in the pages that follow.

There is a considerable literature on marketing history (for recent reviews, see Jones and Shaw, 2006; Jones *et al.*, 2009; Tadajewski and Jones, 2014; Jones and Tadajewski, 2016). Although scholars have studied it as far back as ancient Greece, most of the research has focused on the period running from the eighteenth to the twentieth century. It explores the practices of retailing and channel management, product management (e.g. branding, market segmentation), promotion (e.g. advertising), market research, as well as the marketing strategies used by companies or industries which furnish considerable information about the interplay between all of the foregoing elements (Tadajewski and Jones, 2014).

High profile contributions to marketing history and the history of marketing thought unpack marketing's role in defining our political-economic present. In contributing to this literature, we argue that marketing is a key vehicle in ensuring the ordering of society. It plays a significant role in system maintenance and, in doing so, rethinks and reaffirms capitalist economic relations. In situating marketing within the wider sphere of political economy, we link the intellectual figures connected to the GHSE with the emergence of marketing research and education at the university level. This project consequently requires us to interpret these people, their lives, and writings against the socio-political context in which they were embedded. We are not saying that context simply shapes lived experience. It does this and more, offering up inspiration and problems that require solutions. Context is a background and generative mechanism implicated in the trajectory of marketing thought (Morgan and Rutherford, 1998; Rutherford, 1997; Tadajewski, 2006a, 2006b).

Connecting the influence of the GHSE with marketing education is not as easy as it sounds. There were multiple threads of influence and not all thinkers held the same views about the market, marketing, and the social welfare benefits that flow from them. We will document that one strand takes a more critical stance towards the market, whilst other threads were underwritten by a more optimistic, and psychologically egotistic (Crane and Desmond, 2002) perspective regarding the beneficence of this distribution mechanism.

To set the scene a little, marketing as we understand it today originated in ancient times from about 2700 BCE (Jones and Shaw, 2002), with the Agora (the Greek marketplace), in sixth century Athens, being one of the earliest and most impressive exhibits in the ancient world:

> There were products of every description, meat, fish, fowl, wheat, bread, cakes, vegetables, fruits, wine, oil, flowers, textiles, shoes, slaves, crafts and money lenders. Price was negotiated between retailers and customers, with sellers eager to undercut the competition. Peddlers walked among the shops, and some of the earliest advertisements were market vendors in Athens crying their wares in the Agora. Crying (a cross between talking and singing) was an early form of advertising; and a forerunner of the town criers of medieval

> times. . . . The Athenian Agora of 2,500 years ago probably resembled the hustle and bustle of an American, European, or Asian flea market of today.
>
> (Shaw, 2016, p. 31)

The ancient Greeks also contributed to the history of marketing thought via their written commentary. Naturally, they did not use the term "marketing". Plato and Aristotle, for instance, reflected extensively on buying and selling activities (Cassels, 1936; Dixon, 1978). These were assuming increased importance in society courtesy of the steady differentiation of labor. People were undertaking more specific, more focused work, and were thereby reliant on other specialists for their daily provisions. These effects reverberated throughout society and the economy. As Shaw (1995) explains,

> The division of labor . . . results in a separation of producers and consumers. To bridge this gap, market exchange – selling and buying – is necessary. The exchange process requires work, work takes time, and time has an opportunity cost. Hence, marketing intermediaries emerge because of their increased efficiency in market exchange.
>
> (p. 10)

Nevertheless, marketing thought was, at best, a small part of the Socratic philosophic system, rather than a well-integrated body of knowledge.

After the fall of Rome in about 500 CE, early medieval churchmen such as Saint Jerome, Pope Leo, and Saint Augustine claimed that traders made a social contribution by creating "place utility" and the profit they earned represented nothing more than a wage paid for labor (Dixon, 1979). Later medieval church fathers wrote about the morality of marketing, some condemning as sinful a variety of practices that are illegal today (Dixon, 1979). Others, such as Alexander of Hales and Saint Thomas (thirteenth century), stressed the beneficial nature of marketing (Dixon, 1979, 1980). Thus, from the earliest Greek philosophers to the close of the medieval period, there were scholars who understood the basics of marketing but they framed it within the context of discussions of moral philosophy, rather than as a separate and distinct subject matter.

Moving forward in history, Nicholas Barbon, John Carey, Simon Clement, John Hales, Edward Misselden, Sir William Petty, and others writing from the fifteenth to eighteenth centuries continued to discuss "marketing". This was often undertaken in conjunction with theories of economic development (Dixon, 1981). Dixon credits the late eighteenth century classical economist Adam Smith with a clear understanding of the so-called "marketing concept", a bedrock piece of our discipline to the present day. To demonstrate his argument, Dixon cites a famous quote from Smith's *Wealth of Nations*: "The real and effectual discipline which is exercised over a workman is not that of his corporation but that of his customers" (Smith, quoted in Dixon, 2002, p. 741). During the mid-nineteenth century, "liberal" American economists such as Edward Atkinson, David Wells, and Arthur and Henry Farquhar echoed Smith's position and promoted laissez-faire (i.e. free market capitalism). This was what was known as "classical" economics (Coolsen, 1960).

The late nineteenth century economists differed in their approach to the marketplace. It brought them closer to what we now understand as thinking about marketing. What we mean is that they connected their understanding of the wider macro-environment with the abstract, individual consumer and their attempts to maximize personal utility. Among the most important commentators in this tradition, Alfred Marshall, and Austrian economists such as Carl Menger and Eugen von Böhm-Bawerk, wrote about the consumer, production and exchange, marketing effort, and marketing system-environment interactions in their writings (Dixon, 1999). However, these reflections are still distinct from, and predate, the study of marketing as an academic subject legitimized by its place within the university. And most importantly, excepting Alfred Marshall, their writings were not a key influence on those now viewed as the founders of our discipline.

As mentioned above, most scholarship on marketing history has focused on the period since the eighteenth century. The reason for this is obvious. The industrial revolution had triggered massive changes in business and marketing practice (Boorstin, 1974; Chandler, 1977; Fullerton, 1988; Funkhouser, 1984; Strasser, 1989) – practices that were recorded by those involved in them who wanted to document their contributions to social change, development, and progression. Beyond the ruminations of business people and their associates, there were large numbers of observers eager to express their opinions, some of which were pro-business, others not so certain that the rapid changes taking place were equally benefitting all members of society. This outpouring of literature, in turn, generated a substantial amount of archival material available for consultation at some later juncture.

Strasser (1989), for example, describes how the development of mass production in the mid-to-late nineteenth century *required* the concurrent development of mass marketing in America. During that period, marketing strategies including segmentation, brand positioning, and product differentiation were developed. The refinement of packaged, branded products with sophisticated national promotion campaigns accompanied a dramatic change in distribution channels. In this context, the size and extent of operations were transformed. There was a transition from small, family-owned businesses to large corporations (although the latter did not completely replace the former). Small-scale independent retailers were yielding to mail-order houses, chain stores, and department stores. But this is only a tiny snapshot of the disruptive changes that were engulfing practitioners in the period between the nineteenth and twentieth centuries. Industry, rather than agriculture, assumed greater importance. The division of labor accelerated and this was reflected in functional specialization in production, marketing, human resources, and accounting. Connected to this, there was an emerging management tier hired to help deal with the strategic and operational issues these firms confronted.

Technological changes reverberated throughout multiple sectors. The founding of a national rail system and development of refrigerated rail cars, as well as the mass production of the automobile, all revolutionized distribution. New methods of printing technology and photography, combined with the invention of the telephone and radio, dramatically changed communications and promotion. Even mundane facets of products – the packaging we routinely take for granted – were transformed. This period witnessed the development of paper bags, tin cans, cardboard boxes, and glass bottles (Twede, 2016). Electricity made possible new forms of signage and in-store lighting, creating new methods of attracting and enthralling consumers, with the emergence of national brands (Petty, 2016) and national magazine and newspaper advertising (Beard, 2016) disseminating a consumption oriented view of the world.

Fullerton (1988) describes similar changes in Britain and Germany, including, for example, the branding of Pears' Soap (UK) in the 1860s and Henkel Bleich Soda (Germany) in 1876. Lever UK introduced the first laundry soap carton in the 1880s. All three were active users of marketing communications. They enhanced their marketing insights in the next decade, using their extensive knowledge of customer demographics as an input into lifestyle market segmentation. Given these developments, Fullerton concludes that sophisticated, "modern" marketing began in Britain in the mid-eighteenth century and in Germany and the US around 1830. We are beginning to see how Bartels' initial insights into marketing thinking and practice are starting to unravel with additional research, often research that directs our attention beyond the boundaries of the United States.

To help link these contextual and industrial developments to the university and education sector, we can productively turn to Chandler (1977). He highlights an organizational revolution. The business environment and marketplace were no longer mere factors that move and shape practice without resistance. The management cadre we alluded to above became the "visible hand" that united supply and demand. It was this need for skilled management staff that encouraged attention towards the development of courses of instruction that would generate these workers.

The marketing history literature typically focuses on university-level courses of instruction and this has undoubtedly been a hugely influential conduit for the diffusion of marketing practice and marketing thought, but it was not the only educational outlet. Those unable to access higher education often sought training via alternative methods such as correspondence schools, which played an important role in America as well as in Britain (Tadajewski, 2011; Witkowski, 2010). They were primarily directed towards lower-level staff, but did garner the attention of owners and managers looking to improve their overall operational efficiency.

The first business correspondence course was offered in the mid-nineteenth century and salesmanship courses were soon provided by the YMCA, American School of Correspondence, La Salle Institute, the Sheldon School of Scientific Salesmanship, and Alexander Hamilton Institute, which published a range of marketing books (Tadajewski, 2011, p. 1131). The Sheldon School was established in the US in 1902, issued an impressive collection of marketing and sales education materials, and enrolled thousands of students (Tadajewski, 2011). Correspondence materials were also disseminated in other languages for the immigrant market. For instance, the Palatine Universal Correspondence School circulated numerous salesmanship and advertising texts in Polish (Witkowski, 2012). In the UK, the Institute of Marketing was an early twentieth century source of education for students. Collectively, these drew attention to the large market for business education, underlining interest in these areas. University programs responded by emphasizing their relatively higher rigor and degree granting status. Marketing and sales education was thus on the cusp of a period of growth that continues to the present day.

Collegiate education for business – and marketing

While there are examples of early forms of education for business administration being provided at the University of Oxford in the fourteenth century (Richardson, 1941) and Germany in the early eighteenth century (Spender, 2005), higher education for business and marketing really started to germinate at the turn of the twentieth century. The Wharton School of Finance and Commerce was founded at the University of Pennsylvania in 1881 and comparable programs were launched in 1898 at the Universities of Chicago and California. In 1900, the University of Wisconsin, New York University, and Dartmouth College entered the market. Business courses were also being provided through the economics departments at Michigan and Illinois in 1902. The first American marketing courses were taught in 1902 at the University of Michigan (E. D. Jones), the University of California (Simon Litman), and the University of Illinois (George M. Fisk), soon followed by offerings at the University of Pennsylvania, Ohio State University, Northwestern, the University of Pittsburgh, Harvard University, and the University of Wisconsin. Later in this chapter we take a closer look at Jones's 1902 course at Michigan.

Outside the United States, several British universities formulated plans to offer higher education in business (Sanderson, 1972). The Faculty of Commerce at the University of Birmingham, founded in 1902, was the first university degree program in this topic, followed by commerce programs at the University of Manchester in 1903 and the University of Liverpool in 1910 (Ashley, 1938; Fauri, 1998; Redlich, 1957; Sanderson, 1972). German university instruction in marketing-related subjects such as retailing and advertising may have preceded those in America (Fullerton, 1988; Jones and Monieson, 1990; Jones and Tadajewski, 2015). We know, for example, that as early as 1899 courses in agricultural economics at the Universities of Halle and Berlin included coverage of marketing topics (Taylor, 1906). A 1913 report by the American Consulate General in Berlin noted that courses there were being delivered in agricultural marketing, the methods and psychology of advertising, selling methods, and "the study of various phases of economics bearing in a broad way on the subject of marketing" (Thakara, 1913). Separate from the German universities but loosely associated were *Handelshochschulen* (business schools) established in Leipzig and Aachen in 1898, Frankfurt and Cologne in 1901, and Berlin in 1906. The proposal in 1879 for the *Handelshochschule* in Leipzig was to serve a range of occupations including the retail trade (Meyer, 1998, p. 23). The GHSE, which dominated the economics departments of continental universities, was primarily concerned with macroeconomics (*Volkswirtschaftslehre*, the economics of peoples). The *Handelshochschulen* soon developed a branch of economics that became known as *Betriebswirtschaftslehre* (business economics) or *Privatwirtschaftslehre* (private economics). More micro and managerial than the economic history previously taught, the *Betriebswirtschaftslehre* were more narrowly focused on teaching basic functions such as accounting, production, personnel, and marketing (Locke, 1985; Ashley, 1903a), but accounting overshadowed all others. The study of marketing in American schools soon outpaced provision in Germany.

The emerging marketing discipline

The published history of the discipline is largely a chronicle of books, teachers, university courses, and academic associations. Among the first scholars to bear testament to these important events was Paul Converse (1933), who published a description of "The First Decade of Marketing Literature" in the *Bulletin of the National Association of Teachers of Marketing and Advertising* (*NATMA Bulletin*). His list included material such as Ralph Starr Butler's (1910) *Marketing Methods*, Paul Cherington's (1913) *Advertising as a Business Force*, L.D.H. Weld's (1915) *Studies in the Marketing of Farm Products*, A. W. Shaw's (1915) *Some Problems in Market Distribution*, and Paul Nystrom's (1915a) *Economics of Retailing*, as well as an emerging periodical literature. During the 1930s, several pioneers wrote articles for the new *Journal of Marketing* highlighting the contributions of a limited range of the earliest teachers, courses, and institutions, as well as the key periodical and book literature (Agnew, 1941; Hagerty, 1936; Litman, 1950; Maynard, 1941; Weld, 1941).

Even in early business school programs, the term "marketing", per se, was not used. In its place, "distribution", "trade", and "commerce" were synonyms for "marketing". Each of these referred to the activities that took place during the exchange of goods or distribution of products from manufacturer to consumer (Jones, 1971; Lazer, 1979), activities that were starting to secure attention from the emerging group of scholars interested in the reality of the marketplace beyond the abstractions of classical and neoclassical economic theory. Economic theory was about to be juxtaposed against marketplace activities and found wanting in many ways. It did not accurately reflect the empirical realism of exchange processes and transactions.

In classifying the early literature, the traditional categories included functional, institutional, and commodity approaches. These three are sometimes considered the earliest schools of marketing thought (Shaw and Jones, 2005). Functional analysis was concerned with the activities performed by middlemen or participants in the marketing process. It explicated what they did in moving goods from producers to the ultimate consumer. This was not a neutral exercise. While it may not have been articulated as a political project, it was. Analysis of marketing functions often served as the basis for early twentieth century arguments that marketing "added value" in the circuits of economic exchange. Throughout the twentieth and into the twenty-first century, the definition and understanding of value would shift, but debates about marketing's contribution to society have never been fully resolved (Wilkie and Moore, 1999). Shaw's (1912) article, later expanded in his (1915) book, is one of the first examples of functional analysis. It sketched the rudiments of a vision of marketing's distributive function and the contribution it made to economic and social efficiency.

Institutional analysis refers to the study of marketing agencies or institutions, such as wholesalers and retailers. This body of work often paid considerable attention to determining the efficiencies of industries. Statistics were gathered – notably operating costs and average turnover – which were distributed to interested parties via university research bureaus (among other groups) to enable individual firms in specific locales to determine their efficiency versus their competitors. Nystrom's (1915a) study of retailing is the seminal example in this category. Finally, commodity analysis explores the way a class of goods is marketed. The most frequently examined were agricultural products. There were entire books published on extremely focused topics. For example, Henry Erdman's (1921) *The Marketing of Whole Milk* or Weld's (1915) *Studies in the Marketing of Farm Products*.

However, as Hollander (1980, p. 45) appreciated, it is difficult to classify Weld's work exclusively as representative of any single school of thought. He blended functional, institutional, and commodity analysis. This strategy was representative of most early marketing studies. They tended to examine the institutions in a product category to identify the marketing functions being performed in order to diagnose and treat current problems. In any case, the three approaches dominated our scholarship throughout the first half of the twentieth century.

An early bibliography of marketing that was extensive and representative enough to warrant publication in the *Journal of Marketing* (Converse, 1945a) was compiled by Fred E. Clark during the 1920s. Clark's list included numerous government reports as well as articles from such journals as the *Annals of the American Academy of Political and Social Science*, the *American Economic Review*, and the *Journal of Political Economy*. The first academic periodicals devoted to marketing were the *Journal of Retailing* (launched in 1925), *The American Marketing Journal* (1934), and *The National Marketing Review* (1935) – the latter two merging in 1936 to form the *Journal of Marketing* (*JM*), which, to this day, is generally considered the most prestigious periodical in the marketing discipline. At the same time the sponsoring organizations of those two merged journals, the American Marketing Society and National Association of Marketing Teachers, united to form the American Marketing Association.

By the mid-1930s, the marketing discipline was becoming an institutional force (Witkowski, 2010), a significant presence on campuses, and an essential factor generating the motive power of capitalism. The 1930s were also a turning point for the development of historical reflexivity. But it was Robert Bartels' dissertation of 1941 which formed the basis of an article entitled "Influences on the Development of Marketing Thought, 1900–1923" that has become a key node in orienting many neophyte academics in the development of their subject. Bartels' spadework expanded into three editions of his book (Bartels, 1962, 1976, 1988). In these he traced an extensive range of literature as well as the development of American university courses and the core contributors from their origins circa 1900.

Naturally, a figurehead in any research area will be subject to extensive scrutiny. Bartels has been no exception. We have already gestured to some of this critique. But this is not to deny his titan-like influence and the important energy he exerted in keeping historical self-reflection and appreciation alive with the orbit of marketing scholarship. As such, his narrative provides an appropriate point of departure for us and, while we are aware of the risk of oversimplifying his thinking, the essence of Bartels' work can be summarized in a chart showing the lines of personal influence involved in the development of marketing thought (Bartels, 1962 – see Figure 1.1).

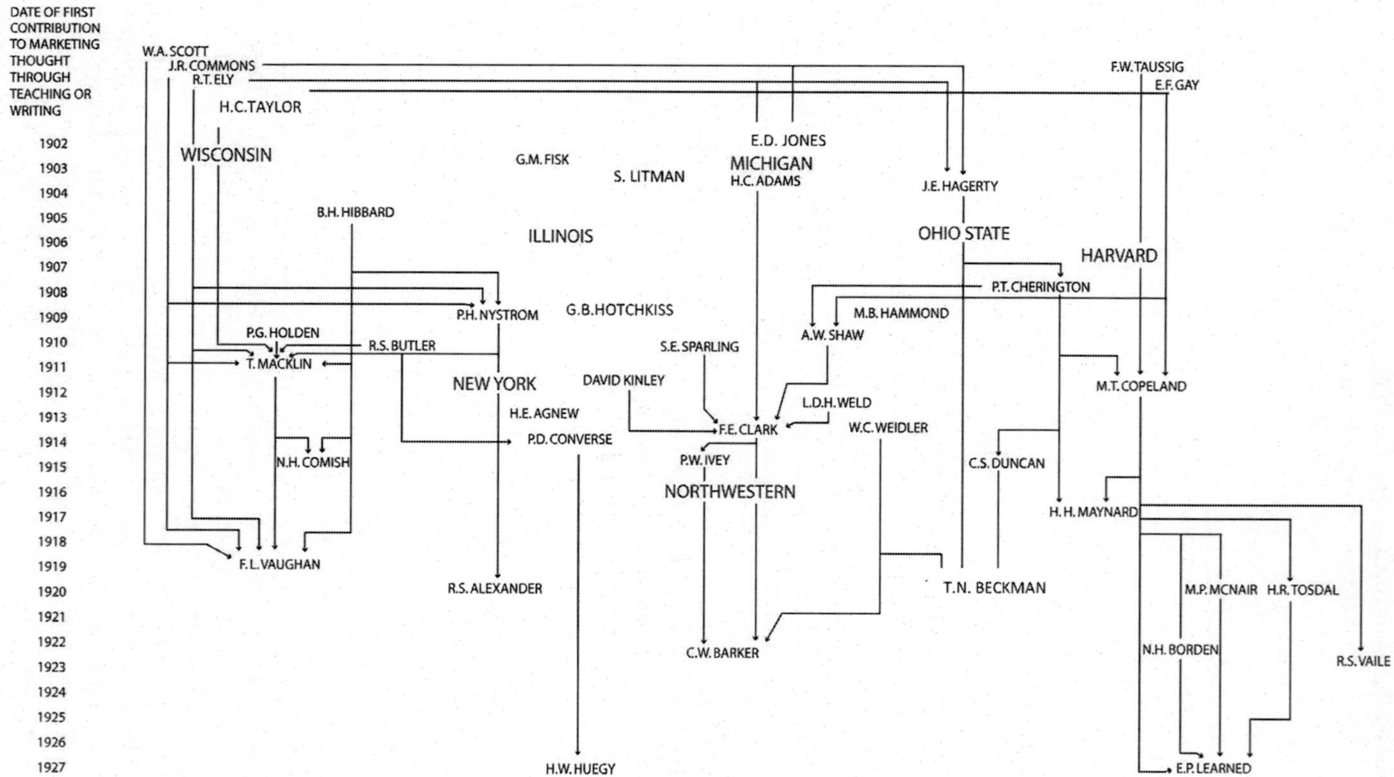

Figure 1.1 Intellectual genealogy of marketing thought

Source: Adapted from Bartels (1951) and Jones and Monieson (1990).

This shows the first collegiate marketing teachers and their networks of influence. It also tracks the institutions at which the subject was first taught as well as the approximate dates when these events occurred. In attempting to trace the origins of these courses, Bartels (1962, p. 29) concluded that "*their backgrounds are not generally known but . . . the idea for such courses did not always originate with the individuals who actually taught them*" (emphasis added). With historical research, it is often a gesture or cursory reference like this that provides the cleavage for rethinking foundational assumptions, theories, concepts, and practices. In our case, Bartels makes a pregnant point. We know about the people and the institutions who delivered the courses. But these individuals did not invent them. This is where Bartels offers us our wedge. For whatever reason, he did not examine the background of these scholars, explaining why they wrote and taught what they did. He did not explore the epistemology, methodology, axiology, pedagogical values, and political principles that influenced their research and teaching. This is a point that has long intrigued us. Who influenced these pioneers? And how did they influence them? These questions are the axes for this book.

The circumstances surrounding the University of Michigan course, offered in 1902, present an interesting case. Jones was encouraged to teach this "first" marketing course by the head of the economics department, Henry C. Adams, who was a strong supporter of higher commercial education. On his return to Johns Hopkins University from studying in Germany in 1880 – an institution that was receptive to continental educational ideas, especially those emanating from Gustav Schmoller (Backhaus, 1993/1994, p. 19) – Adams had made a proposal to the curriculum committee "novel to academic ears . . . for a course on 'American Technics', which would comprise contributions from agriculture, manufacturing and transportation supplemented by abundant illustrations from statistics" (Dorfman, 1969, p. 14). His suggestion was turned down, but it is possible that Adams' plan was a forerunner of the program given by Jones at Michigan.

Shortly after Adams' pitch, his colleague at Johns Hopkins, Richard T. Ely, who was later a teacher and mentor to E.D. Jones at Wisconsin, taught "Commerce and Its Historical Development in Modern Times" to graduate students in economics. Ely provided the following definition of "commerce".

> Commerce we may then say is one branch of human activity and is concerned with the exchange of economic goods. . . . When commerce is defined as a distinct branch of activity it is desired to call attention to the fact that it is not the mere exchange of goods or valuable products but such exchange as a separate business conducted by people called merchants.
>
> (Ely, 1884a)

He distinguished between the functions of wholesalers and retailers, tracing the movement of goods from manufacturer to consumer.

> Before proceeding further the various varieties or kinds of commerce are to be defined. First, there is the common distinction between wholesale and retail

> trade in commerce. It frequently happens that goods pass through several hands between the producer and the consumers. The one merchant buys in large quantities from manufacturers or importers and distributes in smaller lots to another merchant who divides it again into still smaller lots and sells to the consumers. The first kind of trade is wholesale and the second, retail. The trade which distributes to consumers is retail. The trade which precedes that is wholesale. Manufacturers frequently sell to wholesale dealers indirectly through commission merchants who receive as their payment a percentage on sales. Commission merchants deal largely in a few special articles or goods and do not buy these goods outright as a rule but take them "on commission". They are rather agents than merchants. The manufacturer, commission merchant, wholesale dealer, retail merchant – the term wholesale is to be applied to all the trade which precedes that between the retail merchant and the consumer. The combinations differ in various lines of business and also the number of hands through which goods pass. The large packers of fruit in Baltimore, for example, buy of the small packers in the surrounding country and sell these purchases as well as what they pack to merchants. They would have to be regarded as merchants and manufacturers at the same time. As their sales are made generally through agents called brokers who receive a commission, their profits are made on the goods they buy when they sell to a wholesale grocer.
>
> (Ely, 1884a)

Other topics included the means of transportation and communication, commerce and the social question, the influence of commerce on the character of people, and the division between foreign and domestic business, among others. Because of this coverage, it could be credited as a very early marketing program.

The Ely example demonstrates the importance of examining the background of the earliest courses and the people who delivered them. By doing so we can develop insights into the influences that encouraged them to study and teach as they did. An important theme in the writing about the development of marketing thought has been a biographical one. People naturally like to know about other people, their successes, their failures, their recoveries from setbacks, and their personal foibles. Between 1956 and 1962, the *Journal of Marketing* featured 23 biographical sketches about "Pioneers in Marketing" focusing on the first contributors to the discipline. While Bartels – and later Stan Hollander – helped keep historical research alive, the American Marketing Association has demonstrated a limited willingness to attend to their intellectual forebears. The *Journal of Marketing*, as a case in point, discontinued the "Pioneer Series", which Wright (1980) argued had served as a major contribution. Later, *JM* revived the series. In combination with other sources (e.g. Bartels, 1941, Appendix D; 1962, Appendix A; Converse, 1959; Wright and Dimsdale, 1980), this provides a sample of 42 individuals who form a core – but not the total range of contributors available – who helped define, cement, and promote the importance of marketing in the business world (see Table 1.1).

A few of those individuals were pioneers of marketing practice (e.g. A.E. Filene and L. Filene, the retailing magnates) and therefore contributed only indirectly to

Table 1.1 Pioneers in marketing–education/institutional affiliation

***Journal of Marketing* Pioneer Series**	**Converse (1959) additions**
H.E. Agnew – U. Michigan (1902)	E.E. Calkins – Knox College
N.A. Brisco – Columbia (1907)	S. Roland Hall – n/a
Ralph Butler – U. Michigan (1904) / U. Wisconsin (1909)	J.G. Frederick – n/a
Paul Cherington – Harvard (1908)	Wheeler Sammons – n/a
Fred E. Clark – U. of Illinois (1916)	W.H.S. Stevens – n/a
Paul Converse – U. Wisconsin (1915) /U. of Illinois (1924)	A.W. Douglas – n/a
Melvin Copeland – Harvard (1908)	C.S. Duncan – U. Chicago (1913)
Henry Erdman – U. Wisconsin (1920)	Horace Secrist – U. Wisconsin
E.A. and L. Filene – n/a	Fred Russell – U. Illinois (1916)
Benjamin Hibbard – U. Wisconsin (1902)	W.D. Moriarty – U. Michigan
George Hotchkiss – Yale (1906)	
L.S. Lyon – U. Chicago (1921)	**Bartels (1941; 1962) additions**
Harold Maynard – Harvard (1919)/Iowa (1922)	
Edwin Nourse – U. Chicago (1915)/Harvard	T.N. Beckman – Ohio State (1924)
Paul Nystrom – U. Wisconsin (1914)	Neil Borden – Harvard (1922)
C.C. Parlin – U. Wisconsin (1890s)	Ralph Breyer – Wharton (1925)
Stanley Resor – Yale (1901)	N.H. Comish – U. Wisconsin (1915)
W.D. Scott – U. Leipzig (1900)	T. Macklin – U. Wisconsin (1917)
Arch W. Shaw – Harvard (1908)	W.C. Weidler – Ohio State (1915)
Daniel Starch – U. Wisconsin (1906)	E.T. Grether – U. California (1924)
Harry Tosdal – U. Leipzig, U. Berlin /Harvard (1915)	Paul Ivey – U. Michigan (1917)
Roland Vaile – Harvard (1922)	E.P. Learned – Harvard (1927)
L.D.H. Weld – Columbia (1908)	

marketing thought (although A.E. Filene was a prolific author on a range of retailing and social topics). This, we should add, is an arbitrary distinction. Scholarship and practice are not distinct spheres, surgically demarcated from each other. There were substantial numbers of academics who had parallel practice-based careers. Others worked in the mid-ground as consultants. Some worked in close connection or directly with government agencies such as the United States' Federal and Industrial Trade Commissions.

Of the 36 pioneers listed in Table 1.1 for whom educational information is available, 16 attended or were affiliated with either Wisconsin or Harvard. One pertinent conclusion for our present purposes that emerged from Bartels' publications was that the development of the collegiate study of marketing in America was concentrated at those two institutions. They are the peaks of our educational field in this period, the poles which attracted the thinkers who shaped the discipline in the years to come. It is also worth noting that there were connections between Wisconsin and a number of Midwestern schools, including Illinois, Ohio State, and Michigan.

Some seminal contributors to marketing thought such as Edward David Jones, George M. Fisk, Simon Litman, and James E. Hagerty are conspicuously absent from that biographical literature. However, we now have access to information that never figured on Bartels' intellectual radar. To take an example, Jones studied in Germany and later under Richard Ely at Wisconsin, where he subsequently lectured between 1895 and 1902 (Jones, 2012, chapter 2). In 1902, he moved to Michigan. This was where he taught his path-breaking course. Likewise, Litman studied in Germany and then lectured at the University of California, then moved to Illinois in 1908 (Jones, 2012, chapter 3). Both Fisk and Hagerty are known to have studied in Germany and expressly acknowledged the influence of the GHSE on their thinking (Farnam, 1908, p. 26), as did Jones and Litman. The structure of our story is starting to cohere.

Fisk and Hagerty also apprenticed under Ely; Fisk at Johns Hopkins and Hagerty at Wisconsin. Some of those in the "Pioneers" list of biographies in Table 1.1, such as W.D. Scott and Harry Tosdal, were exposed to the cutting-edge educational experience offered in Germany. Ely, in turn, studied under the GHSE. What we have here is a filament that connects the architects of marketing thought. They were either educated on the continent or taught by those who had been exposed to its intellectually rigorous environment. This connection has never been mentioned in any of the literature published prior to 1990 (Jones and Monieson, 1990; Jones and Tadajewski, 2015).

In fact, the historical trail of academic marketing thought, its written history, biographies, and course materials, all seem to point to economics in general (which we might expect) and to the GHSE more specifically (which was far less expected). No fewer than 15 of those individuals determined by Bartels as having had a personal influence on marketing thought studied directly under economists of the GHSE, including Henry C. Adams (who studied in Germany in 1879–80), Richard T. Ely (1877–80), George M. Fisk (1894–96), Edwin Francis Gay (1890–93 and 1902), James E. Hagerty (1898–99), M.B. Hammond (1894), Benjamin Hibbard (1908), Edward D. Jones (1894), David Kinley (1901), Simon Litman (1899), H.R. Seager (1891–93), Samuel Sparling (1894), Frank W. Taussig (1879–80), Henry C. Taylor (1900–01), and H.R. Tosdal (1915). To those we need to add William James Ashley, the founding Dean and Professor of Commerce at the University of Birmingham in Britain. Our story thus navigates the Atlantic Ocean in multiple directions (from the US to Germany; Germany to the US; and Germany to the US and on to the United Kingdom).

Origins in economic thought

In this section, we examine what historians have written about marketing and how it was influenced by economics. Many academics before 1925 agreed that the development of marketing thought was predominantly indebted to economics (Converse, 1945b, p. 15). These views were reaffirmed throughout much of the last century (Kangas, 1966). For example, Bartels (1962) suggested that the most influential systems of economic thought at the beginning of the twentieth century were those of the classical and neoclassical economists. The classical school is closely associated with Adam Smith, David Ricardo, and John Stuart Mill. The major ideas connected with this tradition included a belief in laissez-faire (i.e. limited government intervention in the market), the efficiency of free competition and free markets (i.e. enshrined in Adam Smith's notion of an "invisible hand"), and the assumption that marketplace actors were economically rational and pursued their own self-interest. Assuming all participants were rational in that way, social welfare would be maximized (i.e. via self-interest, people tended to specialize in tasks that they could perform effectively, subsequently exchanging their offerings for money or via barter to the benefit of all). So, while the individual consumer directed the market, he did so in Smith's writings as a disembodied calculator (Dixon, 2002). Classical economics also relied heavily on abstract, deductive thinking – looking at the world through the prism of general theories and laws – in order to determine what should happen in the marketplace. Examples included theories of supply and demand, value, monetary theory, and theories of economic development.

Despite Bartels' claim that these views were widely adopted by marketing scholars, his substantiation is limited, often vague, confusing, and full of caveats. He appreciated that some of the views of classical economics needed to be modified. As a case in point, demand was not simply determined by supply. Adam Smith's economic vision where free markets, unrestricted competition, and the pursuit of self-interest by all would result in efficiency and equilibrium did not match the reality of late nineteenth century competition. The marketplace was, for a pool of observers, characterized by high levels of competition, and a lack of knowledge of production and distribution costs, leading to incorrect pricing strategies. Customers were not necessarily rational in their buying behavior; their emotions shaped the choices that were ultimately made. Nor were they necessarily truthful – they sometimes lied to merchants to secure advantageous prices, occasionally leading merchants to ruin. The pursuit of rational self-interest, therefore, while an appealing picture, was incommensurate with the messy reality of the marketplace. Put otherwise, it was not production cost alone that set prices. There was a complex interplay between production, marketing practice, and subsequent demand that contributed to the prices being set and achieved. The market was not spectrally determined by invisible forces, but by the very real "visible hand" of management (Chandler, 1977). This hand was sometimes overt, sometimes covert. Marketing's role in this context would be one of demand management. Business activity would help shape the market using all the tools and techniques at its disposal.

In that connection, Bartels admitted that by the late nineteenth century when academic marketing was emerging, there was a transition in popular thinking from laissez-faire to the need for some government regulation of business. So-called "cutthroat competition" and the rise of the Robber Barons brought the dark side of business practice to the forefront of government and public attention

(Khurana, 2007; Tadajewski, 2009). Not all business activities benefitted society. On the other hand, it was increasingly apparent that a growing economy offered the promise of work and rising standards of living for many. In view of this, government could be a force for good in terms of limiting problematic practice; at the same time, it might enable the expansion of the business system and the associated benefits which would accompany it. Against this background, marketing practice and education were starting to be considered central to this picture of abundance for all.

In his conclusions about the influence of economics, Bartels averred that at the turn of the twentieth century, students of marketing held

> a general philosophy of optimism, a vision of new frontiers of progress, a businessman's viewpoint of confidence in free play in the market, and widespread agreement that consumers acted rationally in the market . . . [and it was agreed that economists'] concepts of marginal utility, opportunity costs, subjective and objective value, abstinence, hedonism, 'the marginal man', and rationalism were useful tools of thought.
>
> (1962, p. 19)

This constellation of assumptions is used to support his belief that some early marketing scholars subscribed to laissez-faire and the concept of rational economic man. Circumspection, however, encourages us to think otherwise. As Bartels shows, but fails to appreciate the ramifications of, the economists under whom many marketing teachers studied included Richard Ely, John Commons, Henry Taylor, and Henry Adams. As we will see in more detail later in this book, these individuals considered themselves part of the institutional school of economics, which was derived from the GHSE. There were important differences between the GHSE on the one hand and classical and neoclassical economics on the other. This has been largely ignored, dramatically underplayed, or investigated superficially. The influence and the importance of these different schools of thought are confounded by Kangas, who identifies Commons, Ely, and Taylor as "some of the most outstanding neo-classical economists of [the] day" (1966, p. 73, 82). They were not. All three considered themselves as institutional economists.

Institutional economics has been called one of the most influential and distinctively American contributions to economic thought (Dorfman *et al.*, 1963, p. 8). It refers loosely to a method of studying social, political, and economic phenomena that takes a relatively long-term perspective and focuses attention on forces of disequilibrium (i.e. when supply and demand might not actually meet and what can be done to remedy or alter the situation) (Arndt, 1981). It examines the evolutionary processes in the economy and the roles played by institutions in shaping economic behavior. Institutional economics is consequently broader (i.e. takes a more socially holistic perspective) and distinct from the institutional analysis of marketing described above (i.e. the study of specific marketing agencies, such as wholesalers and retailers).

It was a product of the last third of the nineteenth century. This period witnessed tremendous economic growth and industrialization. These brought vast inequalities in wealth and assets, social dislocation, and the rumble of discontent with the political-economic status quo. Growing urbanization, monopoly power, strikes, reckless disposal of western land and resources, commercial crises, and long periods of depression and unemployment all raised concerns over the dominant ideology of laissez-faire. This resulted in increasing government intervention in the form of railroad and corporate regulation and in the organization of farms and trades, especially during the 1880s and 1890s.

Yet, the meaning of institutional economics is elusive. The term itself was used as a label to designate a specific tradition in 1918 (Rutherford, 1997) and has been retrospectively applied to individuals whose contributions are viewed as seminal in this mold (Rutherford, 2010). Generally the works of Thorstein Veblen, Wesley Mitchell, and John Commons (among others) are accepted as representative of this tradition (cf. Rutherford, 2010). Commons was the only one of these prominent institutional economists to write a book (1934) by the same title. To Commons, an institution was "collective action in control, liberation and expansion of individual [trans]actions" (1931, p. 648). Collective action includes unorganized custom. It was also embodied in the activities of the family, the corporation, trade associations, unions, and the state (Commons, 1931, p. 649). According to Commons, transactions are the basic unit of interest in economic study. The emphasis on transactions, rather than commodities and individuals, marked the transition from classical to institutional thinking, since it focused attention on relations and processes rather than on static analysis. Similarly, his emphasis on groups (institutions) and social processes (evolution) gave Commons' work a truly sociological character.

His conceptualizations were grounded in data. He moved inductively, that is, from focused studies of industries and firm practices to more abstract concepts. Obviously, for Commons, field investigation was important as an information source. In equal measure, it was highly salient for his pedagogic practice. He was well known for visiting companies, using this empirical material for research, as well as providing an entrée for his students to the real world of business practice.

Thorstein Veblen and Wesley Mitchell added an anthropological (Veblen, 1899a), evolutionary perspective (Veblen, 1898), and a quantitative, statistical methodological strategy (Mitchell, 1913) to Commons' sociological-legal approach (Commons, 1924, 1934). Each wanted economics to be more empirical, based on solving social and economic problems. Their thinking was interdisciplinary, basic to which was their opposition to various aspects of "orthodox" doctrines (Veblen, 1898, 1899b; Mitchell, 1918). As we will see in Chapter 2, these views are consistent with the GHSE.

It was during the middle of the twentieth century that the institutional approach gained explicit recognition in marketing, largely through the work of Wroe Alderson, and the authorial team of Duddy and Revzan. This work has received some attention in the literature, so we will largely restrict our attention to a brief genuflection here. Alderson (1951, p. 83) borrowed from Commons' work to develop a theory of the marketing process. Arguably, though, Duddy and Revzan (1953, Appendix C) made the most explicit and extensive application of the institutional approach, drawing heavily on Commons' architecture. If we are to summarize their contributions succinctly, they showed how all three traditional forms of marketing analysis – the functional, institutional, and commodity approaches – could benefit from ideas derived from institutional economics.

It is fair to say that a limited number of historians have registered connections between marketing thought and the institutional economics discussed above. For example, Brown concluded that

> whether influenced by the developments in economics or . . . a product of the same forces that led economic theory into institutional channels, the early study of marketing was marked by an effort to describe and measure the exact nature of the activities involved in the marketing of goods. . . . Early study of marketing was strongly grounded in institutional economics.
>
> (1951, pp. 60–61)

Hollander suggested that institutional economics provides a good description of marketing "in general" and pointed to formative marketing institutionalists such as L.D.H. Weld (Hollander, 1980, p. 45). These gestures were largely perfunctory. They remained underdeveloped and offered tantalizing hints of connections that could be excavated with appropriate (archival) research.

In summary, if the professoriate were influenced by their educational experiences in Germany, most notably their exposure to influential intellectuals aligned with the GHSE, their philosophical and methodological assumptions will deviate substantially from those presented by Bartels as emblematic of marketing thought in the early twentieth century. We are arguing, in effect, for a fundamental reorientation of how we understand the origins of marketing thought, undermining the foundations that Bartels postulated as the architecture for modern marketing as we know it.

By calling into question the idea that our pioneers were devotees of orthodox economics we place marketing theory on a very different trajectory by way of the German Historical School. This school of thought had the potential to create a marketing that was not oriented primarily by managerial concerns, but by questions of ethics, social justice, and societal betterment. This, clearly, is a different vision of the discipline to that held by most scholars, who profess the importance of producing instrumental knowledge for one core interest group, namely marketing managers. To question Bartels, we need to understand the philosophical foundations of marketing. This means we need to immerse ourselves in the work of the GHSE. It is only against this backdrop that we can understand what our transatlantic pioneers brought back with them, how their education influenced their ideas, and the ultimate significance of this school of thought for marketing.

Method and overview

In approaching the research for this book, we have emphasized the interpretation and explanation of events so that they form – where appropriate – a coherent story (Fullerton, 2011). This does not, of course, mean that we exclude material deliberately that does not cohere with our narrative. More than that, we seek to lead the reader through the development of marketing thought in a way that is both accessible and rigorous. Clarity and explanation are our watchwords. The story should incorporate as much evidence as possible and our arguments must be derived from the evidential basis we provide.

For Barzun and Graff (2004), historical writing has to be accurate, ordered, and logical. Continual self-reflection throughout the researching and writing process is essential. This means we will follow our narrative trail in whatever direction it takes us. Equally, we will indicate lines of inquiry that we think are worthy of further pursuit for other scholars interested in deepening our knowledge of the foundations of marketing thought.

An awareness of time, continuity, and change is essential to good historical research (Fullerton, 1988). The same can be said of appreciating the internal differences that might make an individual's values and pedagogic practice deviate from peers associated with the same institution or school of thought. This is important given the project we are setting ourselves and the differences that demarcate those trained in Germany. These are a function of their biographies, their intellectual commitments, and political values. Not all academics, even those taught within fairly well specified paradigmatic boundaries, share the same political values, and this will influence how they envisage the impact of their work and the core constituents for their intellectual products.

We are interested in the influence of the GHSE beginning in the late nineteenth century on American and British economists who were the first to study and teach marketing from about 1900 through to the 1930s when the marketing discipline was firmly implanted in its institutional and increasingly fecund intellectual soil. During those 40 to 50 years, there were changes in economics with respect to its axiology, epistemology, and methodology which were a function of the political environment, and these, in turn, impacted upon the emergence of marketing. Those changes were the result of debate and conflict between different schools of thought. To understand how and why the study of marketing emerged as it did, therefore, we must comprehend contextual, intellectual, and biographical factors. This is something, to repeat the point made above, that people have failed to do in the case of the linkages between economics and marketing.

In the rest of this book, we will engage with the development of economics. We primarily focus on the German Historical School, the context in which this strand of thought developed and was eventually disseminated to the first generation of marketing academics. The research and pedagogic practice the latter were exposed to subsequently informed their publications, engagement with students, and public-facing activities. The sort of understanding we seek begins by acknowledging that the idea of marketing existed before the term was widely used. The concept of "marketing" that was taught via courses of university instruction is a twentieth century invention. The various practices that we associate with it – advertising, paying attention to customers and their needs, engaging in market intelligence gathering, and so on – have a much longer genealogy than its institutionalized format.

In our excavation of economics and marketing thought, primary source materials will be an essential part of the evidence we marshal to explore the interconnections between the disciplines. Such content can be defined as material produced – written, published, or stored – during the historical period under investigation. This is where our study differs from Bartels' work. He relied on published, secondary sources (i.e. material already available and not written at the time when the events they described took place). These were augmented by interviews with surviving scholars. By contrast, extensive archival research has formed a central part of the research for this text.

Contextually situated biographical analysis plays an important role in our account. To underscore what we have maintained in this chapter, there was widespread agreement about who first studied and taught marketing. We have *some* idea about the influences that shaped their intellectual development. Academics are literature-generating machines, and many left behind collections of archival materials relevant to their personal, professional, and intellectual biographies. We know a considerable amount about the environmental conditions – the socio-economic, political, and intellectual currents – that shaped the context in which they lived. The material that we use in this project includes unpublished autobiographies, diaries, curriculum vitae, university employment records, minutes of university meetings, syllabi, lecture notes and exams, unpublished correspondence, papers, and speeches. Acknowledging our infatuation with this form of research, for us it is truly a treasure trove of source material. It has been a project that has occupied the first author since the late 1980s and caught the imagination of the latter in the mid-2000s. What is astounding to both of us is that these collections, and there were many, had not been touched. They demanded exploration.

The review of published work on the history of marketing thought that we explored above suggests that there were a small number of institutions which are considered the original centers of influence. This means that the University of Wisconsin and Harvard University were priority sites of primary research. The influence of Wisconsin was significant and spread to other Midwestern schools, including Illinois, which, for other serendipitous reasons as well, fits into the story told in the pages that follow.

In starting to explore these original sites, we had a nagging feeling that there was part of the narrative about the early development of the philosophy of marketing thought that was being missed. Intellectuals trained in the philosophical and methodological assumptions as well as the pedagogic practices associated with the GHSE did not simply remain in the United States. They traveled to other countries, locations where they were probably likely to have been influential in shaping research and educational practice. Admittedly, this was a strong assumption to make. Sometimes historians need to be guided by their gut instinct. This unsettled feeling that we were missing a piece of the jigsaw came to a head in 2013 when we began to seriously explore other sites, most notably locations in the United Kingdom.

During this process of reflection, the Commerce degree program at the University of Birmingham came into the analytic frame. This was designed and implemented by an economist, William James Ashley. Ashley was trained in German Historical Economics (Koot, 1980). A cursory check of the structure and content of the program confirmed that there was a fruitful vein of inquiry via this connection. As such, it became a third priority site for primary research. Secondary research settings included the archives of the University of Michigan, University of Illinois, and Yale University.

The archival collections of Richard Ely, first director of the School of Economics at Wisconsin, of Edwin Francis Gay, first Dean of the Harvard Business School (HBS), and of William James Ashley, first Dean of the Commerce Program at the University of Birmingham, were all rich sources of primary materials. The collections of several other scholars and institutional holdings were also used. Ironically, despite his training as an economic historian, Edwin Francis Gay was not a very thorough record keeper. Correspondence and administrative records pertaining to the founding of the HBS are somewhat sketchy, with the bulk of these located in Gay's collection at the Huntington Library in San Marino, California. However, Melvin Copeland's (1958) history of the HBS, Herbert Heaton's (1952) biography of Gay, and the history of the early years at the Harvard Business School by Jeffrey Cruikshank (1987) were valuable tools for unravelling the foundations of marketing thought at Harvard. At the other extreme, the collection of unpublished papers of Richard Ely is a goldmine. His correspondence alone exceeds 100,000 pieces. It includes exchanges between Ely and 18 of the 39 individuals included in Bartels' genealogy. Ely's extensive records of scholarly organizations and of research and teaching were also useful in providing insights into the origins of marketing thought at Wisconsin and beyond.

The *Farnam Family Papers* at the Sterling Library of Yale University include materials related to the career of Henry W. Farnam, who was an economist. He trained in Germany in the late nineteenth century and in 1906–08 conducted a thorough survey of American economists to investigate the influence of the GHSE. The results were published as "Deutsch-Amerikanische Beziehungen in der Volkswirtschaftslehre" [German-American Relationships in Economics] in *Die Entwicklung der Deutchen Volkswirtschaftlehre*, edited by Gustav Schmoller in 1908. The responses to that survey are included in the *Farnam Papers* and constitute direct evidence of specific influences of the GHSE on US economists, including many who were involved in the sedimentation of marketing.

The *William James Ashley Papers* held at the Cadbury Research Library, University of Birmingham Archives include correspondence between Ashley and individuals such as the German economic historian Lujo Brentano as well as Richard Ely and Henry Adams, photocopies of lecture notes, unpublished papers and presentations by Ashley, as well as the minute books of his commerce seminar. Other relevant sources included course syllabi and exams, minutes of the Commerce faculty meetings, and other unpublished manuscripts including one student's extremely detailed and complete set of notes for Ashley's course on Business Policy. As another student wrote in Ashley's obituary, "As a lecturer his slow speech and long pauses made it easy for students to 'get him all down', and many notebooks must have been verbatim reports" (Heaton, 1927, p. 684).

The focal time period for this research was roughly 1885 to 1930. This encompassed several significant events, such as the migration of American scholars, especially economists, to study in Germany (1870s–1890s), the establishment of the School of Economics at the University of Wisconsin (1892), the founding of the Commerce Program at the University of Birmingham (1902), the organization of the Harvard Business School (1908) and founding of the Bureau of Business Research at Harvard (1911), the popularization of Scientific Management (Taylor, 1911/1998), and the delivery of the first marketing courses at the Universities of Michigan, California, and Illinois as well as publication of the earliest books about marketing thought (1900–1920).

In subsequent chapters, we engage with the individuals associated with the GHSE. We differentiate their assumptions and arguments from the ideas of classical economics. We then turn to examine the foundations of marketing thought at several institutions. In the order of their inclusion in our narrative, we are following – broadly speaking – a chronological approach.

Conclusion

In the chapters that follow, we rely extensively on archival materials. Along the way, we share discoveries of individuals, courses, and literature not previously mentioned by other historians. Some of those discoveries may serve as opportunities for further study. However, our primary purpose is to go beyond the existing patchwork of facts to identify common political-intellectual connections and the sociological as well as philosophical origins of marketing as a discipline.

2 The German Historical School of Economics

Introduction

This chapter begins with a brief account of the popularity of German higher education with Americans during the late nineteenth century. This sets the stage for understanding the nature and scope of interest in German economics. Our overview of the GHSE includes a brief description of the main contributors and their ideas. We do not attempt to provide an original interpretation of their work. Rather, the most important ideas of the German economists who were influential in the US – and Britain – are discussed. The legacy of the GHSE is most evident in institutional economics and, to a lesser extent, in the British Historical School of Economics. These connections lay the foundation for subsequent chapters that focus on the study and teaching of marketing at the University of Wisconsin, University of Illinois, University of Birmingham, and Harvard Business School.

The migration of American students to Germany

During the nineteenth century, especially the 1890s, many American students seeking higher education were attracted to Germany. In 1899 alone, more than 150 American students were pursuing post-graduate studies in German universities (Sheldon, 1889). Various estimates place the total number that studied in the country between 1820 and 1920 as high as ten thousand (Herbst, 1965, p. 1; Thwing, 1928, p. 40). Half of those attended the University of Berlin, about a thousand each at Leipzig and Heidelberg. The most popular subjects were history, economics, and the natural sciences (Thwing, 1928, p. 160). This academic migration was impressive, not only in absolute terms, but also relative to US attendance at other European institutions. In 1895, for instance, there were 200 Americans registered at the University of Berlin while there were only 30 at the Sorbonne in Paris (Herbst, 1965, p. 8).

A relatively small number of US students graduated with German degrees. This was because the habit was to study at various schools in turn under the most famous professors: "They tasted, without drinking deep, of the waters of the Teutonic fount. The influence of the instruction, and of the university life, was, in the case of many students, slight; but in the case of others, it was fundamental and permanent" (Thwing, 1928, p. 45). There were several reasons for the popularity of German education. Ease of entry was one. Cost of living was low, with fellowships available to offset costs. By contrast, the French system required a nine year course of studies leading to a doctorate. And, up until 1871, admission for a degree at Oxford, Cambridge, and Durham required subscription to the 39 Articles of the Anglican Church (Thwing, 1928, p. 76). With these as alternatives, matriculation from a German institution was relatively simple. One could begin a doctorate with little undergraduate training and complete the degree without a thesis (Myles, 1956, p. 102), although many did produce a dissertation.

Most importantly, these institutions were highly respected (Tribe, 2002). They were professional schools, a place to prepare to earn one's living (Ely, 1938). In American colleges, the emphasis was on uniformity and discipline. Instruction followed the lecture-and-recitation method. By contrast, German schools provided an atmosphere of academic freedom and equality between students and professors – and research was much more important in the country than in France, England, or America at that time. Graduate students were treated as junior colleagues and classes in the social sciences took the form of seminars modeled after the laboratory method of the natural sciences. Seminars were incubators in which they were trained to carry out independent investigation of important problems. For example,

> Professor Wagner's [University of Berlin] conception of a seminar is that of a course in which the professor takes for the time the minor role of director and the students themselves become the lecturers . . . There is [also] a social side to a . . . seminar, especially when conducted by Professor Wagner, that must not be overlooked. Here professor and students meet upon a footing of intimacy, the formality of the seminar room is, for the time, put to one side, questions are asked as they arise in the student's mind and answered in detail. Here friendships are made that last through life. And then, occasionally, there is the adjournment to a neighboring beer hall, where the professor divests himself of the last traces of his habitual reserve, where stories are told and discussions engaged in that are, here at least, animated enough.
>
> (Seager, 1893, pp. 246, 248)

These seminars were based on the analysis and interpretation of original sources. For instance, during the nineteenth century the University of Gottingen's library held over 200,000 volumes, ten times the number of the largest college library in the United States (Thwing, 1928, p. 130). When the first business school associated with the University of Berlin began classes in 1906, seminars, rather than lectures, were thought to be a partial answer to the unique educational needs of their cohort (Redlich, 1957, p. 62).

During the 1890s and perhaps even earlier, students in economics often went on field trips to various industrial establishments to study firsthand the institutional forces shaping the economy. Max Sering's seminar included many such "excursions" (Seager, 1893, p. 240). This atmosphere created a commitment to scholarship as a profession, a "craftsman's regard for technical expertise, an unfailing respect for accuracy, and a concern for the application of knowledge and skills to social ends" (Herbst, 1965, p. 19).

American students could also identify with the continental social and political setting of the late nineteenth century. Both countries were struggling for unification. Germany and the United States were experiencing more rapid growth than any other countries in the world. With industrialization came economic and social problems. Changes in the systems of production and distribution brought urbanization, unemployment, poverty, and depression. Social change is not an unalloyed good.

Science in the service of industry

During the last half of the nineteenth century, Germany surpassed all other European nations to become a leading world industrial power, second only to the United States. This accomplishment was due primarily to the economic and political unification of the country and its education system, which focused upon science and economics.

Before its 1871 victory over France, the territory of Germany consisted of 30 loosely interconnected states. This military action resulted in the political unification of much of Germany under Prussian leadership. This might not have been possible without the economic unification which began in 1833 with the formation of the Zollverein or Customs Union. Under the terms of this union, which included most of the major states later forming the Reich, numerous trade barriers were eliminated. This constituted a powerful stimulant to growth (Stolper, 1967; Kitchen, 1978). Enhancing this accelerant, the 1830s witnessed the construction of a railway system which complemented the Customs Union by geographically connecting the states. Economic unification was further assisted by increases in the industrial labor force (Stolper, 1967).

One of the major factors facilitating the industrialization of Germany was the education system. It was reputed to be the best in the world. During the eighteenth century, many states had established elementary schools with compulsory attendance. Thus, by the nineteenth century, it had a higher rate of literacy than the rest of Europe (Craig, 1978, pp. 186–187; Fullerton, 2016). The government also underlined support for the *Realschulen* (trade schools) that were founded to provide basic practical education for businessmen and farmers (Kitchen, 1978, p. 65). These supportive mechanisms were successful. Indeed, Alfred Marshall (1919) used the phrase "science in the service of industry" to highlight the contribution of the education system to its economic vitality.

It is not surprising that the Germanic states took special pride in higher education, as they possessed more and better universities at the beginning of the nineteenth century than most of their neighbors (Craig, 1978, p. 192). Much of the distinction accorded to these institutions was due to their work in the natural sciences. Research by chemists led to the discovery of artificial fertilizers which revolutionized industries ranging from agriculture to dye-making processes, leading to numerous spin-off products (Dillard, 1967, p. 309). Basic discoveries in physics led to innovations in electrical manufacturing businesses (Dillard, 1967, p. 312). For those exposed to the high quality educational provisions in the natural sciences at this point, specialization, objectivity and the importance of evidence were synonymous with scholarship. These characteristics spread to a variety of disciplines, including the social sciences and history.

The German Historical School of Economics

There is some debate whether there was a "school" of German Historical Economics (Caldwell, 2001; Pearson, 1999). Nonetheless, it has been largely ignored by mainstream economists and historians (e.g. Khurana, 2007). Fourcade-Gourinchas (2001, p. 432) indicates that the contributions of the GHSE are "nearly forgotten today". Balabkins (1993/1994, p. 27) points out that most American readers would be completely unfamiliar with the names, ideas, and contributions of the historical school. Milonakis and Fine (2009, p. 71) go so far as to suggest that this group of thinkers have "been relegated to the intellectual dustbin of history". Within the specialist history of economic thought literature, they garner more attention, and their contributions are the subject of considerable study (Senn, 2005). Yet, even in this tradition, academics remain vague about what exactly the students of GHSE pioneers "absorbed" from their mentors (Rutherford, 2006, p. 162). As our contribution, we want to bring their work to the intellectual foreground, connecting it to the emergence of marketing, tracing lines of agreement and points of divergence between a series of scholars and their writings. Where Rutherford sees vagueness about what was being communicated, we want to illuminate the ideas, theoretical perspectives, and methodological tools being passed from generation to generation.

We do not assume that this "school" was homogenous in intellectual or political terms. There were variations of the GHSE (older, younger, youngest, or newer) depending on the source. Still, we can simplify our narrative somewhat. General consensus divides the school into two traditions: the "older school" and "younger school". Nor were these mutually exclusive. A substantial amount of their writings and activities overlapped, particularly from the middle to late nineteenth century. As expected, the younger school were slightly junior to the older school in age and their work continued into the twentieth century.

In the early nineteenth century, classical economics ruled the intellectual waves in Germany, England, and the US (Mitchell, 1969). It was based on a search for natural, universal laws and followed a deductive logic in proposing abstract theories of economic behavior. As we mentioned in Chapter 1, the classicists believed in laissez-faire (minimal government intervention in the economy) and assumed that economic man was perfectly rational and motivated by self-interest. In short, the orthodox school was conservative, individualistic, and non-interventionist with respect to marketplace activities, and assumed that one set of universal laws could be applied to all economies and countries.

The dominant textbook used in Germany during the early to mid-nineteenth century was Karl Heinrich Rau's *Lehrbuch der Politischen Oekonomie* [Textbook of Political Economy], first published in 1826 and reprinted in nine editions until 1876. Rau's text was heavily based on classical economics, especially on the work of John Stuart Mill (Tribe, 2002), as were other German texts by von Thunen and von Hermann (Mitchell, 1969). However, in 1841 Friedrich List published *Das Nationale System der Politischen Oekonomie* [The National System of Political Economy], which included a critique of Adam Smith's *Wealth of Nations*. List wrote that Smith's abstract, universal economic theories could not account for national and historical differences between Britain and Germany (thereby introducing historical and contextual relativism into theoretical rumination). For List, classical economics did not provide guidance about how to manage the German economy. It did not provide solutions to the economic and social problems then being experienced. List's critique signaled a shift in economic thinking. It was followed in 1843 by Wilhelm Roscher's *Grundriss zu Vorlesungen uber die Staatswirthschaft nach Geschichtlicher Methode* [Outline of Lectures on Political Economy according to the Historical Method]. Roscher is considered to be the founder of the older GHSE.

Towards the latter part of the nineteenth century, an historical approach began to inflect the study of theology, history, jurisprudence, political science, and sociology (Herbst, 1965), but was most pervasive in the field of political economy or economics. Notable German economists whose work reflected and refracted the historical approach include Wilhelm Roscher, Bruno Hildebrand, Karl Knies, Johannes Conrad, Ernst Engel, Gustov Schmoller, Adolph Wagner, Lujo Brentano, Kary Bucher, Gustov Cohn, Adolph Held, G.F. Knapp, Erwin Nasse, Albert Schaffle, Georg Schanz, Gustov Schonberg, and Werner Sombart (Myles, 1956, p. 81).

To clarify what follows, it is worthwhile to further differentiate the classical school and GHSE. We are doing so at a high level of abstraction and generalizing across numerous different thinkers, each of whom articulated slightly different positions. With this proviso in mind, in contrast to the classical school, the GHSE was liberal and nationalistic and believed in social welfare. Connected to this, they articulated an active role for the state in the national economy. They were reformers who believed that ethics and morality were central issues in economics. It was not value-neutral. It was conceptualized in political terms as world-shaping and impactful. In other words, empirical research and theorizing had to play a role in shaping the economic system so that it benefitted all concerned, not just a small number of vested interests. They also maintained that economic behavior was contingent on the social and political environment. These were interconnected spheres of activity. They formed the conditions of possibility that enabled, affected, and placed boundaries on the practices associated with other spheres. Economics was not just something that took place in the Ivory Tower of the university. It was part of an integrated whole; part of a larger science of society.

We mentioned above that the older school introduced a degree of relativism. They had questioned the universalism of classical economics – in this case, the idea that an economic theory or law applied irrespective of the historical and cultural specificities of the location under consideration. In preference, they stressed that economists had to be attentive to the historical, cultural, social, and economic circumstances of the environment they sought to examine, reflect upon, and – it was hoped – improve through the application of their scientific insights. To put this in more concrete terms, these economists believed that to understand the German economy, or any economy, one had to understand its distinctive history (hence German "Historical" School). Such an understanding could yield theories. But these would be contingent theories.

More formally, we can say they subscribed to temporal (time) and locational (place of inquiry) relativism. This meant that their theories were not intended to remain unchanged in perpetuity. They had to be subject to periodic revision as the political-economic situation ebbed and flowed. In developing these theories, intellectuals associated with the older school tended to draw upon the tools of inductive logic (moving from reflecting on specific circumstances to more general statements), observation, description, and statistics about actual economic behaviors and events – in short, economic theory had to be developed using an historical method and heavily informed by empiricism (a theory of knowledge which privileges understanding generated by studying the actual marketplace).

The older school

The founders of the GHSE included Wilhelm Roscher, Bruno Hildebrand, and Karl Knies. Wilhelm Roscher (1817–1894) studied history and political science at the Universities of Berlin and Gottingen. At Berlin, he was deeply influenced by Leopold von Ranke, who focused on archival research and used the seminar method in his teaching (Thompson, 1942, p. 413). The ideas on jurisprudence developed by Friedrich von Savigny similarly helped shape Roscher's views on political economy (Ashley, 1895, p. 100). Roscher started teaching history at Gottingen in 1840, but his interest shifted to political economy. In 1848, he moved to the University of Leipzig, where he remained until his death in 1894.

Roscher's *Grundriss zu Vorlesungen uber die Staatswirthschaft nach Geschichtlicher Methode* [Outline of Lectures on Political Economy according to the Historical Method] served as a manifesto. It presented a program for his own work as well as a bedrock for the GHSE (Ashley, 1895, p. 100). In his *Outline*, Roscher distinguished between two classes of method. The first he termed the philosophical or idealistic; the second, the historical or physiological. The objective of the philosophical method was to deductively produce a system of abstract concepts or theories (e.g. orthodox economics). Furthermore, Roscher differentiated two forms of inquiry (positive and normative) in political economy: what is (what has been; and how it became so); and what should be (Roscher, 1878, p. 105). The philosophical method addressed the normative – what ought to be the case. Of the answers yielded by this method, Roscher wrote, "any one of them may be right, but, of course, only for one people and one age . . . the only error would be if they should claim to be universally applicable" (Roscher, 1878, p. 110). The latter point demarcated the German approach from the universalistic aspirations of classical economics.

The purpose of the other class, the historical method, was to trace the development of human relations and economic developments as accurately as possible (Ashley, 1895, p. 103). This focus on "real life" or an empiricist orientation and valorization of the world was a reaction against the abstract, deductive method of classical economics in favor of an inductive, historical one. While such a method was basic to their approach, this was merely one part of a different way of viewing the economy and the role of economics in society. This is not to suggest that the older school saw nothing of value in the economic orthodoxy. Their findings and insights were always available as an input for the critical thinking that the GHSE sought to embody. Roscher felt that both what is and what should be required reflection. But each demanded a different method or approach to study.

For Roscher, political economy was an historical science, but one that should follow a particular approach.

> [O]ur aim is simply to describe man's economic nature and economic wants, to investigate the laws and the characteristics of the institutions which are adapted to the satisfaction of these wants, and the greater or less amount of success by which they have been attended. Our task is, therefore, so to speak, the anatomy and physiology of social or national economy.
>
> (Roscher, 1878, p. 111)

Throughout his writings, Roscher referred to the "natural laws" of the economy. However, he explained his use of "natural law" in reference to political economy as an economic organism. This was not an organism subject to completely deterministic laws and effects. "I do not, indeed, by any means pretend that the public economy of nations is governed by natural necessity, in the same degree as, for instance, the human body" (Roscher, 1878, p. 82). By "natural law", Roscher meant the regularities which are in evidence in a given economic context. To trace the "physiology" of an economy, therefore, he was setting himself a focused epistemological problem. He had to be attentive to context and political-economic points of difference. The dynamism inherent in this position called for the use of an inductive, comparative, observational method (Streissler and Milford, 1993/1994) – the historical method (this dynamism would be a feature that spans the older and younger schools, getting steadily more dynamic and relativistic as we move to the younger, more socially activist generation). Furthermore, Roscher observed that

> the natural laws governing the public economy of a people, like those of the human mind, are distinguished in one very essential point from those of the material world. They have to do with free rational beings, who, because they are thus free and rational, are responsible to God and their conscience, and constitute a species capable of progress.
>
> (Roscher, 1878, p. 84)

Progress was defined by the development of the economy and he attempted to explain this using a stage theory of economic evolution based on a cycle of rapid growth, maturity, and decay. These events were infinitely complex so they could only be used as categories or concepts rather than as natural laws (Weber, 1975, p. 77). In other words, his stages were a step removed from universal laws.

The second of the founders of the older school was Bruno Hildebrand (1812–1878). In addition to his academic career, he served in the German parliament and founded the first statistical bureau in Switzerland at the University of Berne. While in Switzerland, he championed the building of railroad lines. In 1861 he returned to Germany, taking a position at the University of Jena to teach political economy and two years later added the editorship (co-edited with Johannes Conrad) of the *Jahrbucher fur Nationalokonomie und Statistik* [Yearbook for National Economics and Statistics]. While serving in the Hessian parliament, Hildebrand was very cognizant of serious economic problems, especially the widespread poverty that plagued the country. Thus, he became interested in social change and led a reform movement in the state parliament. These involvements led to a practical emphasis in his work (Myles, 1956, p. 44).

Hildebrand's major contribution to the older school came with the 1848 publication of his *Die Nationalokonomie der Gegenwart und Zukunst* [Economics of the Present and of the Future]. His other work was highly empirical, including "Zur Geschichte der Deutschen Wollenindustrie" [The History of the German Wool Industry] (Hildebrand, 1866). In fact, his teaching appointment at Jena was not a popular stop for US students, as is evident in Figure 2.1a. This resulted in his influence being confined primarily to his published scholarship.

Hildebrand was critical of orthodox economic theory for its disconnection from reality. He questioned its pretensions to universalism and its failure to provide solutions to the economic woes facing Germany. For instance, the economy had developed more rapidly and more recently, and was in a different stage of development than England's. English free trade theories did not provide his country with a program for its industrial development. More generally, because of the orthodox prioritization of theoretical reflection, there was little discussion of practical economic problems and possible solutions. The most pressing of these in Hildebrand's view were poverty, the development of industrial independence, and an adequate banking system (Hildebrand, 1866, p. 45). Within the older school, his work marked a transition from what had been conservative criticism to active reform.

The major themes in Hildebrand's recommendations for political economy are consistent with those of Roscher and recur in the writings of Karl Knies. The first of these themes deals with formulating "laws" of economic development. Hildebrand agreed with Roscher that an economy evolved through certain stages. This said, his stage theory was less complex than the latter's and he differentiated his use of the term "laws" of development from the laws of orthodox doctrines.

> The whole Smithian school regarded the science of economics as a natural theory of commerce in which the individual was viewed as a purely egoist force which, like every natural force, always operates in the same direction and always produces the same effect under similar conditions. For this reason, in Germany as in England, its laws and rules were called economic

> natural laws, and eternal duration was ascribed to them just as it was to other natural laws.
>
> (Hildebrand, quoted in Myles, 1956, p. 67)

Hildebrand was even more critical than Roscher of the claimed universality of classical economics. He felt that economic science

> need not attempt to find unchangeable, identical laws amid the multiplicity of economic phenomena. Its task is to show how humanity has progressed despite all the transformations of economic life and how this economic life has contributed to the perfection of mankind. Its task is to follow the economic evolution of nations as well as of humanity as a whole, and to discover the basis of the present economic civilization as well as of the problems that now await solution.
>
> (1863, p. 145)

A third theme within the work of the older school was that the state should play an active role in the economy. Like Roscher, Hildebrand did not completely reject the role of individual self-interest in driving exchange activity, but felt that this was not adequate as a basis for theory development.[1] Economics was not an ethically neutral science for Hildebrand. It was and should be ethically oriented. Societal betterment in terms of economic justice was a feature of his writing. Poverty amidst plenty underlined that the economy did not self-correct. It needed intervention to ensure that all prospered and this is where historically and activist-oriented economists, ideally with connections to government, could facilitate progressive social change.

Self-interest did have some role to play in ensuring economic vitality. Hildebrand did not doubt this. But he did seriously qualify it. It was not necessarily a secure guarantor of our commitment to the wider ethical responsibilities that all members of society should demonstrate. It did not always lead people to be public spirited. To be sure, self-interest can motivate, but it can induce unethical practice as well. Trusting economic justice to self-interest was therefore a dubious basis upon which to ensure a fair and ethical distribution of the benefits of industrialism. In making this line of argument, his point was that our assumptions about the functioning of the economy had to be subject to critique; that we needed to have a realistic understanding of human behavior; that this was possible via attention to the empirical world; and social reform was necessary to reorient the political-economic system where it diverged from a normative vision that underwrote the values of the nation.

The third founding member of the older school, Karl Knies (1821–1898), was professor of political economy at the University of Heidelberg between 1865 and 1898. His influence may have been the most significant of all the scholars associated with the older school. Knies was described by Myles (1956, p. 48) as "the most profound of the three" older school economists. Richard Ely (1906a) considered him to be "one of the ablest of German political economists and the one from whom more modern influences have proceeded than probably any other man". In that connection, Knies' influence may have been felt more from his teaching over a period of 30 years at Heidelberg than from his writing (Tribe, 2002). He was a significant figure in the intellectual development of both John Bates Clark and Richard Ely, and both became prominent US economists.

The most important of Knies's ideas were included in his (1853) *Die Politische Oekonomie vom Standpunkte der Geschichtlichen Methode* [Political Economy from the Standpoint of the Historical Method]. This was described by Ely as "an elaborate and complete exposition of the historical method as applied to economics" (Ely, n.d.a, p. 4). He fundamentally subscribed to the view that the structure of a given economy was shaped by history (Betz, 1988). In addition to temporal relativism, Knies underscored the locational dimension by pointing out that geographic, climatic, and cultural factors were involved in economic development.

> The truth of all theories which have their foundation in empirical life rests upon concrete hypotheses. Relativity in the validity of their conclusions or judgments is a necessary result of the circumstance that these hypotheses do not remain identical nor occur constantly in all times, places and circumstances.
>
> (Knies, quoted in Ely, n.d.b, p. 5)

According to Ely, this relativism became one of the lasting contributions of the GHSE (Ely, n.d.b, p. 5). In explicitly proposing this principle, Knies paved the way for the younger school. Signifying the transition from the older to younger Historical school were two notable economists, Ernst Engel and Johannes Conrad. Engel (1821–1896) became famous for his laws of consumption which dealt with the income elasticity of demand for food. These laws were based on extensive statistics that were collected during his tenure as director of the Royal Prussian Statistical Bureau at the University of Berlin from 1860 until 1882. There, Engel taught statistics to many American students.

Johannes Conrad (1839–1915) was influential via his work in what was later called agricultural economics. Examples of his research include "Die Statistik der Landwirthschaftlichen Production" (1868) [Statistics of Agricultural Production] and "Der Konsum an Nothwengigen Nahrungsmitteln im Berlin 1781 und 1881" (1882) [Food Consumption and Demand in Berlin from 1781 to 1881]. With their emphasis on the use of statistics and empirical research, these economists intellectually connected the older and younger schools.

The younger school

The leader of the younger school was Gustav Schmoller (1838–1917), who taught at the University of Berlin (1882–1917). While studying at the University of Tubingen under Max Duncker, Schmoller developed a passion for historical research. Like Hildebrand, he had a keen practical interest in politics. He campaigned privately and later publicly for the unification of the German provinces under Prussia. In his later years, he was called to the Prussian State Council (Ely, n.d.b, p. 7).

Some suggest that Schmoller carried Knies's emphasis on relativism to the extreme. He proposed that the main tasks of economic science were observing correctly, defining, and classifying, along with explaining typical patterns and causal relationships (Abraham and Weingast, 1942, p. 22). We must not associate this emphasis on causality with universalism.

> [A] perfect and complete classification of phenomena in economics is impossible, anyway, because these phenomena and, therefore their definitions, as well as the terminology which these definitions employ, are in a constant state of flux and transition and never can be absolutely grasped.
>
> (Abraham and Weingast, 1942, p. 23)

Reflecting this epistemological position, Schmoller led a generation of economists in the belief that no theory was possible *until* detailed historical investigations had been carried out. As a science, political economy was relatively new. But it had a longer-term mission, which was

> to describe and define economic phenomena; to design and portray these phenomena as part of a system and pattern by employing scientific terminology to do so; to understand these phenomena as a connected whole and as a part of the total life of a people; to explain particular events from their causes; and finally to predict a future on the basis of our knowledge as regards the developmental process of the past. It therefore becomes the task of political economy to arrive at a complete and perfected picture of economic life in terms of time and space, and in terms of the relationship and historical sequence of economic phenomena. This is accomplished by subjecting observations to comparative and differentiating thought, by checking the veracity of these observations for the sake of scientific accuracy, by grouping these observations into various classes according to their similarity or difference, and at last, by trying to understand such a classification in terms of a typical and regular pattern and an all pervading causal connection.
>
> (Abraham and Weingast, 1942, p. 22)

In his emphasis on relativism, evolution and political intervention, Schmoller's thinking, like that of Knies, was close to the positive philosophy of Comte (which, in its later forms, stresses links between knowledge and the modification of the order of society and thus echoes the younger GHSE). Whereas Comte rejected the "vain search for the causes of phenomena", Schmoller believed the search for causes, whilst difficult to establish, was important. He admitted "not to know historical laws", but rather:

> economic and statistical laws by which we mean to express nothing more than an ever recurring regular and typical sequence of phenomena. . . . [A] uniform

> and ultimate [natural] law does not exist in economics and never shall. The institutions and the phenomena operating in a given economy constitute only an individual picture, are representative only of the epoch and the place where they have occurred, and can only be explained through the historical evolution of that economy and its people.
>
> (Abraham and Weingast, 1942, p. 25)

Following Schmoller's example, during the last quarter of the nineteenth century the younger school produced numerous publications hallmarked by an historical, descriptive, and statistical focus. These included studies of agricultural economics (Conrad, 1868; Scheel, 1887; Knittel, 1895), the history of industrial and labor organization (Bucher, 1892; Schanz, 1877; Schmid, 1896), economic statistics (Conrad, 1882; Scheel, 1882), and industrial and trade history (Hildebrand, 1866; Schmoller, 1890–1893; Schone, 1899). Besides their empirical work, two events related to this outpouring of intellectual virtuosity are noteworthy. The first was the so-called *Methodenstreit* [Battle over Method]. By the 1880s the younger school had a virtual monopoly on economic thinking and research in Germany. In 1883 Schmoller (1883) came under attack from an Austrian economist, Carl Menger, for the extreme stance of the younger school against deductive theory (Menger, 1883). This was misplaced. Few in the GHSE rejected the need for theory, deductive or otherwise.

Their vision of theory was multifaceted. For starters, the GHSE engaged with many different forms of theory. They questioned and reworked it. This point is much more significant than it appears at first glance. The GHSE critically evaluated Say's law, that is, the notion that supply will generate demand (Milonakis and Fine, 2009). This, of course, was inconsistent with marketplace reality for many goods and services. Theoretically, its importance cannot be understated. While later writers would try to clarify the misconceptions surrounding this "law", they did not resolve the point that many economists were neglecting to appreciate the seminal role of marketing in constituting demand (e.g. Hutt, 1974).

Roscher, in the first place, submitted that orthodox economists had focused too much attention – despite Adam Smith's dictum about the relationship between production and consumption – on production at the expense of the consumption of products. He was acutely aware that production was contingent upon effective demand; "wants" had to be stimulated if the economy was to continue to expand (Hagemann, 1995). Most importantly, he was not a naïve theorist who believed that supply drove demand (see also Streissler and Milford, 1993/1994). In an economy where money was the driving force rather than barter and immediate usage, demand and exchange could be delayed; a stimulus was consequently necessary to keep the wheels of capitalism turning. In fact, the GHSE went further than this, arguing there were no natural human "needs". Rather, all "needs" were cultural constructions (Prisching, 1993/1994). On their reading, the market was underpinned by the cultural value system operative in society. It did not define it. What this means – very simply – is that the market is not a natural phenomenon.

Among the many other factors that foregrounded the emergence of our discipline as a university subject, the fact that the GHSE effectively cleaved a space for the function of marketing to assume a more central stage in economic theory should be appreciated. After all, if supply generated demand, what role would there be for marketing in an economy apart from distributing information? By the time marketing was being actively promoted within the university by a proponent of GHSE ideas, Edwin Francis Gay at the Harvard Business School and Arch W. Shaw, an early pioneer in our discipline, both echoed contestations of Say's law (e.g. Cuff, 1996, p. 16).

Beyond engaging with extant theory, the GHSE were forceful in expressing their vision that prior to theory development, appropriate descriptive and empirical research was a necessity. Any theory would be historically based. This implied context and time specificity, thereby introducing contingency rather than universalism as a guiding assumption. Epistemologically, it was expected to be holistic in emphasis, conceptualizing the nation and core institutions as ontologically real and forming the conditions of possibility for social action. Embedded within this, they distanced themselves from abstractions of economic man. Their view of human nature encompassed psychological and sociological influences that took them away from the idea of the self-interested, utility maximizing individual. People were driven by their desires and passions, and their opportunity for action was curtailed by very real cognitive and personal limitations. In other words, they appreciated – as Richard Ely articulated in the 1880s and 1890s – that we are all shaped by the context in which we live in conjunction with our psychological and physiological gifts. With all this complexity, undertaking empirical research with the expectation of theory development which promised universal and unchanging laws of the economy and society was unrealistic. At best, any "laws" would be "short-run relative laws, specific to the given type of society and relative to time and space" (Milonakis and Fine, 2009, p. 84). As a result, conceptual development and whatever abstraction was presented had to be firmly grounded in empirical data.

Still, the younger school, especially Schmoller, felt that the older school had not gone far enough in demanding or producing an adequate data base on which to develop theory. As is typically the case with a great deal of academic labor, extreme positions are often negotiated by those seeking a middle ground upon which to productively forward knowledge production. Schmoller is an exemplar in this regard. Recalling any claimed incommensurability between deductive and inductive approaches, he admitted that "there is no science which can employ one to the exclusion of the other" (Abraham and Weingast, 1942, p. 25).

In addition to the *Methodenstreit*, between 1870 and 1872 several affiliates of the GHSE publicly called for social reform (Sheehan, 1966, pp. 59–60). This earned them condemnation from members of the National Liberal Party as "*Kathedersozialisten*" or "socialists of the chair" (Oppenheim, 1871). Several of the so-called *Kathedersozialisten* met during 1872 to consider collective action and in 1873 they formed the *Verein fur Sozialpolitik* [Society for Social Policy] under the leadership of Schmoller. There were two criteria for attendance at these meetings. One was an interest in social policy. The second was a rejection of extreme laissez-faire liberalism. The *Verein* "saw as its special mandate the proof of the necessity of state activity [in the economy], particularly for the protection of the lower classes, and an investigation into the extent of requisite state interference in practical affairs" (Conrad, 1910, p. 430). Some of the policies recommended by members included social insurance schemes, factory inspection laws, state ownership of railroads, progressive tax measures, minimum wage regulations, public works programs, and collective bargaining (Ringer, 1969, p. 147).

Alongside Schmoller, the *Verein* included Roscher, Hildebrand, Wagner, Knapp, Brentano, Mithoff, Conrad, and Engel. Although philosophically it was dominated by the Historical School, the membership differed in their political beliefs, ranging from the almost liberal position of Lujo Brentano to the near socialist views of Adolph Wagner. The group was united, nonetheless, in emphasizing historical laws and ethics, in their subscription to the importance of state interference with economic processes in the interest of social welfare, and in their belief in evolution (Herbst, 1965, p. 145). Stimulating group dynamics and the pressing nature of the economic and political problems they perceived, all made for intellectual ferment, leading to an active publication strategy. Thus, the *Verein* increased the reform character of the Historical School and allowed economists to combine ethics with their scientific ideals.

Influence of the German Historical School of Economics

The epistemological, methodological, and political influence of the GHSE was strongest in America, leading to the development of institutional economics. Students also valued the pedagogical pragmatism characteristic of this foreign educational system which was manifested in the use of seminars and field trips. The ethical inflection of this variant of economics was appealing to idealistic young people who were inculcated with the idea that the state had a constructive role to play in economic life. As part of this, they were encouraged to envision the challenges involved in policy-making in terms of how their knowledge could help shape potential economic futures. They viewed economics (and by extension, marketing) as committed to distributive justice; the idea that all involved in the distribution of goods and services should receive their due reward. The customer, likewise, should receive quality products at a fair price. Some shared the axiology of their continental professors and became highly reform-minded.

A steady stream of German-trained economists began returning to America during the 1870s. These included F.W. Taussig and Edwin Gay, both of whom went to Harvard, as well as Richard Ely and Henry Adams, who joined Johns Hopkins. After beginning their academic careers at the latter, Ely and Adams moved to Wisconsin and Michigan respectively. For our purposes, these four individuals were among the most influential figures to train under the GHSE. Certainly, this is true in terms of their impact upon those who later specialized in marketing. Others followed, until the onset of World War I, but the influence was strongest during the 1870s and 1880s (Dorfman, 1955, p. 24).

Figures 2.1a and 2.1b illustrate where those who apprenticed under the GHSE took up teaching positions on their return. Each is listed under the institution where

	University of Leipzig	University of Heidelberg	University of Munich	University of Halle	University of Berlin		
	Roscher (1848–94)	**Knies** (1865–98)	**Brentano** (1891–1914)	**Conrad** (1872–1915)	**Sering** (1897–1925)	**Wagner** (1870–1917)	**Schmoller** (1882–1917)
University of Birmingham (UK)							
W.J. Ashley		•					•
Harvard University							
F.W. Taussig (1879–80) †						•	•
W.Z. Ripley (1893–94)							
A.P. Andrew (1898)				•			•
C.J. Bullock (1902)				•		•	
E.F. Gay (1890–93; 1902) †	•		•		•	•	•
H. Tosdal (1915) †						•	
University of Michigan							
H.C. Adams (1879–80) †		•				•	
E.D. Jones (1894) ††				•	•		
University of Wisconsin							
R.T. Ely (1877–80) †		•		•		•	
H.R. Seager (1891–93) ††				•		•	
S.E. Sparling (1894) ††				•		•	
B.H. Meyer (1894–1895)						•	•
H.C. Taylor (1900–01) ††				•	•	•	•
B.H. Hibbard (1908) ††							
E.A. Ross (1888–89)						•	
University of Illinois							
E.J. James (1875)	•			•		•	
G.M. Fisk (1894–96) ††			•	•		•	
M.B. Hammond (1894) ††				•		•	
E.L. Bogart (1898)				•			
D. Kinley (1901) ††							
Ohio State University							
J.E. Hagerty (1898–99) ††				•		•	

† Early Contributors to Marketing Thought cited in Bartels (1962)
†† Early Contributor / Student of Richard T. Ely

Figure 2.1a Students of the German Historical School of Economics

they spent most of their career and the date(s) in parentheses indicate the year(s) they studied or undertook education in Germany. Each student is also connected to the GHSE scholar(s) under whom he studied. It is worth registering that fifteen of the individuals in Figures 2.1a and 2.1b were included in Bartels' chart indicating personal influences

	University of Leipzig	University of Heidelberg	University of Munich	University of Halle	University of Berlin		
	Roscher (1848–94)	**Knies** (1865–98)	**Brentano** (1891–1914)	**Conrad** (1872–1915)	**Sering** (1897–1925)	**Wagner** (1870–1917)	**Schmoller** (1882–1917)
Columbia University							
J.B. Clark (1873–75)	•	•					
R. Mayo-Smith (1876)	•	•				•	
E.R.A. Seligman (1879–81)		•				•	
S.M. Lindsay (1891–94)				•		•	
Wharton School							
E.J. James (1875–77)	•			•		•	
S.N. Patten (1876–77)				•			
R.P. Falkner (1885–88)				•			
E.R. Johnson (1891–92)			•	•		•	
New York University							
J.F. Johnson (1875–76)				•			
J.W. Jenks (1885)				•			
University of California							
B. Moses (1873)		•					
W.C. Mitchell (1897)				•			
S. Litman (1899) †			•				
C.C. Plehn (1889–91)							•

† Early Contributors to Marketing Thought cited in Bartels (1962)

Figure 2.1b Students of the German Historical School of Economics

in the development of marketing thought (Bartels, 1951, p. 4; and Figure 1.1, Chapter 1 herein). The substantial importance of Ely for early marketing professors is highlighted in Figure 2.1a.

The number of economists trained in Germany during this period appears to have been substantial. For instance, Myles (1956) compiled a list of 79 German-trained economists based on pre-1905 membership in the American Economic Association. Thirty-three earned degrees in Germany and 46 others had some training there. In 1906, Henry Farnam conducted a survey of 126 North American economists (115 respondents) to determine the influence of the GHSE. Fifty-two had no training in Germany, but 6 of those were influenced in a positive way courtesy of their professors, and they cited Ely and Adams approvingly. Sixty-three had some training in Germany, including 20 who earned degrees. Seven of those who did study in the country felt that they were not influenced at all and only 3 had a negative reaction to their training. So, overall, the reported influence was very positive. Based on the number of students who referenced them, the most popular professors were Wagner (Berlin), Schmoller (Berlin), Conrad (Halle), Sering (Berlin), Roscher (Leipzig), Brentano (Munich), and Knies (Heidelberg) – in that order. Their influence helped spread appreciation for the "historical method" followed by the general "point of view" they espoused. These included the functions of the state and – perhaps most obviously – a general "stimulus" to study economics (Farnam, 1908). Many of the respondents commented upon the pedagogic influence exerted by this school courtesy of the seminar method and use of field trips by their tutors.

Ely responded at some length, citing the influence of Conrad, Wagner, Schmoller, and Knies, whom he considered his "master" (Ely, 1938, p. 44).

> I took my A.B. at Columbia in 1876. There I had political economy for one term. . . . The instruction that we received did, I think, more harm than good. I really feel that it is no exaggeration to say this, because it probably gave us an idea that we knew something about the subject whereas we really knew nothing. You can imagine then when I went to Germany, studying first under Conrad, then under Knies – under whom I took my degree – and then under Wagner, a whole new world was opened to me. The broad scope of political economy was presented, the idea of relativity as opposed to absolutism, the insistence on exact and positive knowledge, all made a strong impression upon me. . . . Knies I regard as one of the ablest of German political economists and the one from whom more modern influences have proceeded than probably any other man. . . . I may also mention that the ethical view of economics impressed me strongly. I think the Germans under whom I studied had a sufficiently clear perception of the difference between ethics and economics. They had a feeling, however, that ethical influences should be brought to bear upon our economic life, and they believed also that those ethical influences which were actually at work shaping economic life to a greater or less[er] extent should be examined carefully as existing forces.
>
> (Ely to Farnam, 1906a)

He continues,

> I overlooked mentioning the influence of Schmoller which, after all, has been considerable in my work. I did not study under Schmoller, but I have read [his writing] many times . . . [and it] proved helpful to me when I was giving my first course of lectures at the Johns Hopkins University.
>
> (Ely to Farnam, 1906b)

Not all were influenced in a positive way, nor were they influenced in the same ways. Frank Taussig (1906) was particularly lukewarm.

> When I went to Berlin in 1879, I got great stimulus – new points of view – from Wagner. I got little from Held, whom I heard also. On the whole I think

> I have been influenced not more by the Germans than by others. Latterly I have got most from Marshall and Bohm-Bawerk – less from Schmoller than I had expected.
>
> (Taussig, 1906)

On the other hand, his colleague at Harvard, E.F. Gay (Figure 2.1a), reported that he "owed much to Schmoller in the way of general suggestion" (Gay, 1906). Upon arriving at Berlin in 1891, Gay found Schmoller and his students involved in the collection of facts upon which to base new economic theory.

> He [Gay] soon felt that here was the intellectual home he had been seeking. Here were the things he believed in: the devotion to history as the key that might unlock many doors; the attempt to see the interaction of all manifestations of the human spirit, economic, legal, political, social and intellectual; the rigorous criticism of evidence and the hope that from it all would emerge a science of economics which would serve as a sure guide for policies of social betterment.
>
> (Heaton, 1952, p. 39)

One of Ely's colleagues at Wisconsin, B.H. Meyer (Figure 2.1a), believed that the methodological approach used by the younger GHSE was highly valuable for a progressivist oriented economics.

> Wagner influenced me chiefly with reference to the variations in the limits of state functions, and in the view that financial (or fiscal taxation) reform can be made the fulcrum of social and political reform. In a word, certain aspects of Wagner's philosophy influenced me deeply. Schmoller influenced me in method. As you know, he is historical, analytic, concrete, intensive, and yet circumspective. I believe Schmoller's method is the method for us in the US.
>
> (Meyer, 1906)

As mentioned above, the most cited influence taken from the GHSE in Farnam's survey was the inductive, historical method. By calling attention to the importance of this approach, these students were underlining how their German teachers influenced their epistemological position. By making reference to the necessity of history in helping unravel the structure of the economy, they illuminated the transmission of methodological values from generation to generation.

Earlier in his career, Edmund J. James was a professor at the Wharton School of Commerce at the University of Pennsylvania (Figure 2.1b) – an environment hospitable to GHSE ideas as a reflection of the support for German business instruction articulated by Joseph Wharton, the industrialist who funded the institution (Spender, 2005). Later James became President of the University of Illinois (Figure 2.1a) and was a staunch supporter of business education (see Chapter 4). He wrote the following to Farnam.

> The German economists . . . gave me an historical and comparative point of view. . . . I got my first idea of the value of detailed investigation before attempting to generalize in the world of economic phenomena and also my first conception of the relationship of law to economics.
>
> (James, 1906)

James E. Hagerty (Figure 2.1a), who first taught marketing at Ohio State in 1905 and later contributed to the literature with *Mercantile Credit* in 1913, was one of those who studied in Germany. As we will go on to discuss in further detail in Chapter 3, he did so as part of his doctoral work at Wisconsin under Ely. In his response to Farnam, Hagerty wrote, "I believe that I have been influenced as much by American as by German teachers in the methods of the German economists. I . . . mention Professor Ely especially whose influence has been in that direction" (Hagerty, 1906). Several others responding to this survey singled out Ely as a strong, secondary conduit for GHSE ideas. George M. Fisk, a student of Ely's at Johns Hopkins, later in Germany under Brentano, Conrad, and Wagner, and the first teacher of marketing at the University of Illinois, referred to the historical approach, the systematic method of presentation, and the tools of instruction as formative. He claimed that "the difference in point of view was of great value" (Fisk, 1906). Although not listed in Farnam's ranked summary of response categories, many of his correspondents commented upon the teaching methods of their professors. For example, Robert Brooks of Swaithmore College responded with the following.

> From Professor Conrad I learned how exceedingly interesting and profitable it was to take students to visit mines, factories and public institutions of various sorts – a bit of experience that I have employed myself in my own teaching.
>
> (Brooks, 1906)

As indicated above, seminar instruction was modeled after the laboratory method in the natural sciences. Books, periodicals, and documents were treated like specimens to be examined. "The economic Seminar library is contained in two large rooms furnished with desks, writing materials, etc., adequate to supply the needs of all the members. . . . Along the walls are shelves containing a very complete collection of economic works, some five or six thousand in all" (Seager, 1893, p. 252). F.W. Taussig and H.C. Adams may have been the first Americans to apply the seminar methods taught in Europe in their teaching.

Two events during the 1880s signified, more than anything else, the impact of the GHSE on US economic thought. Not surprisingly, these events reflected the values and ideas underlying the formation of the *Verein* and the *Methodenstreit*. First, in 1885, the American Economic Association (AEA) was formed. The motive force behind the founding of this organization was a group of German-trained economists, including E.J. James, Simon N. Patten, and Richard Ely. The latter described this event as their "hegira – the flight from the old to the new" (Ely,

1936, p. 148). The AEA was a protest against the system of laissez-faire and reflected the need to secure a platform for free discussion about alternative economic arrangements, including how economics could influence policy and the desirability of ethics and social justice informing the political agenda (Ely, n.d.b, p. 197; see also Ely, 1898).

The first proposal for the association came from Patten and James under the title "Society for the Study of National Economy" and used the *Verein fur Sozialpolitik* as its model (Ely, n.d.b, p. 198). Their initial constitution stressed the necessity for government intervention in the economy, and while there was some support for this, that principle proved to be too narrow for adoption. This led to Ely's proposal. He retained the central idea of governmental activism and broadened the principles of the association to include an emphasis on scientific research, including historical and statistical study (Ely, 1936, p. 144). As Ely characterized formative publications of the AEA, "in their insistence on observation, they show the influence of the German Historical school" (Ely, 1936, p. 149). He added that a "warm humanitarianism" imparted by their continental teachers led them to be concerned with labor problems and poverty. These conditions were part of the evolution of the fundamental institutions of economic life, but this did not mean they could not be ameliorated (Ely, n.d.b, p. 211).

The second development paralleled another debate associated with the younger school. The *Methodenstreit* between Schmoller and Menger was reprised in the United States between representatives of the orthodox school and the emerging new school. It included, on the side of classical economics, Simon Newcomb, who was critical of the alleged socialist tendencies of the new school; A.T. Hadley, in favor of a specialized study of economics separate from normative (i.e. what ought to be, that is, social change) considerations; and F.W. Taussig, who railed against excessive state intervention. Arguing the views of the "new economics" were Seligman, who underlined the relativity of economic theory; E.J. James, in favor of state interventionism; H.C. Adams on the inseparability of ethics and economics; and Richmond Mayo-Smith on the advantages of the historical method.

This new approach to economics (i.e. what later became known as institutional economics) was a direct legacy of the GHSE. The founding of the AEA and the continuing battle over method were the most obvious signs of influence. Offering us insight into the genealogy of translation, Ely observed,

> Institutional economics began in this country in 1885. Read the 'Statement of Principles' by the founders of the American Economic Association as given in Volume I of our publications. I do not know where you will find a better statement of those principles which characterize institutional economics.
>
> (Ely, 1931)

Beyond the methodological innovations of the GHSE, Ely argued that the most influential ideas they forwarded were those of evolution and relativism (Ely, n.d.b, p. 212). This position is consistent with the younger school. Schmoller wrote in 1900 that the GHSE's distinct contributions were the recognition of the process of evolution, an ethical-psychological view of human behavior, and a *critical attitude to both extreme individualism as well as socialism* (socialism being characterized by the desire for an egalitarian society, shared ownership of the means of production, cooperation between people, and social solidarity) (Abraham and Weingast, 1942; Ely, 1885, 1886c; Salley, 1993/1994). To that we might add the pedagogical pragmatism they manifested. In time, these axiological, ontological, epistemological, methodological, and sometimes deeply political values would find expression in the early development of marketing thought.

Despite the fact that the influence of the GHSE appears to have been strongest in America, there were more modest connections to other countries. During the mid-to-late nineteenth century, there were already challenges within England to the social ideals, methodology, and claims of universality articulated by classical economics. Richard Jones (1790–1855) criticized Ricardo's deductive method and urged the uptake of inductive, historical research (Koot, 1980). T.E. Cliffe Leslie (1825–1882) and John Kells Ingram (1823–1907) were advocates of an inductive, historical approach as well. These economists and a handful of others are sometimes positioned beneath the umbrella of the English School of Historical Economics (Bolton, 1976; Koot, 1980; Tribe, 2002). While not all drew their paradigmatic inspiration from studying in Germany, one exception to this point was William James Ashley – a figure of importance for the development of marketing education in the United Kingdom.

As a student at Oxford University, Ashley was influenced by Arnold Toynbee.

> [Toynbee's] short and meteoric career at Oxford played a significant role in making that university and its extension movement into the most important breeding ground for an historical approach to economics in England. . . . Inspired by Toynbee and guided by the scholarship of the German Historical School, Ashley was the most promising figure among English historical economists. . . . Perhaps only Ashley was fully in sympathy with the German historicist aim of laying a foundation for a new and historical economic theory to be derived inductively from patient historical research.
>
> (Koot, 1980, pp. 186, 188, 202)

We study Ashley for two reasons. His contributions in terms of institution building and pedagogic practice have not been appreciated to the extent they deserve. Secondly, they expand the focus of this study beyond the American-centric nature of the marketing thought literature – an expansion that is highly desirable. He occupied a position of seminal historical importance due to his role as the founder of university business education in Britain. As the Dean of the Faculty of Commerce at the University of Birmingham, Ashley's contributions to marketing are a central element of our story.

Conclusion

During the nineteenth century, the GHSE was motivated in large part as a reaction to orthodox economics, which, the Germans believed, was not relevant to their economic context. It failed to offer solutions to the problems caused by rapid industrialization, social dislocation, and rising inequality that were exacerbated by the economy and legal system (e.g. laws regarding private property). As a result, the GHSE developed an approach that was macro and interdisciplinary in focus. It drew inspiration from a variety of social science disciplines and the humanities in order to provide workable solutions based on historical and contemporary empirical evidence to guide policy-makers. This move firmly embedded economics within the domain of ethics. It was not a value-neutral science; it was normatively oriented. It wanted to change the world, not just describe it. Perhaps given the vaguely Marxist flavor of this type of sentiment, it is no wonder they were sometimes called socialist in orientation.

Depending on which element of the German Historical School was the focus of attention – the older or younger – their ideas were, in varying degrees, historically minded, empirically grounded, (largely) inductively constructed, epistemologically relativistic, and socially activist. It was primarily among the younger school that we see these characteristics most explicitly displayed. Their academic productivity was combined with a commitment to solving then-current economic problems that were foregrounded by their ethical and moral axiology. At the same time, German universities earned a reputation as the best in the world. This led to a large migration of US students to study at the feet of some of the finest scholars working in the field of economics. That included a significant number of individuals who became prominent in American economics during the late nineteenth and early twentieth centuries.

Some of these neophytes became pioneers in the early development of marketing as an academic discipline. Some trained other economists, who, although they did not study directly under the GHSE, were indirectly shaped by this approach to intellectual labor and political activism, and they too, eventually, were well recognized for their contributions to marketing pedagogy and the emerging literature base.

Marketing was – in effect – a subfield of economics that sought to take the logic of the GHSE to its endpoint. Pioneers in our discipline wanted to study the marketplace and the progress of goods through its networks and supply chains in considerable detail. They sought to rework economic theory by reconnecting it to the empirical realism of day-to-day marketing activities. Marketing, in a succinct summation, became even more empirically oriented than German Historical economics, with some members of our community loading themselves on to trucks that ferried goods to the marketplace to study how products were moved, where costs were added, and where inefficiency crept into the process. This is about as far removed from the abstractions of demand and supply diagrams that pepper economics textbooks as can be imagined. The chapters that follow will trace this intellectual history, outlining and explaining the importance of their contributions.

Note

1 David Kinley (1949, p. 141), one of Richard Ely's former Ph.D. students, and later President of the University of Illinois, articulated a reasonably similar position to that found here. Kinley's work is nuanced and developed throughout his academic life. Out of the figures we explore in this book, his work is informed by an extensive knowledge of the German literature, but continues to demonstrate traces of orthodox economics (e.g. references to equilibrium, the price mechanism, arguments that merge Adam Smith and institutional perspectives) (see Kinley, 1949, p. 142). For Kinley, individualism was a force for good in some situations; but the incentive structures that fostered it needed careful formulation, monitoring, and control by government. He was not averse to government control, indeed viewed it as necessary given the complexity of the economy, but he did underline that limits to government power were highly desirable. This partly reflects his antipathy to "planned economies" (i.e. Communism) and his awareness that politicians might not necessarily be the most intelligent, skilled guides to economic activity (e.g. Kinley, 1949, pp. 142–144).

3 Foundations of marketing thought at the University of Wisconsin

Introduction

One of the centers of influence on the development of marketing thought was the University of Wisconsin. As Bartels explained,

> Wisconsin, at the turn of the century, was the residence of such economists as W.A. Scott, J.R. Commons, R.T. Ely, and H.C. Taylor, to whom were attracted such pioneer students of marketing as Jones, Hagerty, Hibbard, Macklin, Nystrom, Butler, Converse, Comish, and Vaughan. Among the contributions to marketing thought made at Wisconsin were the conception of the field of 'marketing' and the offering of the first course in co-operative marketing of agricultural products. The contributions and influence of men who went out from that school to teach and write throughout the country were immeasurable.
>
> (1962, p. 35)

This chapter traces the origins of teaching and research in marketing at Wisconsin. They began in the School of Economics and included the Course in Commerce and the Department of Agriculture, both of which evolved from the former. The nature of this development was largely driven by Richard Ely, who was the first director of the School of Economics as well as a vocal and enduring disciple of the German Historical School. Under his influence the study and teaching of marketing developed as an applied branch of economic science shaped by the GHSE. This point, of course, develops the line of thought unpacked in the last chapter. Classical economics was highly abstract and deductive. The GHSE were more empirical and inductively oriented. However, where the GHSE really differed from the orthodox school was in terms of their axiology. This accentuated political and activist engagement to stimulate social change. Their epistemological and methodological positions assisted in the realization of progressive improvements in the welfare of all members of society. And marketing, we submit, was another mechanism whose utility came from its ability to assist in the greater operationalization of the axiological, epistemological, methodological, and political vision of the GHSE.

Over the course of the early twentieth century, the ideas and politics of the central figures associated with the GHSE, its inflexion in economics, and subsequently in marketing, would move through various stages (Herzberg, 2001). All of them underwent their own specific shifts in thinking. Some moved from greater levels of militancy and activism (Khurana, 2007) to more "conservative" positions. Ely was an exemplar in this case (discussed below). Others were always relatively mainstream in their political positions (Rutherford, 2006). H.C. Taylor, for example, does not seem to have associated with more radical causes (Gilbert and Baker, 1997). He was not a prolific reader of alternative scholarship, nor engaged in the extended study of alternative political regimes characteristic of Ely. Rather, he envisioned his life as working in "professionalized public service" (Gilbert and Baker, 1997, p. 294). Expressed slightly differently, Taylor had witnessed the hardships of life on the farm and had insight into the difficulties this community faced. He wanted to assist them via his research, training of doctoral students, and the elevation of agricultural and farm marketing to a distinct research area with its own books (including his own) and department at Wisconsin (Department of Agricultural Economics). This was not the end of his endeavors; Taylor enacted his commitment to linking theory and practice in government, undertaking extensive public service.

These "scholar-activists" (Gilbert and Baker, 1997) enrobed themselves in convenient labels like "conservative" as a way of underlining that they did not want to see the radical overthrow of society akin to some anarchist and communist movements (Ely, 1886c). It did not mean they were committed to the status quo. They did not want society and the organization of the market to remain static, unchanging, and serving the interests of some groups over others. Certainly, their views were "progressivist" in tenor. They wanted to use their scientific expertise to help inform policy-making and maximize distributive justice. This meant fostering a system of business practice that helped all participants achieve their aims – as much as was feasible – whether they were farmers (a focus at Wisconsin); working in industrial and retailing contexts (a special interest of those at Harvard); or the ultimate consumer seeking value for money (Wisconsin and Harvard dealt with these issues). Such a progressivist project has much to commend it. It was highly ambitious. Ambitions can sometimes be realized. Seldom do all aspects of our plans come to pass, however.

To justify the place of marketing in the curriculum and enable the successful delivery of the programs that this first generation of teachers were called upon to deliver or which they promised to senior colleagues, they had no choice really – initially for partly pragmatic reasons (i.e. to produce resources like teaching materials) – but to get heavily involved with field research. Naturally, their training by the GHSE or by second-generation advocates predisposed them to this empirical approach. But, it is undeniable that they had to study the market if they were to have something important, relevant, and timely to say to their students. What should be fundamentally appreciated is that the academic study of marketing was an even more applied discipline than the economics of the GHSE.

Bearing all the above in mind, this chapter will outline the distinctive character of economics at Wisconsin which Ely had established by 1900. The focus then shifts to some of his students – Samuel Sparling, Edward David Jones, Henry Charles Taylor, James Hagerty, M.B. Hammond, Benjamin Rastall, and Paul Nystrom – all of whom took up careers specializing in marketing, some at Wisconsin, some moving on to other universities. The impact of the GHSE is demonstrated through their intellectual genealogy and via the acknowledgements by Ely's students about how and why they approached the study of marketing.

What contemporary readers might want to notice – and heed very closely – is how far removed these pioneers' ideas are from some of the rhetoric that continues to underwrite marketing theory today. The arguments we present firmly undermine the unconvincing rhetoric that we see associated with the marketing concept or relationship marketing (i.e. about "win-win" relationships and equal power relations). In the context of the time, the power of corporations was starting to become seriously disconcerting and this led socially minded academics and teachers to challenge these shifts in power, using their empirical reflections to rethink extant theory and ideology (e.g. laissez-faire). Some mainstream academics in the present day prefer the production of rhetoric to the intellectually aware, empirically realistic, and politically activist stance our ancestors demonstrated. This calls into question the progressive narratives that are repeated *ad nauseam* in our discipline (Hollander, 1986). Our acuity to inequality and unequal power relations might even have devolved. Corporations are more powerful today, yet myopic scholars still invoke concepts and assumptions that new students can explode with brief subjective personal introspection.

The conditions of possibility for Richard T. Ely at Wisconsin

In 1892 Ely moved to an institution whose axiological foundations – as cultivated by John Bascom, the fifth President of Wisconsin (from 1874–1887) – were commensurate with his own. Bascom, like many in the mid to late nineteenth century, was increasingly concerned about the changing nature of American society. Materialism, greed, and the pursuit of financial wealth were undermining traditional, Christian values, he believed (Hoeveler, 1976).

Bascom, indeed, was a man ahead of his time. He rapidly adopted the views of Darwin, subscribing to evolution with a twist. Applying the theory of evolution to society led him to theorize that the latter could be progressively improved. The nature of humankind had not been perfected. But, with effort – that is, educational and moral uplift, combined with economic growth – the trajectory of society could be dramatically elevated. In articulating this position, we see his subscription to the Social Gospel – a religious perspective that would impact upon Richard Ely and John Commons respectively – which held that it was the responsibility of educators (among others) to help create the Kingdom of Heaven on Earth (or as close as we could get to it). Economics – in concert with other disciplines – was fundamental in achieving the social change objectives that underwrote Bascom's vision for "the modern university" (Hoeveler, 1976).

Unusually, Bascom was a firm critic of laissez-faire; he was supportive of the labor movement; argued for women's rights and suffrage; and was attuned to the unequal nature of the marketplace and business system, directing his ire at John D. Rockefeller, among others. As Hoeveler (1976, p. 291) summarizes Bascom's position (which positively resonates with the later ideas of Ely, Commons, and related GHSE thinkers):

> He spoke for labor organizations because they too were vehicles of power that could redress the unfair balance in an age of industrial corporations. The greatest danger to any society was precisely this imbalance, and the consequent spiritual and physical deprivation by oppression of great numbers of the population.

For Hoeveler (1976), Bascom can be credited with helping generate the kernels of what became the Wisconsin Idea – the notion that the university should work in conjunction with government. The role of the state consequently loomed large in his mind (it would grow to assume an even more substantial role – i.e. in terms of balancing capital–labor interests – in the work of the institutional economists). Here Bascom was keying into a discourse that was disseminated widely in the late nineteenth and early twentieth centuries, namely "service".

This concept has a complex genealogy – often being linked to various religious perspectives, particularly Christianity – and was frequently called upon in the business literature of the period. For some commentators, when it was used by practitioners – and it was a refrain often heard at the Harvard Business School (HBS) in the 1920s – they doubted the sincerity underwriting its use. As a concept, though, service is internally differentiated. It did not mean the same thing to all people. Most clearly at Wisconsin (it was picked up by university Presidents Bascom and Van Hise, for example), it was linked very firmly to social and government service. By contrast, at the HBS, as we will see later, the agenda was far more managerial and focused upon economic expansion.

To preempt our later arguments, this agenda – especially as conveyed by Arch Shaw – was underwritten by the (far too) optimistic assumptions most commonly associated with orthodox economics, seeing psychological egotism as generating positive social outcomes (Crane and Desmond, 2002). Shaw, in effect, reversed the logic found at Wisconsin. Government existed to serve business, which would subsequently benefit society (cf. Kinley, 1949, p. 144). And his preference was for minimal intervention beyond the provision of market intelligence (e.g. census studies and large-scale research individual firms could not conduct). By contrast, the GHSE influenced academics at Wisconsin (e.g. John Commons) and elsewhere conceptualized the marketplace as unequal. Those involved in exchanges were presented as having differing abilities to successfully negotiate the market, with exchanges structured by power relations that did not always benefit all participants equally (Rutherford, 1994). This is not to say that these scholars were not optimistic about the future of society or the potential benefits of growth. Ely was quick to stress that he had faith that the social world could be managed to help people live better – but certainly not perfect – lives. Hardships of various kinds would not disappear, irrespective of the rhetoric of radical groups. In other words, the GHSE were aware that growth, high levels of competition, corporate consolidation, attempts to secure quasi-monopoly power, and the proliferation of products and services were accompanied with costs of their own; costs that were transferred to or imposed upon the ultimate consumer and other stakeholders.

Bascom used terminology that sounds far more status quo oriented to contemporary ears than it should. He talked about academics and students alike becoming "servants of the State" (Hoeveler, 1976, p. 294). They were not uncritical observers of government activities; nor were they mere functionaries intended to help research and implement policies determined by politicians distant from their constituents. In line with progressivism, staff and students alike were expected and encouraged to help serve the state, enabling it to improve the life chances and circumstances experienced by the citizenry. In effect, Bascom articulates a philosophy of the state, a politics of academic practice that those who studied in Germany, like Ely, would find consistent with their axiology, ontology, epistemology, and political leanings.

For Bascom, the university should study the business system. It must identify problems and their causes, determining paths for social change that would prevent powerful groups (e.g. corporations) from pursuing profit without concern for the "public interest". Ensuring that social welfare was prioritized over private gain was the nub of the contribution that the university could make in support of what became known as the Wisconsin Idea.

One of Bascom's students, Robert M. LaFollette, became the governor of Wisconsin during this period and personified the progressive movement (i.e. using science to enhance government decision-making and social welfare). Under LaFollette, the state government prioritized social efficiency through rational administration based on expert decision-making. This provided the opportunity for the university to supply that expertise. Courtesy of its extensive program of social and political reform, Wisconsin came to be described as "a laboratory for wise experimental legislation aiming to secure the social and political betterment of the people as a whole" (Roosevelt, 1912, p. vii). Ely, later described as a "barometer of Wisconsin Progressivism" (Rader, 1966), was a perfect choice for directing the newly created School of Economics.

Ely arrives at Wisconsin

In 1891, the administration of the University considered a proposal to establish a chair in "commercial science" much like that in existence at the Wharton School. However, during the following year the proposal was broadened, resulting in the formation of a School of Economics, Political Science, and History under the direction of Ely (see Figure 3.1). The two individuals most responsible for bringing him to the university in 1892 were the President, T.C. Chamberlin, and professor of history, Frederick J. Turner. Chamberlin had hired Turner in 1888 from Johns Hopkins, where he had been a student of Ely's. Both Turner and Chamberlin

Figure 3.1 Richard T. Ely, ca. 1910

Source: University of Wisconsin–Madison Archives, image#S04055, with permission.

wanted to build up advanced work in the social sciences and they believed that Ely was the person for that task.

During eleven years at Johns Hopkins, Ely had established a reputation as one of America's preeminent reform-minded economists. These were probably the most productive years of his career (Rader, 1966). He published many journal articles and seven monographs, served on the Baltimore and Maryland tax commissions, and was instrumental in founding the American Economic Association (AEA). Many of his students became leading economists, historians, sociologists, and politicians. They included John Commons, Frederic Howe, and Woodrow Wilson. The two dominant themes in Ely's work during that time were the "New Economics" and class warfare, especially how the latter could be defused through various mechanisms, including individual education, unionization, and government action (Rader, 1966, Chapters 2, 3).

Ely became the leading spokesman for a new approach to the study of economics and this was evident when the AEA was formed. He led the attack on orthodox doctrine, ideology, and methodology. He criticized the rigidity and determinism of classical economics, its oversimplified notion of economic man, and its thesis of "natural laws", including the idea of laissez-faire (Ely, 1886a). This was endowed with an almost religious status, which advocates supported largely irrespective of the inequities and harm it caused (Ely, 1884b, pp. 10–12).

Letting the market do its work unimpeded by government or other forms of intervention was deemed by subscribers to the orthodoxy to result in less harm than active modification to the economic system. Ely's perspective, on the other hand, was underwritten by his religious, ethical, and theoretical commitments (Ely, 1886b). It was characterized by a substantial degree of hope – that things could be different, that they could be better for all members of society, and that we must be willing to scrutinize our assumptions and ways of life. We must never, he submitted, assume there was nothing to learn from the past or that the future was path dependent. He made this apparent in his studies of socialism, for example. Ely and the marketing students associated with him would later be described as trying to envisage an economics that worked the "middle" ground (Ely, 1902), treading a "middle way" (Coats, 1985) "between state socialism and laissez faire capitalism" (Gilbert and Baker, 1997, p. 281). They were very cautious about uncritically heralding efficiency and the growth of corporations. This is one of the areas where their views contrast markedly with those articulated at Harvard.

David Kinley (1914), one of Ely's students, expressed the commitments being inculcated at Wisconsin especially well in one of his later publications. The economic system had grown increasingly complicated. Monopoly and concentrations of economic power were becoming normalized (Ely, 1910b) – issues that John Commons explored in considerable detail. The legal system was finding it difficult to adequately control the expanding corporate universe and financial capitalism (Ely, 1902). The man on the street, the individual who lived from paycheck to paycheck, was subject to "economic coercion" by groups with far more power than they could marshal or easily resist (Ely, 1902). The state, GHSE pioneers believed, had to operate at least partially as a countervailing power alongside unions and related groups.

Questions about economic efficiency in the hands of people like Ely and Kinley had a much darker side than was later articulated by Frederick Taylor (1911/1998). Large companies with huge capitalizations were not sublimely efficient organisms operating for the welfare of society.[1] With far reaching decision-making responsibility and little oversight, corporate management and executives were effectively being placed in an unenviable position (Kinley, 1906). It invited temptation. But, and this is important to note, this was not an anti-capitalist argument nor a diatribe against bigness and efficiency per se. Rather, GHSE-minded thinkers like Ely, Commons, Kinley, and so forth wanted to foster critical reflection about the current organization of society. Business had provided benefits such as lower priced products that brought satisfaction and improved quality of life. Still, it must not be assumed that efficiency always resulted in social welfare. Economists and marketing scholars alike had to be alert to the changing nature of the economic system and be willing to question who was benefitting and whether legislation might be needed to equalize the benefits in a more pro-social fashion.

Marketplace complexity, combined with their desire to investigate the economic landscape, led Ely and colleagues to read widely, drawing from any sources that promised to offer inspiration. There was no literature that he discounted a priori. If sources were useful, they informed Ely's scholarship. If they were not, criticism would be forthcoming. This intellectual openness can be termed "social objectivity" (Gilbert and Baker, 1997). Objectivity in this vein is effectively a commitment to "even-handedness" (Morgan and Rutherford, 1998), that is, a willingness to treat each source with respect, scrutinizing it, and accepting, rejecting, or revising the arguments being presented. In other words, being "non-partisan" was encouraged within the *Verein* (Salley, 1993/1994) and the AEA (Coats, 1985). This did not obviate the interest in working class causes and alternative methods of production, distribution, and exchange.

At Wisconsin, his focus on economics and ethics was consistent with the orientation the university had taken under the leadership of Charles R. Van Hise, who became President just after Ely arrived. Van Hise conceptualized education, scholarship, and service to government as a means of helping foster economic growth and informing community decision-making so that his institution could maximize its impact upon the state.

Education was meant to help people make decisions that would better enable them to negotiate an increasingly unequal marketplace. It was a stimulus to question the status quo, not simply accept, reaffirm, or support vested interests. An extended quote will help us fully comprehend the vision that shaped what they wanted to accomplish at Wisconsin. Van Hise understood the mission of the university in the following way.

> Religious concerns were not prominent in his thought, but emphasis on the moral and social responsibilities of the scholar to the public interest loomed very large. . . . Van Hise's version of the Wisconsin Idea was the most materialistic . . . transforming into a doctrine of economic growth. This dogma then defined the state university's research activity, for new knowledge must be applied directly to the improvement of the lives of the people. The *service ideal* meant especially the invigoration of extension – the new "missionary" work of the university . . . so that virtually every home or business in the state, from machine shops to model dairy farms, would feel the long outreach of the state university.
>
> (Hoeveler, 1976, p. 298; emphasis added)

As a major exponent of the GHSE and a visible member of the university, Ely proclaimed enthusiastically that the seeds initially planted in German soil were starting to productively germinate with great potential for economics and – later – marketing: "the younger men in America are clearly abandoning the dry bones of orthodox English political economy for the live methods of the German school" (Ely, 1884b, p. 64). Those "live methods" included the use of experience, observation, descriptive statistics, and comparison.

Economics was viewed as a social science dealing with constantly changing social phenomena. The social view took precedence over individualism and self-interest (Ely, 1884b, pp. 43–48). Consistent with this approach, Ely declared that the purpose of studying economics was "to train people to an intelligent understanding of economic phenomena, so that they may be able to solve concrete problems as they arise" (Ely, 1884b, p. 49). In short, economic science could provide the basis for reform. This is why Ely and his students have been labeled "activist-intellectuals" (Gilbert and Baker, 1997, p. 281). Their work formatted the outlooks of their students, peers, and influential members of government and impacted upon seminal legislative events like the New Deal. Ely's work as well as that of many of his graduates, especially H.C. Taylor, was praised for having made notable contributions to the national economic, industrial, and agricultural planning undertaken in the 1930s.

Back to classical economics and beyond

But let us not get ahead of ourselves too much. Ely envisioned the new school at Wisconsin as the West Point of the civil service (Ely, 1938, p. 181). The educational offerings being provided had to help graduates earn a living. To facilitate this, he encouraged his students to "look and see", citing his continental education for his appreciation that book knowledge and practical experience must be combined (Ely, 1938, p. 187). He liked to quote John Commons on the purpose of this "look and see" method. As Commons was fond of repeating, "academic teaching . . . is merely brains without experience. . . . [T]he practical extreme is experience without brains. . . . [O]ne is half-baked philosophy, the other is rule of thumb" (Ely, 1938, p. 186). What all of this basically means is that Ely and his colleagues felt that theory and practice had to be united in forming well-rounded economics and business graduates (Ely, n.d.c). In explaining the relationship between knowledge and action, he wrote, "this is a world full of work to be done and knowledge should bear its fruit in better citizenship. This was the principle which determined the development of the economics department at Wisconsin" (Ely, n.d.c, p. 187).

One way of achieving this pedagogical aim was by using the seminar method of teaching. In fact, the economic seminar, described in the university catalog as an exemplary feature of the school, was "designed to embrace discussions of periodical literature, recent works and original papers" (University of Wisconsin Catalog, 1892/93, p. 145). Turner had used the seminar method, after having experienced it while a student at Johns Hopkins. Ely traced his own knowledge and engagement with this method to the University of Halle, where it was widely employed. By using the seminar as a laboratory in which primary materials (e.g. government documents) were examined and discussed, students experienced aspects of empirical realism in the classroom.

John Commons (1964) adopted a related strategy by inviting various civil servants, union officials, and other practitioners including capitalists, communists, and anarchists, to speak to his charges. This both anticipated and reaffirmed the benefits of field trips, that is, it brought them closer to the real-world situations they were exploring, would experience as practitioners, or have involvement with as future law-makers. In this case, as with the use of seminars, pedagogical pragmatism and social objectivity were being followed. As one of Ely's pupils described it, "Ely stated problems and then taught students how to wrestle with them by gathering facts related to the problem" (Taylor, 1960, p. 28). The broad parallels between the seminar and later use of the case method in business teaching should be obvious, albeit the interest groups who were to be provided with solutions to their problems differed. There was less pluralism in business cases at Harvard.

When it came to graduate research, Ely felt that the most appropriate topics were historical and descriptive in emphasis (Ely, 1891). This focus was a function of his GHSE training. But his approach to academic labor at this point was influenced by factors outside of his own intellectual interests. They were affected by the political climate in which he was operating. In 1894, for instance, Ely was subject to a trial for "economic heresy" at Wisconsin.

Ely's trial: economic heresy

The late nineteenth century was a period of turmoil. Radical groups were making headlines through their calls to overthrow the status quo; strike action had, in some cases, grown violent; economic turbulence was responsible for uncertainty and hardship; and the gap between the very wealthy and the extremely poor was becoming all too vivid. In this context, academics taking unorthodox positions, that is, those that were perceived to align themselves with working class groups, labor activism, union activities, or alternative economic perspectives, were ready targets for opportunistic critics. It may be hard to appreciate it in the present day, but economics at the time was perceived in dramatically different terms. It was a hotbed of radicalism, leading students to look at the status quo in terms that their parents and elders found disconcerting. As Goodwin (1998, p. 55) underscores, the emerging cadre of economists who had returned from Germany with new, novel, and creative solutions to the social problems confronting the US

> were vocal, iconoclastic, and publicity seeking. Inevitably they came to be seen by many college and university authorities as troublemakers, disrespectful of the status quo and of traditional social, political, and economic values. Persecution of radical economists came to characterize the era.

Richard Ely already had experience of the intolerant nature of the political climate when colleagues at Johns Hopkins questioned him about whether he subscribed to socialism (Bateman, 1998). His response was perhaps expected. He started to temper overt public statements, presenting his analyses as those of an interested observer seeking to advance the frontiers of knowledge, rather than promote a political ideology. This did not prevent him facing related charges in the mid-1890s. As Ely recalled,

> In 1894 the nation was in the throes of a depression; unemployment and misery reached new heights; radical sentiment was rising. The tide of the workingman's discontent swept about 750,000 employees in the various industries into a series of strikes. . . . I was aware, however, that in some quarters outside

> of the university, I had aroused antagonism. Had I not written on Marxian socialism, a topic as full of dynamite as Darwinian ideas had been twenty years earlier? Had I not conducted and written about labor investigations? Had I not attacked corporate abuses? For these activities, such periodicals as Godkin's *Nation*, which was a citadel in all matters affecting property and labor, branded me as a radical and dangerous man.
>
> (Ely, 1938, pp. 218–219)

Ely, as a prominent figure, came to the attention of the Superintendent of Public Instruction in Wisconsin, who alleged that he was a conduit for "utopian, impractical, or pernicious doctrines" (in Rolnick, 1955, p. 200). Ely was publicly criticized for associating with radical individuals and for allegedly making threats against a non-unionized local printing shop. His accuser, Oliver Wells (in Ely, 1938, p. 220), presented him as Janus.

> Professor Ely, director of the School of Economics, differs from Ely, the socialist, only in the adroit and covert method of his advocacy. A careful reading of his books will discover essentially the same principles, but masked by glittering generalities and mystical and metaphysical statements.

In short, Ely was subject to scrutiny for teaching values inconsistent with the economic and social mores of the United States. His German training was subject to denunciation in the national presses as a source of un-American "doctrines" (Schlabach, 1963–1964), that is, he articulated "anti-laissez-faire" perspectives. Even so, the timing of this trial was unfortunate. Ely was weighed down by a personal crisis. He had just lost a child and his wife was undergoing a bout of ill health. What this trial does underline, however, is a connection that Bartels and other writers have failed to register (e.g. Jones and Monieson, 1990). Bartels (1962) did not connect Ely with another early contributor to marketing, David Kinley, in his genealogical chart of "personal influence in the development of marketing thought". This is a major error. Ely was a precondition for the emergence of marketing scholarship and education. Let us explain.

Counterfactually oriented historians might wonder what would have happened if Ely's career had halted prior to his extensive and prolonged supervision of the important figures that Bartels highlighted. In some respects, historical contingency nearly headed in that direction. Ely was under serious pressure in his "trial": "I felt that my career which had just fairly begun at Wisconsin was being threatened. I realized that all my hopes and ambitions to play a significant role in the educational history of the country were in danger of frustration" (Ely, 1938, p. 222). Yet, he was not in a completely fit and well state to defend himself. In this task, he was assisted by David Kinley (among others), a former student of Ely's who had studied under him at Johns Hopkins and Wisconsin (Rutherford, 2006) and was then professor of economics at Illinois. Kinley spoke to the press, maintained a stream of positive letters to Ely, buoying his spirits when they were at a low ebb, something that Schlabach believed he "no doubt needed" (1963–1964, p. 153).

While Ely had indeed been educated in Germany and was well versed in the economic and political literature emerging from this nation, Kinley was abundantly clear that he "could not regard him as a socialist" (Kinley, 1949, p. 31). Interestingly, one of the lines of defense mounted by Kinley and colleagues to the charges that the regents of Wisconsin had to investigate – that of Ely teaching "pernicious" doctrines – was to highlight how quotations taken from context can be used to paint even orthodox – apparently highly desirable – perspectives in a dim light. Recalling this time, Ely writes,

> Some of my friends, especially Professor Turner, Kinley and my brother-in-law, had compiled a series of extracts from the works of Adam Smith and John Stuart Mill which, considered by themselves, conclusively proved that both Smith and Mill must have been radical socialists! Of course, the extracts, in their proper context, had no such significance. The point was that Mr. Wells' evidence that I was a socialist rested largely upon isolated extracts and statements from my lectures and writings. The parallelism at once broke the strength of his charge.
>
> (Ely, 1938, p. 229)

Indeed, in articles written prior to this genealogical point and in the period around the trial, Ely was cautious, but clearly not always careful enough for some, about the way he represented alternative systems of economic management such as socialism. His large exegesis on "Recent American Socialism" (Ely, 1885) was an exemplar of the approach associated with the GHSE. It was historical, relied on a substantial amount of primary source materials, and exhibits considerable nuance in its didactic approach.

Ely seeks to educate his reader, differentiating more moderate streams of thought which seek a peaceful transition to socialism (e.g. the socialistic labor party) from extremely radical and destructive groups (e.g. anarchism) which sought the overthrow of society. He states that he is interested in presenting political-economic ideas, neither advocating nor refuting them. This said, he does adopt a moralistic tone in places, critiquing excessive consumption and waste. One of the problems with the public parading of wealth is that it presses home to those who do not possess sufficient resources the unequal nature of society. This was dangerous. It creates a market for radical ideas and foments the desire for social change.

Ely, in effect, was not the conduit for utopian or radical notions that Wells maintained and for which he was subject to scrutiny. He was a warning bell who tried to articulate the feelings and experiences of the less privileged in society. The existing system was unequal and would reach a tipping point sooner or later if something was not done to ameliorate its excesses. On occasion, his remonstrations must have irritated. This was potentially dangerous given the numbers of "industrial capitalists" sitting on university boards (Bateman, 2005) who were not averse to removing faculty whose views diverged from their own.

> While it is extremely unpleasant to be called an alarmist, it is foolish to underrate the possible disasters in store for us; and it is precisely what people have, from time immemorial, been wont to do. Again and again have leaders of social forces behaved with the wisdom of the ostrich, which buries its head in the sand and believes there is no danger, because it can see none. The Philistine – and the greater majority of the ruling middle class are Philistines – loves the dangerous narcotic.
>
> (Ely, 1885, p. 60)

Equally, though, he submitted that revolutionary ideas will face "inevitable defeat" whilst still possibly causing considerable harm for class relations. This harm, in turn, will halt economic growth and development, which will benefit no one. It is this tempered approach which was characteristic of his self-described "progressively conservative" axiology (Schlabach, 1963–1964). A progressive conservatism was not a dogmatic "creed", more an embodiment of his evolutionary and relatively optimistic conception of society. In a paper written in the aftermath of his academic trial, he outlines his theory of society which chimed with the views of the GHSE and Bascom alike.

> No sane man can claim that in our social arrangements we have yet reached perfection. . . . There is no royal road to a happy condition of society, but the road is long, arduous, and often painful. There is no possibility of escape from toil and suffering. Mitigation and gradual improvement are the utmost we can hope for, and it is the duty of all those who have the ear of the masses to tell them this plain truth even if it is not altogether palatable. At the same time there is enough which can be accomplished, to stimulate all to put forward their best efforts, and to give encouragement in the midst of the weary struggle for better social conditions.
>
> (Ely, 1894, pp. 182–183)

Depending on who is consulted, Ely's trial had varying effects. He made his position clear to avoid misinterpretation: "I am a conservative rather than a radical" (Ely, 1894, p. 183). This conservative stance entailed saving what was best about society and the economic system and removing what was dysfunctional. He was looking for the middle ground. In staking his intellectual territory, he expressed his support for a biblically inspired version of "social solidarity". In doing so, he comes close to the ideas of the socialistic labor party, albeit now the citations to the vast range of socialist literature that he had at his fingertips in the 1880s were absent. In their place, Ely's writing speaks to solidarity and cooperation between classes (a perspective that links his work with that of Frederick Taylor and may possibly be a reason why Ely was interested in the engineer's work).

> As society becomes real and vital, and means more and more to us all, it becomes apparent that no one class exists for itself, and that no one class can exist apart from all other classes. While there is such a thing as vicious legislation in behalf of a few favored individuals, whatever promotes the interests of any one of the great and numerous classes in society, either in matters physical, mental, moral, or spiritual, advances the interests of every other class.
>
> (Ely, 1902, p. 78)

He continues,

> The true ideal . . . may be termed the principle of social solidarity. According to this principle, the great institutions of society must be conserved, but developed in the interests of liberty. . . . There must be a carefully elaborated, and wisely executed regulation of economic relations.
>
> (Ely, 1902, p. 77; see also Kinley, 1949, p. 141)

Although presented as a "progressive conservative", he continued to argue that scholars had to help deal with the social problems which faced society (Ely, 1910b). The resources of the United States were plentiful and could be better utilized; economic concentration deserved critical examination, as did the "injustices" which accompanied it (Ross, 1977–1978); and the wastes of the distribution system could be reduced, with access to products and services improved according to "one's notions of justice" (Ely, 1885, p. 51). Distributive and economic justice were ongoing themes in his writing.

But Goodwin (1998, p. 55) is not accurate in claiming that people like Ely emerged "largely unscathed" from the academic trials of the period. Numerous scholars lost their jobs or had to find employment outside of academia or modify their positions to evade ongoing criticism. Ely makes the effects on his psyche perfectly apparent. The outcome of the trial did shake him for at least six years (Rolnick, 1955, p. 203). Extending this point, Dorothy Ross (1977–1978, p. 52) indicates that in this period Ely's "views grew more conservative". Rutherford (2006, pp. 163, 165) makes related arguments. Like many other actors in politically turbulent times, he looked for shelter in less controversial areas (Bateman, 2005; Herzberg, 2001).

One such avenue involved paying close attention to the workings of the market, where he advocated the "look and see" method. As he put it, "We are surrounded by the most wonderful economic phenomena and are blind to them" (Ely, 1910b, p. 439). Taking a close look at the market, questioning existing economic theory (Ely, 1902), and with the refutation of Say's law in the back of his mind, progressives like Ely were interested in the "workings of the market where it could be made to work equitably and efficiently" (Ross, 1977–1978, pp. 52–53). The theses he supervised in the immediate aftermath of his trial certainly reflected these more "conservative" predilections (Ross, 1977–1978) and it is at this point that we see him supporting the intellectual labors of some of the most influential contributors to our discipline.

Turning to marketing topics in this way can be understood as a politically safe strategy. Historically oriented theses that studied highly specific markets were effectively describing the status quo. This can, of course, be a political move. Yet, in equal measure, it does not look immediately threatening to the institutional gatekeepers of the time. Even the titles of the dissertations that Ely supervised sound relatively innocuous. Consider, for example, A.G. Fradenburgh's (1894) "The Petroleum Industry in the United States", Charles Bullock's (1895) "A Financial History of the United States 1775–1789", B.H. Meyer's (1897) "History of Railway Legislation in Wisconsin", H.C. Taylor's (1902) "The Decline of Landowning Farmers in England", B.H. Hibbard's (1902) "The History of Agriculture in Dane County, Wisconsin", B.M. Rastall's (1906) "The Labor History of the Cripple Creek District", Paul H. Nystrom's (1914) "Retail Distribution of Goods" (later published as *The Economics of Retailing*), and Theodore Macklin's (1917) "A History of the Organization of Creameries and Cheese Factories in the U.S.". Note that Bullock, Meyer, Taylor, and Hibbard all studied in Germany (see Figure 2.1a in Chapter 2) and Taylor, Hibbard, Nystrom, and Macklin were featured in Bartels' genealogy of marketing (Figure 1.1 in Chapter 1).

Ely's graduate courses almost always included readings from the major works of Roscher, Knies, Schmoller, and Wagner. A typical exam taken by those enrolled in his course on the "Distribution of Wealth" in 1899 included questions on "Wagner's views about the distribution of wealth and the socioeconomic order as compared with the Classical English economists", the "ethical laws of ownership", and the "modification of distribution by self-conscious social efforts" (Ely, 1899). For that module, Ely maintained a book that listed suitable topics for student papers. These included "The Economic Effects of Changes in Fashion", "Advertising Considered from an Economic Standpoint", "Competition in Advertising and Effects of Trademarks", as well as numerous examples of industry analyses. Following his "trial", then, but before the turn of the century, marketing was assuming a significant presence in Ely's teaching and supervision. He was building up cognitive capital in politically safe waters which he could continue to leverage going forward.

By the close of the School's first decade, a number of developments were noteworthy. First, it had grown very quickly. There were 62 graduate students in economics in 1900/01 and 90 the following year. Wisconsin had become a major source of American PhDs in the subject. Since most of the early marketing scholars were trained as economists, that explains, in part, why Wisconsin was a center of influence on our discipline. Secondly, Ely had a tremendous impact on many of these students. And for some of them this was not just book-level immersion. They studied on the continent on his recommendation.

Wisconsin students of the German Historical School

Among the first students in economics at Wisconsin were David Kinley, Edward David Jones, Samuel E. Sparling, James E. Hagerty, M.B. Hammond, Henry Charles Taylor, and Benjamin H. Hibbard (see also Figure 2.1a). They were among the earliest notable contributors to the development of marketing thought (see Figure 1.1). Each spent time studying in Germany, reflecting Ely's habit of encouraging them to do so whenever possible. In this way, a direct link was formed between the GHSE and marketing.

For example, in 1894, Jones, Sparling, and Hammond traveled together to study economics at the Universities of Halle, Berlin, and Tubingen (see Figure 2.1a). Sparling returned from Germany to complete a thesis on public administration in 1896, then taught the subject at Wisconsin until 1909. His (1906) *Introduction to Business Organization* was cited by Bartels as the first book to deal with marketing in general (1962, p. 267). In it, Sparling explained how a science of business could be developed.

> Science is based upon accumulated experience. Classification is the result of a comparison of differences and similarities. . . . We may describe and classify the facts of business in such a way as to indicate their underlying tendencies and principles.
>
> (Sparling, 1906, pp. 3–4)

Epistemological affiliations between the GHSE and what he is writing are obvious. He also conceptualized all business activity as extractive, manufacturing, or distributive. Distribution was subdivided into marketing activities along with those practices which facilitate exchange, such as banking and credit. Marketing, itself, was understood as "those commercial processes which are concerned with the distribution of the raw materials of production and the finished output of the factory. . . . Their function is to give additional value to these commodities through exchange" (Sparling, 1906, p. 17).

Sparling's book contained chapters dealing with the "Evolution of the Market", "Exchanges", "Direct Selling", "Wholesaling and Retailing", "Traveling Salesmanship and the Mail-Order Business", "Advertising", and "Credits and Collections". More importantly for our purposes here, he viewed marketing as part of a science of business that could and should be developed following the inductive, comparative, historical approach of the GHSE.

Hagerty taught the first marketing course at The Ohio State University in 1905 and studied at Wisconsin for a year, then in Germany from 1898 to 1899 (Figure 2.1a). When he became the head of the economics department at Ohio in 1905, one of the first individuals he brought in to teach marketing was M.B. Hammond, who had accompanied Jones and Sparling to the continent (Hagerty, 1936). Hammond completed his Masters' in Economics under Ely at Wisconsin and his PhD at Columbia. Today, he is credited as the first author to use the term "marketing" in a manner consistent with its modern meaning in an 1897 article that appeared in the proceedings of the American Economic Association (Bussiere, 2000). That paper was based on his Master's thesis.

Edward David Jones

Together with Sparling and Hammond, Edward David Jones (Figure 3.2) returned to Wisconsin from Germany in 1894, completing his thesis on "Economic Crises" (Jones, 1894) under Ely's supervision. In Germany, Jones studied under Conrad (University of Halle) and Sering (University of Berlin) (see Figure 2.1a). For six years after his graduation in 1895, he taught economic geography and statistics at Wisconsin and for a while it appeared he might stay long-term. Nonetheless, in 1901 he was offered a full-time position in the Department of Economics at Michigan by Henry C. Adams, head of the department, a friend of Ely's, and once again, a student of the German Historical School. Adams was a strong supporter of developing university instruction in business.

He was interested in having Jones teach a course called "The Physical Basis of Industrial Organization", which subsequently came to be titled "Industrial

Figure 3.2 Edward David Jones, ca. 1906

Source: *History of the University of Michigan* (Hinsdale and Demmon, 1906).

Resources of the United States". Ultimately those plans led to what is widely recognized today as the first university course in marketing (Bartels, 1962). Promoted as "The Distributive and Regulative Industries of the United States", it was outlined in the University of Michigan Catalogue (1901) as

> a description of the various ways of marketing goods, of the classification, grades, brands employed, and of wholesale and retail trade. Attention will also be given to those private organizations not connected with money and banking, which guide and control the industrial process, such as trade associations, boards of trade and chambers of commerce.

In 1903/04 this course was expanded into three others, all taught by Jones and apparently popular, as they were offered in both semesters. "The Distribution of Agricultural Products" focused on the various systems of marketing agricultural items and included an explication of commission selling, cooperation, public and private market contracts, and speculation. "The Wholesale Trade" looked at "the requirements of marketing as they affect the technique of manufacturing . . . the principles governing the determination of price and quality . . . the outlets employed in direct and indirect selling and the methods of stimulating trade" (University of Michigan Catalogue, 1903/04). Finally, "The Retail Trade" covered the following:

> the general position of the retailer followed by an analysis of location, stock-keeping, selling and advertising. Special attention is paid to the principle of departmentizing [*sic*]. Department stores, mail-order stores and special stores are studied.
>
> (University of Michigan Catalogue, 1903/04)

According to Jones, retail practice was confused, often lacking ingenuity and imagination (barring the obvious theatrically minded stores like John Wanamaker's). Drawing from the history of US trade, he registered that since the Civil War there had been a scarcity of goods and that shielded retailers from competition, making it relatively easy to generate profit, resulting in many firms treating customers with indifference (Jones, 1905). "The result has been to cramp the growth of the retail industries as a whole, and render them unsatisfactory to the manufacturers as the distributors of their products" (Jones, 1905, p. 10). According to Jones, dissatisfaction was a stimulus for the rise of nationally branded goods being sold directly to consumers. Rendering the picture even more dynamic, the industrial revolution had dramatically improved the means of transportation and communication, leading to the creation of larger markets and "keen and relentless competition" that demanded higher education in commerce and marketing (Jones, 1904). Education promised to furnish the intelligent neophyte with guidance about the best methods of meeting this new "cutthroat" competition, with the newly minted professoriate and their assistants drawing on the insights offered by industry observers and practitioners who had managed to succeed against all odds. Even so, at the turn of the twentieth century, there were very few suitable textbooks on commercial subjects, so the best sources of published information for pedagogic practice, in Jones's opinion, were trade magazines (Jones, 1903a). There were many available; they repeated the practical wisdom accumulated by retailers, traveling salesmen, and other groups, all wishing to share their trials, tribulations, and warnings with those eager to follow in their footsteps (Friedman, 2004). In that connection, he cited as examples *The American Agriculturalist*, *Northwestern Miller*, *Iron Age*, *Engineering and Mining Journal*, *The Manufacturer's Record*, *The Textile Record*, *The World's Work*, and *The Commercial and Financial Chronicle*. Indeed, most of Jones's published research later appeared in trade magazines such as *Mill Supplies* and *The Engineering Magazine*.

He believed that marketing courses, in connection with administration, finance, and accounting, were an essential part of business education (1913a). To teach these subjects, scientific investigation was first necessary to discover general principles. He made this clear when he wrote that the "chief function of this generation of college men associated with business administration will be recognized to be, not teaching, but scientific investigation" (1913a, p. 190). It should, of course, be expected that his prior training provided a model for research, and Jones employed an inductive logic by gathering historical, statistical data, using this in his descriptive case studies of marketing practice.

In 1903, the Carnegie Institution of Washington undertook the publication of a multi-volume history of the American economy. The project was structured into eleven divisions, one of which was the history of foreign and domestic commerce. Jones felt that it should include a related topic that had been ignored, the "evolution of methods of marketing products – wholesaling, retailing, etc." and was eager to contribute materials on this topic (Jones, 1903b). In 1907, he assumed responsibility for writing a chapter on the "American Domestic Market Since 1840" (Carnegie Institution of Washington, 1907, p. 78). The plan included having students at the university undertake various aspects of the history of the marketing of agricultural products (Jones, 1907). Although that volume was never completed, Jones published a series of 23 articles between 1911 and 1914 which were a trial run for the project. Taken together, they constitute an impressive contribution to marketing thought.

The articles were published in the trade journal *Mill Supplies*, which introduced Jones to its readers as an associate editor. "No person who wishes to keep abreast of the times, improve the conduct of his business and aid in reducing to a minimum the abuses and complexities apparent in the trade should fail to observe the conclusions reached by Professor Jones, who has made the solutions of these problems his life's work" (Crawford, 1911, p. 2). This collection of Jones's thoughts had common threads and was remarkable for the tone in which it was presented, as well as for the principles and concepts of marketing it sketched. What is salient given the background training he experienced is his explicit articulation of social ethics and distributive justice. In the opening piece, entitled "The Larger Aspects of Private Business" (1911a), Jones explained that his purpose was to "examine some marketing problems" and the apparent inefficiency connected with the process.

He pinpointed three separate movements for greater industrial efficiency. The Conservation movement sought to reorganize industries concerned with the production of raw materials. Scientific Management had improved the organization of manufacturing and transportation (and eventually, in turn, impacted upon marketing). Jones labeled a third current the "cost of living movement", which would "reform the distributive system to secure efficiency in the merchandising of products from producer to consumer" (1912d, p. 284). He argued that greater efficiency in marketing could be achieved via the application of Scientific Management principles to industrial purchasing and consumer buying. What this meant in summary was the scientific study of the marketing process, elimination of unnecessary actors and waste, and efficient transportation of products to where they were needed in a timely fashion. Another vehicle for improving efficiency was the organization of industrial and consumer cooperatives and the standardization of products (i.e. reduction in variations to help standardize production, distribution, and selling processes, as well as to help improve consumer decision-making. With respect to this last issue, less thought requires less cognitive energy at the same time as reducing the risk of the misallocation of funds to products inconsistent with the needs of the buyer).

Jones determined that retailing activities added 50 percent or more to the cost of goods, and this was mainly "waste" due to advertising and an overabundance of retail stores (1912f). The ratio of population to stores was decreasing and this seemed, he opined, to be an unnecessary trend. Advertising, he proposed in a manner consistent with the position of Thorstein Veblen, was almost entirely a waste.

> A distributive expense of great importance is the modern advertising campaign. Although I am willing to grant what the modern business man says about the necessity of advertising for his individual business it is true in my opinion that advertising is one of the great blood-suckers of modern industry. Very largely it is a waste of money so far as the customer is concerned, as it is merely a usurpation by the manufacturer of the function of recommending and guaranteeing products which previously the local retailer performed. And in the change there is waste, for the retailer is still necessary and the manufacturer must spend immense sums to gain the attention of the customers.
>
> (Jones, 1910, p. 139)

The overriding concern in this analysis related to distributive justice, which reflected an interconnected set of views that Jones articulated over various publications. To put this into perspective, he felt that the emergence of large retailers had set different classes of merchants, the local jobber-small retailer system and the general jobber-department store system, against each other as representatives of rival systems (1911f, p. 245). This introduced excessive competition, growing advertising expenditure, and sometimes deep price-cutting. The marketplace was consequently riven with conflict, waste, and inefficiency. Articulating these kinds of concerns was, while not entirely idiosyncratic, somewhat unusual when read against his family background. Calling it ironic might even be an understatement, since his father-in-law, Z. L. White, owned a large department store in Columbus, Ohio.

A critical tone thus permeated Jones's assessment of the performance of markets. A market should provide an opportunity for the consumer to purchase a good mixture of reliable merchandise in the required quantity at a fair price. The problem was that he did not believe this happened. The picture Jones painted was more turbulent, less beneficial for those involved with trade or buying, and overall he concluded that the system of distribution was excessively expensive (1912c, p. 121).

Greater efficiency was only part of the solution to distributive injustice. Jones advocated the education of consumers as well as producers in the techniques of marketing. For instance, he proposed that people should study and learn the differences in quality between brands and determine the "appropriate service level" which should be purchased (1912e, p. 408). Farmers, he underlined, were in need of marketing education and the "development of a theory of the choice of crops and products from the market side" (1912d, p. 285). He also advocated the organization of consumer and farm cooperatives (1912c, 1912d, 1912e). This cooperative orientation was a reflection of his focus on general welfare over individual self-interest (1911k) – a perspective consistent with his GHSE education and socialization. Extending this ethical axiology, Jones made a plea for the greater development and use of codes of ethics in business (1911g, 1913a).

What these elements signify when read in conjunction (i.e. Jones's promotion of ethics in business and the wider invocation of the Golden Rule) is that core contributors to our scholarly community have sought to reorient major participants in the capitalist system (Tadajewski, 2017). It is remarkable given that the discipline is all too often lambasted for its amorality. Within marketing and sales practice, Jones clarified his position by proclaiming that he hoped a "moral ideal" would replace *caveat emptor* as the standard of merchant behavior:

> *Caveat emptor* will not excuse moral deficiency in [a merchant] because he sells goods, any more than it will in a physician because he leaves medicines with his patients. . . . The moral conception of the merchant as one who selects his stock of goods in the spirit of a friend selecting a present for a friend; who preserves the merchandise as one who feels that it already belongs to another, and is held in trust; who awaits trade with the spirit of accommodation in his heart; who charges for his service with that justice tempered with humanity which characterizes the best class of physicians; and who advises with that fidelity which makes the best attorneys, is the only conception which will attract the highest talent into this profession and will leave the pathway open for growth in functions and in efficiency.
>
> (1912g, p. 577)

Aside from his promotion of an ethically inflected axiology, another concept originating in the articles published in *Mill Supplies* was that of the functions of marketing. A "functional" approach was evident in at least three of Jones's articles (1911k,

1912g, 1913b). They were most vividly expressed in his paper "Functions of the Merchant" (1912g). The list he provided included those now reeled off in rote-like fashion by most historians when discussing this school of thought – although usually the source being cited is Arch Shaw. They were transportation, bulk-breaking, assorting, storage, buying, selling, and risk taking. These activities provided various "utilities", namely, time (getting the product to the market in a timely fashion), place (ensuring the correct locations received their ideal assortment of goods – an area where errors were easy, often common, and obviously expensive), and quantity (i.e. the correct amount) (1912g, p. 575). Let us be clear, Shaw (1912) is often credited with originating the functional approach, but Jones deserves equivalent praise for his insight and ability to distil the manifold relations mediating the activities of business professionals. True, his article was published (in November 1912) three months after Shaw's (August 1912). But we must not forget that Jones had written on functional themes in December 1911 and appears to have developed the idea independently of Shaw's work.

Both pioneers – Jones and Shaw – appreciated that certain functions were always performed in the marketing process and that these added value for consumers. Where the former goes further than most – although he is writing about a set of activities that were often undertaken by practitioners of the period (e.g. Jones and Richardson, 2007; Tadajewski, 2008, 2015b, 2016) – is that his 1912 article outlined a basic version of the marketing concept. In his case, he called for practitioners to focus on serving customers' needs and not simply on sales. Being attentive to Jones's scholarship – combined with the wider reflections of practitioners – thus gives the lie to the problematic periodization schemes that later appeared (e.g. Keith, 1960) and whose contents are swallowed wholesale by even the most prominent writers of the recent past (Vargo and Lusch, 2004).

> Many merchants narrow their field of enterprise by placing undue emphasis on the sale itself as the object of study and the field of retail activity. The field of the retail expert is self-training, the establishment of the principles and policies of action, proper equipment, selection of stock etc.; and the establishment of a reputation for reliability and efficiency. Sales are the natural consummation of these things; and sales only come steadily, and in satisfactory amount, as consummations. In short, then, the proper thing for the merchant to emphasize, as an expert, is preparation for service, rather than the act of sale itself.
>
> (Jones, 1912g, p. 577)

Jones's articles from *Mill Supplies* consequently provide an important source of insight, a collection that is modern in aspects of its content and reflects high ethical ideals. We have offered only a brief analysis of this collection. Further lessons undoubtedly await those curious enough to investigate.

In 1913, Jones was promoted to Full Professor at Michigan. After focusing his teaching and writing on marketing for over a decade, he shifted his attention to business administration. This was marked by the diversification of his teaching portfolio to include courses such as “Principles of Administration”, “Problems of Production”, and “Business Organization and Management”, as well as his publication of a series of articles in *The Engineering Magazine* that were collected and republished in *Business Administration – The Scientific Principles of a New Profession* (1913f), *The Business Administrator, His Models in War, Statecraft and Science* (1914b), *The Administration of Industrial Enterprises* (1916), and *Industrial Leadership and Executive Ability* (1920). In inductive fashion, Jones held fast to the idea that the underlying principles of business would be discernible from studying the work of successful administrators. This point raises the specter of a slightly more strongly positivistic vein in his academic work. Success, here, can be boiled down to the attributes demonstrated by a number of highly successful people and these would hold – presumably – for the future. Here we see a slight recoil from the idea of temporal and locational relativism that was emblematic of the GHSE.

As many researchers attempting to study successful business people have rapidly come to appreciate over the last century, they might like to brag at an abstract or vague level, but they are more careful about letting a researcher peek behind their Oz-like curtain. Those who Jones wanted to study were not willing to reveal the methods and practices that undergirded their ascension of the capitalist ladder. Jones, if we are being fair, did minimal consulting that we know about, and effectively trying to cold-call a business titan was not likely to result in a garlanded welcome. If the living will not reveal their secrets, there are always other sources. The dead can speak volumes given the right kind of academic luck. The careers of leaders in military, government, and scientific ventures had been studied and written about for centuries. They were the subject of published biographies; their campaigns a matter of public record. Studying these might prove fertile for those wanting to succeed in business.

Nor was the comparative leap wholly unexpected. As he well understood, the lexicon of business was peppered with military metaphors. References to “captain of industry”, “strategy”, “tactics”, “campaigns”, and so on were common – they still are. By exploring the literature bequeathed by the Romans, Frederick the Great, Napoleon, and more contemporary military history, Jones mined the core competencies of these leaders. Their skills had led to superlative performances. Perhaps, then, they would stand the test of time. Among the core “administrative principles” he excavated were the abilities to make decisions, to take initiative, and to undertake preliminary planning and the subordination of detail, discipline, and concentration of effort for efficiency.

In *The Administration of Industrial Enterprises* (1916) Jones expounded upon “the process of mercantile distribution” (aka marketing). There were chapters dealing with purchasing, selling, advertising, physical distribution, and credit. Pricing was discussed extensively. He was aware of the limitations of the book, calling his treatment an “outline”. Each of the chapters on purchasing, selling, and advertising points out the functions performed by each of those elements. These initial explorations were, it appears, meant to ripen into a much more detailed engagement with marketing.

> The methods of mercantile distribution are presented in outline, without entering upon a criticism of the vast wastes entailed by the modern evolution, for

> the reason that it is becoming customary to separate the discussion of industrial organization from that of commercial organization, and for the further reason that the Author hopes at a later time . . . to present a work upon the American domestic market.
>
> (Jones, 1916, p. vi)

Something in his personal or academic life must have intervened because the promised volume was never penned, although he did teach a course by that title at Michigan from 1914 to 1917.

Academics who believe today that the marketing concept and relationship marketing are of recent origin will be surprised to read Jones's description of successful selling.

> The basic rule of efficiency in selling is to know thoroughly the properties of goods and the needs of people. The reason why this rule is not universally accepted is that it is possible to make a brief record which appears like success by cutting prices, or by applying the arts of salesmanship and advertising to goods without distinctive merit of design or the attraction of low price. Misfit sales do not maintain themselves, however, for each of such sales installs in the possession of the buyer an article which begins at once to educate him as to the error he made in acquiring it, and which re-emphasizes the point steadily and concretely as long as it exists. Intelligently directed sales campaigns aim, therefore, at selling service or satisfaction, by which alone *permanent trade connections* can be formed.
>
> (1916, p. 365; emphasis added)

The notion that firms should maintain a focus on customers and the development of long-term relationships is not a new idea (Tadajewski, 2008, 2009, 2015a, 2015b). Consistent with this view, it was a central part of Jones's perspective in the early twentieth century.

Interestingly, the chapter on advertising draws on several classic works by Walter Dill Scott, Harry Hollingworth, Harry Tipper and George Burton Hotchkiss, E.E. Calkins, and Paul T. Cherington. And he continues to devote attention to the waste in advertising. Practitioners had bemoaned it and critically minded observers regularly deconstructed it as a feature of the growing consumer-driven economy.

> Besides the waste of labor and material agencies, advertising involves a waste of the nervous energy of the public. It demands perception and an act of judgment from the majority of street-car patrons, to discover the few who want Spearmint gum. It flashes a dazzling array of electric lights before the eyes of the thousands who pass on a great city highway, to sift out a couple of hundred patrons for a ratskeller [a bar or restaurant]. In spite of a wastefulness . . . advertising has established itself as part of the machinery of competition which is indispensable for the time being in many branches of industry.
>
> (Jones, 1916, p. 383)

Evident in the passage above, the first lecturer of marketing admitted that the practice of marketing was a necessary evil. This may have contributed to his decision to shift his primary focus to business administration and ultimately to quit full-time teaching.

In 1918, Jones reflected on his career in a letter to Ely.

> I want to tell you how your advanced thinking in so many lines (which American social evolution has since confirmed) and your matchless productivity have been an inspiration to me. My own program can be briefly told. When I went into business administration I did not realize what an unsurveyed wilderness I was going into. Having had little business experience I took usual precaution to ground myself in technique. But the main object has long been to formulate the underlying principles of administration, especially with reference to what, in the phrase of the moment, is spoken of as 'the handling of the human factor'. To get the data for this has required the observation of non-economic joint action, especially military administration and diplomacy. The ethical purport is the same as if I were studying distribution or the labor movement. I hope to see industry made more just and generous not only through a democratic process, but by the formation of a code of ideals of professional competence for administrators. . . . I hope to see the general welfare promoted, not only by the use of the national dividend outside of industry but by the transformation of the life in industry itself, by fitting men to their tasks, interpreting the tasks in terms of service and elegance of method, by control of fatigue, by the sociability and aesthetics of welfare work etc. . . . What I should like from Providence, more than anything else, is the opportunity to push the development along these main lines in which, chiefly, business administration is capable of being deepened and worked into something of a philosophy.
>
> (Jones, 1918)

Jones was convinced that a philosophy or science of business, and by extension of distribution or marketing, was a possibility. He had the process well mapped out. Initially, this necessitated unravelling the core principles underwriting each area. These would be generated by empirical data and the induction and distillation of the ideas. These could subsequently be disseminated through higher education, via closer connections between academe and industry as well as pursued by more traditional routes such as publication (book, journal articles, and periodical literature). Those practitioners who adopted these principles would then be well placed to ensure the maximization of the welfare of society (while meeting, obviously, their own corporate, firm, or personal needs at the same time).

Henry Charles Taylor

Shortly after Sparling, Jones, and Hammond returned to Wisconsin from Germany in 1894, Henry Charles Taylor (Figure 3.3) began graduate studies (1896) at Wisconsin. He was a faculty member from 1901 to 1919. For the first eight years he

Figure 3.3 Henry Charles Taylor

Source: Wisconsin Historical Society, image number WHi-26621, with permission.

was employed as an instructor under Ely's leadership in the Department of Economics, followed by ten years as the founding Chair of the Department of Agricultural Economics. He was eventually appointed Chief of the Federal Office of Farm Management (1919–1921) and Director of the Bureau of Markets and Crop Estimates (1921–1922) and the Bureau of Agricultural Economics (1922–1925) before resuming his academic career as Professor of Economics (joining Ely) at Northwestern University from 1925 to 1928. He later returned to civil service as Managing Director of the Farm Foundation from 1935 through to 1945 and continued with that organization as an agricultural economist until 1952. A significant part of Taylor's work included marketing.

Bartels gestures to Taylor as an influence in the development of marketing thought, calling him one of four influential economists at Wisconsin (1951, p. 4). Taylor's distinctive contribution was that he pioneered the study and teaching of agricultural marketing.

Taylor was drawn to Wisconsin to study economics because of Ely.

> Professor Ely was a social economist . . . [believing that] human institutions were the determining factor in the distribution of wealth. Ely taught that the

> distribution of wealth could be improved by modifying economic institutions. He stressed that in modifying social economic institutions the general welfare is always to be kept in mind as the goal. He taught that private property is not absolute; it is a 'social trust' and may be modified in the interest of the general welfare. . . . [T]he general welfare became the center of interest about which all other problems revolved and in terms of which the problems were to be ultimately solved.
>
> (Taylor, 1960, pp. 26–28)

It is not surprising that Ely's approach would appeal to Taylor, whose father was a member of the Grange (i.e. the "Farmers Movement" which sought to improve the education of this group, their position in a changing economic system, and ensure they were not disadvantaged by the burgeoning cadres of middlemen), and believed he was only a custodian of the land, that it should be managed for "the cause", and who wanted to promote legislation intended to help farmers gain a fair share of the distribution of wealth. This, at its core, indicates subscription to the value of distributive justice.

Ely had been looking for a graduate student to specialize in agricultural economics. Since the subject was not well developed, he advised Taylor to go to Europe, "where agricultural problems were in a more advanced stage because agriculture had been carried on there longer than in the United States" (Taylor, 1960, p. 31). Following Ely's suggestion, in 1899 Taylor went to England, then to Germany, where he studied agricultural economics under Conrad and Sering (see Figure 2.1a). At Berlin, Taylor took courses from Wagner and Schmoller. At Halle, Conrad's courses were described by Taylor as "historical and descriptive in character", concentrating on the political economy of agriculture, rather than on the technical aspects of farming (Taylor, 1940, p. 95).

Taylor returned to Wisconsin in 1901 to complete his doctoral thesis. It was an historical, comparative study of land tenure which drew from archival materials, from personal observations made while visiting farmers and estate agents in England, and from the writings of Roscher, Conrad, Sering, and Brentano. He later cited his own thesis, along with dissertations by Hibbard (1902), Hammond (1897), and Thompson (1907), as landmark contributions to Wisconsin's reputation as the leading center applying the historical approach (Taylor and Taylor, 1952, p. 287). He credited Ely as the primary stimulus for their work and genealogically appreciated that "the roots of that Wisconsin background may lead back to the German Historical School" (Taylor, 1939, p. 2).

On his return to Wisconsin, Ely offered Taylor the position of instructor. A "Course in Commerce" (i.e. a major in commerce) had been started in the economics department under the direction of William A. Scott. Scott made the offer, requesting that Taylor teach economic history and economic geography (Taylor, 1992), taking over those classes from Edward David Jones, who was heading to Michigan. "Teaching the commercial courses was no drawback. Agricultural history and the economics of agricultural marketing were made to loom large in the two commercial courses which I was giving, much of which I moved over to agricultural economics [later, in 1909]" (Taylor, 1960, p. 50).

Taylor's 1901 course in economic geography was a foundation for the agricultural marketing offerings that followed. One of his first moves was to place emphasis on agriculture and marketing. This focus on one industry and a limited number of commodities would later be labeled the commodity approach: "From two-thirds to three-quarters of the time in the course in economic geography was spent in describing where each of the important agricultural products was grown, where it was consumed, and the transportation, merchandising, and processing which it underwent as it passed from producer to consumer" (Taylor, 1941, p. 23).

The course text was Volume VI of the Report of the US Industrial Commission of 1900. Snappily entitled "Distribution and Marketing of Farm Products", it was cited as the first "textbook" used in US marketing courses (Bartels, 1962; Hagerty, 1936). It described the distribution of cereals, cotton, dairy products, the marketing of livestock, and drew out the significance of cold storage and refrigeration when selling perishable products. In Taylor's words, Volume VI was "by all odds the best book on agricultural economics at the beginning of the twentieth century. . . . The facts assembled and the methods of presentation made it possible for the reader to develop in his mind a fairly clear picture of marketing processes and price-making forces" (Taylor and Taylor, 1952, p. 517). Offering the highest level of praise, he suggested that it demarcated the emergence of the "scientific study of marketing" (1922, p. 13). It "had much influence upon my course in economic geography and in turn suggested the method used in studies from 1912–17 in the marketing of Wisconsin farm products" (1941, p. 24). Other government publications which explicated marketing practices were assigned in the 1901 course, including "The Grain Trade of the U.S.", "The Cotton Trade of the U.S." and several bulletins of the Department of Agriculture's Bureau of Statistics (Taylor, 1908).

The materials he developed dealing with agricultural economics eventually formed the basis of his *An Introduction to the Study of Agricultural Economics* (1905). This was most likely the first book in the English language to tackle the subject and would possibly have been one of the first to deal with agricultural marketing had it not been for the pressures of the tenure clock. Taylor explained the omission of content in this way.

> It will be noted that the first edition of *Agricultural Economics*, published in 1905, did not include the subject of marketing, although there was a chapter on prices. My interest in the fields of farm management and land tenure was greater at that time than my interest in marketing. I had not written up my ideas on marketing so carefully as I had those on these other subjects, and since, for practical reasons, it was necessary to publish the book in the spring of 1905 in order to get the promotion to an assistant professorship [and a raise in salary to $1,400 a year], I published the material on the economics of farm management and land tenure which was ready, omitted the discussion of

> marketing, and called the book *An Introduction to the Study of Agricultural Economics*.
>
> (Taylor, 1941, p. 2)

The next edition (1919) remedied this neglect with emphasis on the relationship between the farmer and middlemen.

Tracing the sources that informed Taylor's (1905) book yields an interesting, if not unexpected, path to earlier German courses. In responding to Farnam's 1906 survey, Taylor wrote that many of the subjects he engaged with were covered in the lectures by Sering and Conrad (Taylor, H.C., 1906). Furthermore, a report sent to Benjamin Hibbard (University of Wisconsin) from the American Consulate-General in Berlin indicates that courses in agricultural *marketing* were offered as early as 1912, and probably prior to this, at Berlin, Halle, and other institutions.

> In most, if not all, of the universities there are, of course, opportunities for the study of various phases of economics bearing in a broad way on the subject of marketing. In several there are specialized courses on cooperation. The Universities of Leipzig and Halle pay particular attention to this field. A course of lectures on agricultural cooperation will be given at Leipzig during the approaching (1913) summer semester.
>
> (Thakara, 1913, p. 2)

And, as far as marketing was concerned, the report mentioned the following courses listed in the 1912/13 catalog of the University of Berlin:

> General course in business management. Includes credit, competition, speculation, the methods and psychology of advertising, selling methods and organization tariff technique, etc. Organization of commercial establishments in particular branches. The grain trade and the marketing of grain.
>
> (Thakara, 1913, p. 5)

We are left wondering how much of the material covering marketing at Wisconsin was borrowed from previously delivered content in Germany. Whatever its source(s), Taylor's lecture series marked the beginning of instruction in agricultural marketing at Wisconsin and quite likely in the United States.

Gradually, he expanded the number of courses provided by the Department of Economics. In 1904/05, he taught "The Elements of Agricultural Economics", "Historical and Comparative Agriculture", and "Agricultural Industries" (University of Wisconsin, 1904/05, p. 117), in addition to the module on "Economic Geography". In 1907, he added "Commercial Geography", which provided "a description of the production and marketing of the principle agricultural products, and a study of the conditions which determine the geographical distribution of the centers of production of each of these products; a discussion of the production and consumption of the leading products of mines and of forests" (University of Wisconsin, 1907). He felt that a model program of study in agricultural marketing should include courses in marketing functions and institutions that would

> develop in the student's mind a clear picture of the transactions that take place at each stage in the progress of the product from producer to consumer. It should develop an understanding of the forces which determine the bargaining power of buyer and seller, the part played by the official standards for farm products, by the great news services, by credit systems, and by organized markets.
>
> (Taylor, 1924, p. 24)

A Department of Agricultural Economics – the first such department established on American shores – was formed within Wisconsin's College of Agriculture in 1908, with Taylor appointed as the first Chair. As a result, teaching and research in this area received substantial impetus. He had already encouraged several of his students to undertake marketing topics (Jones, 1907). With the formation of the new Department, thesis work and the publication of research on marketing accelerated.

A phrase that became popular in agricultural circles after the turn of the twentieth century was "the marketing problem". This referred to the suspected manipulation of prices for farm products by middlemen (an issue that would further cement the link – in some minds at least – of marketing with mendacious practice). One result of this widespread concern was the 1903 formation of the American Society of Equity, for the purpose of helping farmers secure a fair share of national income (Taylor, 1941, p. 4). The Society was very critical of a "price-making system" which was "tyrannical", and reduced farming to "commercial slavery" (Everitt, quoted in Taylor, 1941, p. 5). What we should appreciate is that Taylor's attitude was much more moderate.

> I was tolerant towards but not enthusiastic about the Equity movement in Wisconsin. . . . While I was fully aware of the opportunity for dishonesty in the middleman service, I believed that hired men of cooperative associations working in central markets, remote from the farmers, might also succeed in being dishonest. I believed that, so far as the central market was concerned, the best control the farmers could exert was by understanding clearly what took place.
>
> (Taylor, 1941, p. 6)

The last part of the sentence – that the best control farmers could exert was by understanding what happened in the marketplace – is key to comprehending Taylor's motivation, whether it related to his teaching or government service. He was unhappy that farmers did not receive a fair share of the nation's wealth. The remedy for this was education and information provision. With these armaments, the farmer would be better placed to negotiate a just reward for his labor.

In 1906, as the interest of Wisconsin farmers in the activities of middlemen and the price-making system grew (and this interest obviously reaffirms the fact that the price-making system was not being viewed as a "natural" phenomenon, but one manipulated by visible actors), Taylor devoted attention to the cooperative creameries and cheese factories in the southern part of the state (Taylor, 1941, p. 7), later publishing a bulletin on "The Prices of Farm Products". His conclusions about the prices of eggs, butter, and cheese were consistent with the notion that middlemen served an essential function for which a price had to be paid (Taylor, 1941, p. 8). In other words, marketing added value for consumers. His empirical research, whilst being open to a potentially critical account, ended up legitimating the value-adding practices he had witnessed.

In 1911, two of Taylor's senior students, W.A. Schoenfeld and G.S. Wehrwein, explored the marketing of cheese. With Taylor, they published the results of their investigations with the inspired title "The Marketing of Wisconsin Cheese" (University of Wisconsin, 1913). The paper noted where cheese was produced and consumed and explained the activities of middlemen in the process; the advantages and disadvantages of a cheese-maker versus a sales agent carrying out the selling function, the types of retailers and wholesalers, the operation of dairy boards, retail prices, and the services rendered by various middlemen. Taylor commented that "while our findings tended to sober those persons who had been speaking excitedly about the marketing problem, they made it perfectly clear that, in certain stages in the marketing of Wisconsin cheese the agencies were not functioning satisfactorily" (Taylor, 1941, p. 16). Deflation of excessive criticism was nonetheless connected with an appreciation that the status quo could not continue unchallenged. These views would be communicated to relevant political decision-makers, potentially helping to shape legislation and the field of action available to suppliers in the marketplace. This research was important for a number of reasons. It led to a flurry of studies being conducted by doctoral candidates in the department, with this output helping elevate its profile in political circles (Taylor, 1941). It also signified division specialization in marketing and cooperatives which is considered today to be a major contribution to the study of agriculture (Pulver, 1984).

As the Department of Agricultural Economics grew, Taylor recruited two alumni to specialize in agricultural marketing. In 1913, Benjamin Hibbard joined the faculty, having taught at Iowa since graduating from Wisconsin in 1902. In 1917, Theodore Macklin returned from Kansas State College. Macklin was originally a student of Taylor's. Hibbard, Taylor, and several of the graduate students in the department published a series of investigations, including (among others) "The Marketing of Wisconsin Butter" (1915) and (1917) the "Marketing of Wisconsin Milk". The second of these led to a thesis and book on *The Marketing of Whole Milk* in 1921 by H.E. Erdman, another pioneer in marketing education (Mehren, 1960). That book, as well as Hibbard's (1921) *Marketing of Agricultural Products* and Macklin's (1921) *Efficient Marketing for Agriculture*, are imbued with seminal status (Bartels, 1962).

Of the series of articles published between 1913 and 1917 and the books that followed in their wake, Taylor observed that they all followed a common pattern.

Each was designed "to picture the marketing process clearly in order that the true character of the problems of marketing might be discovered" (1941, p. 22). They all "followed through stage by stage the different [marketing] functions . . . not using the term functions although studying functions" (Taylor, 1944). It was in recognition of that fact that Converse thought Taylor might have had prior claim to Arch W. Shaw as originator of the functional approach to studying marketing (Converse, 1944). In his efforts to understand the discrepancy between the prices paid to the farmer and those paid by the consumer, Taylor – as indicated above – unpacked the valuable activities being performed by middlemen. He never lost his compassion for the farmer, however. To the extent that there was a "marketing problem", in Taylor's mind it seemed to be one of educating the farmer in the techniques of marketing so that they might perform essential functions themselves and collect the value added.

Taylor experienced tension between his desire to maintain scholarly detachment and his interest in social reform. This is the same tension that the members of the *Verein* had experienced some 40 years earlier. When he hired Hibbard in 1913, Taylor expressed his views to the Dean of the College of Agriculture.

> The function of the University, in the field of marketing, became clearly defined in my mind. As I see it, our function is to investigate and educate and not to agitate or organize marketing institutions. . . . It is especially important just at this time because Hibbard will be called upon to go before the public on various occasions dealing with the subject of marketing. It seems to me entirely proper for him to give a historical and descriptive lecture on cooperation, pointing out its strengths and its weakness, but not his function to go to a given place to tell people specifically how to organize for a specific purpose.
>
> (Taylor, 1913)

For Taylor, teaching and research should be "scientific" – in this context, this means inductive, historical, and descriptive in nature. Nevertheless, it should result in practical insights for state and federal legislation. While there are obvious parallels, he did not completely accept the Wisconsin Idea. Taylor preferred to do his lobbying outside the university, that is, until he accepted a post in government later in his career. Negotiating political circles gave him the chance to mobilize his considerable talents to improve production and distribution efficiencies, with the intention of contributing to the overall economic health of the nation. As a function of his government work in the 1920s, he made important strides in helping organize US agriculture, substantially assisting farmers with their marketing activities, all with an eye to improving farm life. In these endeavors, his desire to pursue science is interlinked with a political position that wanted to ameliorate social conflict. From Taylor's perspective,

> [T]he new science of agricultural economics, joined with positive state action, could moderate class conflict and radical policy proposals. In 1923 Taylor

> declared to the land-grant colleges that radicalism represented a pathological condition somewhere which should be diagnosed and prescribed for by an expert who, because of his training and experience, is best able to render this service.
>
> (Gilbert and Baker, 1997, p. 298)

These values were long standing. In 1917 Taylor and Ely founded the American Association for Agricultural Legislation (AAAL) for the purposes of making recommendations on policy matters to the government (Taylor, 1917). In a study program intended to catalyze future research that was distributed to members, the following topics were included:

- History of state marketing bureaus and departments;
- The essentials of an efficient state marketing bureau;
- Present status of standardization and grading laws;
- Relation of state marketing organizations to national regulation;
- Cold storage legislation;
- Laws governing cooperative organizations of producers and consumers;
- Federal marketing legislation.

(Ely, 1917)

This scholarly roadmap reflected a concern for land use, prices and credit, transportation, and the role of education in enhancing agricultural decision-making. Importantly, it addressed marketing as an area of concern and, notably, the essential role of the state in the marketing process. Two years later, in a manner analogous to the *Verein*, the AAAL moved towards becoming a more academic, and less political, organization when it was consolidated with the American Farm Management Association to form the American Farm Economics Association (Taylor, 1939).

During his time in government during the 1920s, Taylor oversaw empirical research that studied local and international markets and disseminated relevant information via the radio, and as analytic sophistication improved, the experts employed by Taylor "forecast the future supply, demand, and price of agricultural commodities" (Gilbert and Baker, 1997, p. 298). Providing this kind of information was a real service to the community. The cost of doing so independently would have been prohibitive. Despite this, Taylor left government service in 1925 due to internal political changes which forced his hand.

As difficult as it was, the ideal of a union of the interests of the state, the university, and economic institutions was easier to maintain with respect to agricultural marketing than with more industrial types of activities. For example, in 1916 the School of Economics hosted the First Wisconsin Commercial and Industrial Congress. The stated purpose of this event was "to create an open forum for the discussion of serious and growing economic and social problems involved in the development of the industrial resources of the state . . . touching on significant practical and theoretical aspects of present-day business methods and relations"

(University of Wisconsin, 1916, p. 2). The presentations included "Advertising and Salesmanship", "Education for Business", and "Scientific Management" (University of Wisconsin, 1916, pp. 3–4). In Ely's address, he outlined the connections between practice, academia, and government.

> Business is becoming, if it is not already, a profession. . . . [W]hen we speak of business as a profession, it implies that higher standards are necessary for those who enter the profession and succeed in it. This is the reason why our Universities are getting into closer and closer touch with business and preparing men for business. . . . [T]o do its work . . . the University must be in close touch with business men. That is what the present Congress signifies – a closer touch and I want to add also a closer fellowship with the business interests of the State of Wisconsin. . . . It has been recognized again and again . . . that we cannot have good business without good government. It may be added that we cannot have good government without good business. . . . Business, the University and the State must all pull together for common ends.
>
> (Ely, 1916)

Whether it was applied to business problems or agricultural issues, economic science, and hence marketing theory, was assumed to represent the interests of the profession and the state, which were further theorized to coincide with the general welfare of society.

Economics and commerce at Wisconsin

The Course in Commerce was originally an informal program within the School of Economics, but was officially separated in 1901

> for the training of young men who desire to enter business careers . . . in the belief that in order to achieve the largest measure of success at the present time, and in order properly to perform his duties to himself and to society, the business man needs not only a college education, but a course of study adapted to his peculiar needs.
>
> (University of Wisconsin Catalog, 1900/01, p. 170)

When William James Ashley was designing the Commerce Program at the University of Birmingham, he cited the Wisconsin course as a model of collegiate business education: "Let anyone who knows how we plume ourselves in England if we can appoint just one professor to organize commercial teaching, turn to Wisconsin and Cologne, and he will see what a commercial training means when people are really in earnest" (Ashley, 1903c, p. 272). Like agricultural economics, commerce at Wisconsin was considered an applied branch of economics. As we pointed out at the start of this chapter, in 1891 when the university was first considering the establishment of a Department of Economics (as opposed to the School being placed within the College of Letters and Science), the plan called for separate departmental status for Commerce. Ely objected to that strategy.

> There is no separate and distinct science of commerce. This [within the Economics Department] is where it belongs historically and where it belongs at present according to the practice of the best American and European Universities. . . . [A]n arrangement creating in the same University a Department of Commerce and a Department of Economics must in the nature of things prove unsatisfactory, for a Department of Commerce can have a field only as it encroaches on the proper field of economics.
>
> (Ely, 1903)

A separate program for commerce was inevitable. Within the course, individual modules in business were developed as early as 1904/05 and were offered by the University Extension Division (what we would call "distance learning" today) as early as 1907. One such course, "The Sales, Purchase, and Shipping Methods", was offered in 1910 and credited by Bartels as the first course in marketing at Wisconsin (Bartels, 1962, pp. 29–32). The following year, the instructor, Ralph Starr Butler, issued a series of pamphlets under the same title which later appeared as *Marketing Methods* (1917). Unfortunately, when he claimed that this was the first book to use the term "marketing" in its title, Bartels relied on Butler's recollections given some 30 years later. Wisconsin records suggest a somewhat different interpretation.

Marketing had received attention in a different series of pamphlets prior to Butler's publications. The 1910 module, for example, was taught jointly by Butler and Benjamin M. Rastall (University of Wisconsin, 1909/1910). The latter managed all business administration courses in the Extension Division. These two men also jointly taught "Advertising Campaigns" and Rastall delivered "Credits and Collections". Six months previously, before Butler had even been hired, Rastall authored a pamphlet entitled "The Business Sciences", which included a "Chart of Business Courses" showing the organization of the entire field as he understood it (Figure 3.4a, Figure 3.4b). The educational offerings mentioned above were collectively grouped under the subdivision "Marketing", which, in turn, was part of a division labeled "Business Organization and Management".

Overall, the curriculum mapped out in the "Chart of Business Courses" included five major divisions: Business History, Material Basis of Business, Business Technique (with subdivisions for business law, business mathematics, and accounting), Business Organization and Management (combined with the marketing material mentioned above, including production and industry-specific courses that dealt with marketing content), and Business Finance. Business History was included in the belief that "human knowledge grows as a summation of painfully worked out experiences and experiments" (Rastall, 1909, p. 7). "Materials of Business" explored commercial geography to provide a "general knowledge of the materials of the class with which they deal, and of the sources of such materials, of their production and transportation and marketing" (Rastall, 1909, p. 8). In spite of the

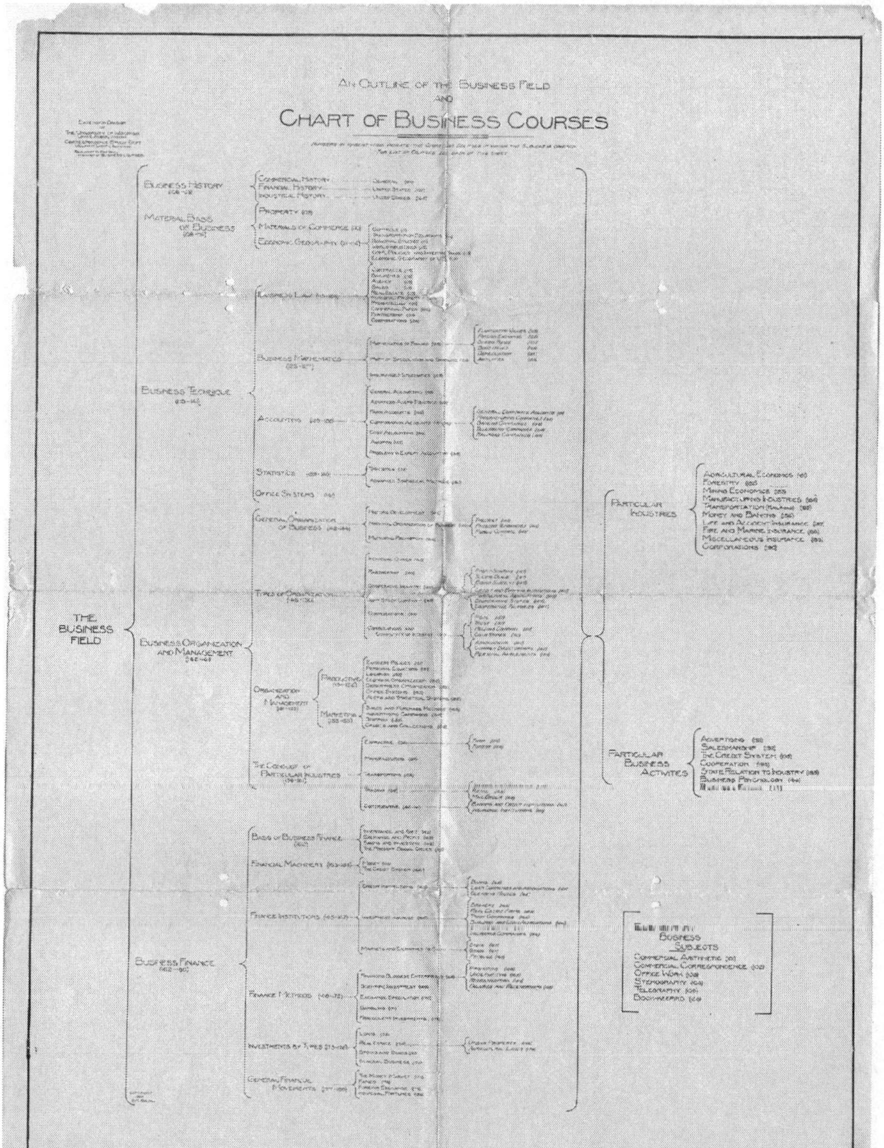

Figure 3.4a Chart of Business Courses, Extension Division of the University of Wisconsin

Source: University of Wisconsin–Madison Archives, Series 18/5/00/5–1 Box 1, with permission.

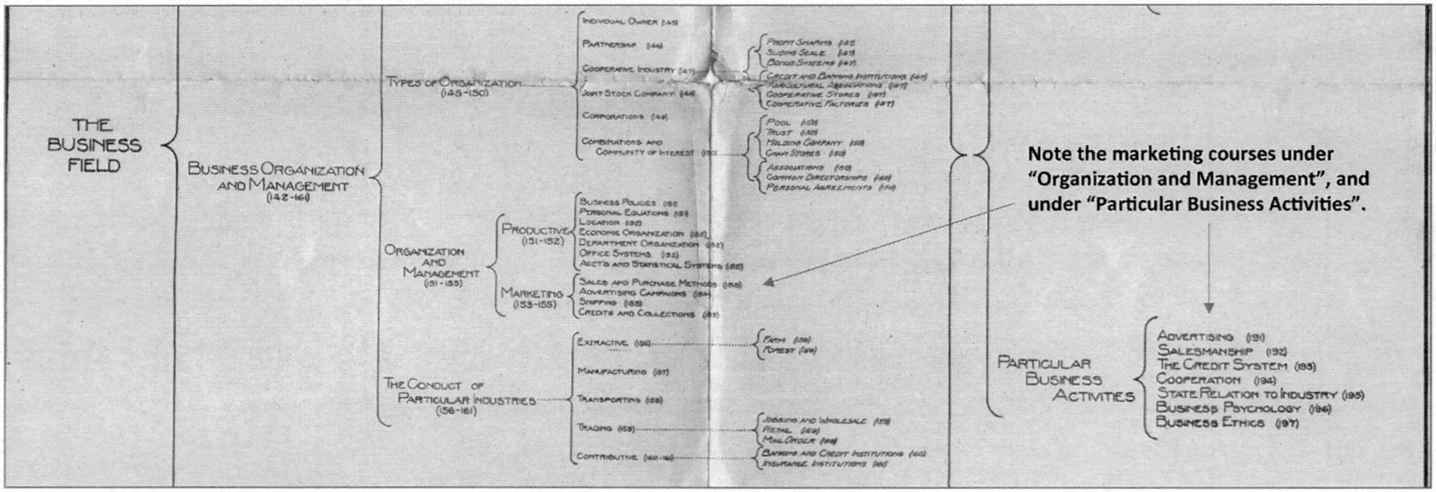

Figure 3.4b Rastall (1909) Chart of Business Courses – Outline of the Business Field

Source: University of Wisconsin–Madison Archives, Extension Division Series 18/5/00/5–1.
This subsection of the full chart highlights the central role of marketing courses and the extensive offerings in marketing.

fact that he has never been mentioned in this connection, Rastall is not without claim to architecturally orienting marketing at Wisconsin. This chart is a major artifact in our history.

Of course, Rastall was a student of Ely's, completing his thesis in 1906, and in the pamphlet on "Business Science" he evidenced his Wisconsin training. He wrote that steadily more complex economic conditions created contrasting requirements for success. On the one hand, they demanded advances in systemization and specialization (this view calls forth the division of labor articulated by Adam Smith and developed further in the recommendations made by Frederick Taylor). This had a narrowing effect on personal ability and vision. On the other hand, higher positions required general training (something Harvard and Birmingham would become noted for delivering). Whereas science had yielded developments in system and specialization, Rastall felt that it could produce greater "business ability". Just as economics training generated the tools for social reform, business science offered the potential to create adept practitioners.

The modules in business administration provided by the Extension faculty were developed from those in existence as far back as 1904/05. Even then "purchasing, marketing, advertising and credit business" were mentioned in the course description for "Business Administration" (University of Wisconsin Catalog, 1904/05, p. 115). This included "in addition to lectures on organization, management and duties of officers, students [with the opportunities to] organize and manage fictitious business concerns" (University of Wisconsin Catalog, 1904/05, p. 116). Clearly it anticipated the common practice a century later of business and management simulations; just one of a number of features of GHSE-type practices and educational opportunities being provided that prefigure many of those in use or called for today.

Paul Nystrom was another of Ely's students who contributed to marketing theory. His focus was the field of retailing. Nystrom's thesis on "Retail Distribution of Goods", completed in 1914, was quickly published as a book about which he later commented to Ely:

> There are a number of chapters . . . that grew directly out of my work in your classes, particularly those on rent in the retail business. You will find the arguments familiar, I'm sure. Chapter XIX, Public Regulation of the Retail Business, was first prepared as a topic in Professor Urdahl's summer session class in Taxation. Other chapters were prepared in Professor Commons' classes, and the seminary discussions contributed throughout.
>
> (Nystrom, 1915b)

He stated that his purpose in writing the book was to describe the retailing business "as it actually was" (Nystrom, 1915a, p. v) by proceeding from personal observations and experiences. Taking induction extremely seriously, he supplemented his empirics with those of over a thousand retail store managers and salespeople who attended his classes between 1909 and 1915.

Starting with a description of the history of distribution and retailing, Nystrom frequently uses statistical tables to depict retail employment by industry, retailing expenses, wages, turnover rates, and so forth. Statistics on consumer income and expenditures were used, for instance, to test Engel's laws of consumption (Nystrom, 1915a, Appendix I). This is all logically structured and developed in a manner consistent with GHSE tenets. Nystrom ultimately aspired to contribute to a "science of distribution". Echoes of his position are found in the later "science debates" (e.g. Hunt, 1976).

> An organized, systematic treatment of the subject is becoming possible. With the adoption of educational courses in schools and colleges dealing with distribution, the establishment of experimental distributive stations, the investigation of specific problems by careful unbiased methods, the accumulation of business facts by means of censuses conducted by the government, all of which have been proposed, and some of which are already under way, the hope of a science of distribution of goods stands a chance of realization in the near future.
>
> (Nystrom, 1915a, p. 22)

Conclusion

All in all, what we see with the work of the scholars explored in this chapter is the permeation of their thought with the axiological, ontological, epistemological, and methodological assumptions associated with the GHSE. To be sure, there were some slight deviations. In one case, there was less evidence of a subscription to temporal and locational relativism. Overt political leanings were less radical and activism took more moderate forms in the hands of H.C. Taylor.

Ely, his colleagues and students did not promote the overthrow of the capitalist system. Nor did they envisage their role as helping advance the interests of one stakeholder in society such as management. They stressed the interlinked nature of the classes, encouraged cooperation, and sought to forward the economic interests of all participants in the marketplace. To help improve the functioning of the economic system, the ethically minded economist and marketer had to be objective. The professoriate and the education they offered was not a force for ideological indoctrination. They should not promote one perspective – such as laissez-faire – to the exclusion of all others. This was not scholarly, it did not help develop the critical thinking abilities of the student, and fostered a mono-dimensional view of the economic world which inculcated mental processing that ran along set tramlines. Intellectual pluralism was the order of the day for the GHSE and embodied in Ely's notion of social objectivity.

As was apparent, Ely appreciated the potential limitations to academic freedom that confronted those who challenged the status quo. He came through his multiple academic trials having felt the pressures that circumscribed scholarly practice (see also Tyler and Cheyney, 1938). To be sure, they are attributed with making him more careful in his published statements, but his core concerns with social and distributive justice remain equally apparent in later work as they were in his earlier publications. Being the subject of public complaint does, however, remind us that simplistic coherence theories of truth are not an especially accurate reflection of intellectual life. Ely's epistemology left room for the politics of knowledge production and reception. Debates about the organization of society and the best methods for structuring and supervising the economic system were always likely to trigger emotive responses from varied interest groups. In this regard, Ely was lucky. He had landed at Wisconsin, an institution whose regents did have to attend to public criticism of their professoriate, but who came down firmly in support of Ely and the value of academic freedom.

By contrast to existing accounts of the emergence of marketing thought (e.g. Bartels, 1962; Jones and Monieson, 1990), we highlighted two significant factors that have escaped the notice of otherwise assiduous historians. In the first place, we made the case that Ely's trial at Wisconsin was an important event which encouraged him to pursue more conservative research for at least six years after the 1894 trial. This was a period when there were multiple seminal dissertations conducted on marketing topics under his supervision.

Our second point is that one of the recognized pioneers of marketing thought helped support Ely during a period of personal crisis that occurred in conjunction with the trial. David Kinley was one of Ely's close friends – and a former student – who helped defend and psychologically support him during a stressful period in his life. Bartels fails to link Ely and Kinley in this fashion. This may seem like a relatively inconsequential matter. But, since Ely was one of the main conditions of possibility for the early development of our discipline, Kinley's assistance shored up one of our intellectual foundations. Of course, we do not know what would have happened without this succor. But this was a dangerous point in Ely's career and he fully realized it. His position was so precarious that Ely worried that he was going to fail to accomplish the tasks he envisaged pursuing at Wisconsin.

One result of this politically fraught period in his life was that Ely sought solace and political shelter in less contentious research areas. Marketing was one of the subjects that he pursued with vigor in the aftermath of his trial. The emergence of the marketing discipline in the inflexion it received at Wisconsin is therefore a function of multiple historical contingencies. Precarity hardly covers it.

Under Ely's direction, the School of Economics, Department of Agricultural Economics, and Course in Commerce were all influenced by the GHSE. His subscription to social objectivity, the evolutionary nature of society, temporal and locational relativism (between countries and states), and a view of human intellectuality and performance which stressed its unequal nature all reinforced an image of the social world which held much potential, but was not being realized. Societal and human imperfections could be partly overcome. Here religion might play a role alongside the emerging social sciences (Ely, 1898). The management of the business system was amenable to description and modification, with the aim of distributing the fruits of economic growth to greater numbers of people than had previously been possible. In all of this, the ethically oriented economist who was willing to explore all avenues of intellectual inquiry and engage in original, critical, and constructive research, offering up his findings and skills to the state without fear of persecution, had a role to play in helping enact piecemeal social change.

Theory, empirical research, and practice were thus firmly conjoined for Ely and those he trained. Pedagogy and research were fused. And education was a means to improve the management of government and policy-making. Ely and the pioneer marketers that followed in his footsteps did not view their activities through the prism of merely advancing business and management interests. Their spectrum of action was much broader than this; equally, though, their research did have implications for practitioners and they did not eschew this part of their role.

Many students listened to their teacher's recommendation to study at the feet of Conrad, Wagner, Sering, and Schmoller. In this chapter, we have unraveled the evidence of influence between these various individuals, stressing the similarities and differences in their paradigmatic positioning. Simply because they often shared a related paradigmatic background did not mean they all approached their scholarly or governmental work in the same way, or that they held their beliefs in stasis as they progressed through their academic and personal life-cycles.

The graduates exposed to the GHSE were pioneers in the development of marketing. They took the GHSE axiology, ontology, epistemology, and politics in a direction which continued the trajectory enabled by the "younger school". Whether in commerce or agricultural economics, marketing became an important branch of applied economics. Their work consistently combined the inductive method with an evolutionary perspective and often exhibited pronounced ethical concerns.

While some marketing historians have recognized parallel ideas in institutional economics and marketing, the more common background in the GHSE has escaped their attention. As this chapter describes, teaching and research in marketing at Wisconsin enables our discipline to counterpoint accusations that it lacks ethical and moral fiber. This has not been true historically, nor does it accurately reflect contemporary research in our subject. To be sure, more ethically oriented and activist research is highly desirable. But that is the nature of academic work. There is no terminal point when we can truly say that all we need to accomplish has been achieved. With such egotism comes blindness; with blindness, we necessarily ignore the distributive and social injustices that will rear their heads while we live within an economic system that prioritizes the pursuit of profit over human welfare (Bakan, 2005). Saying that, what is certain is that our subject did not avoid engagement with these issues at the founding moment of its establishment as a university subject. Nor does it have to sideline it for any reason in the future.

Note

1 It is probably a good thing that Schmoller's writings about firm management were not widely circulated in English-speaking countries. He puts Frederick Taylor's (1911/1998) ideas about discipline firmly in the shade. He invokes the language of "cooperation" and "profit-sharing", but the undercurrent enabling this success is far darker than anything Taylor conjured up. Indeed, there is little truly cooperative about Schmoller's scheme. His remarks sound like Henry Ford's sociology department on steroids, where he encourages workers to keep each other in line, monitor their habits and those of their co-workers outside of the factory or firm realm. "Paternalism" puts his view far too benignly (see Schneider, 1993/1994, pp. 360–370).

4 Foundations of marketing thought at the University of Illinois

Introduction

As the previous chapters have made apparent, Ely's influence on marketing has been profound. One of the students he taught at Johns Hopkins was George M. Fisk. Fisk delivered one of the first university courses in marketing in 1903 at Illinois (Bartels, 1962; Maynard, 1942). Entitled "Domestic Commerce and Commercial Politics", it covered the methods of buying and selling, discussing "the various forms of wholesale and retail trade organizations; department, mail-order and co-operative stores; markets, fairs, auctions, stock and produce exchanges, etc." (University of Illinois, 1908–09, p. 236).

Fisk explored economics as an undergraduate in 1886–87. Following Ely's advice, he undertook graduate work at the Universities of Berlin, Munich, and Halle, where he graduated in 1896 with his PhD (see Figure 2.1a). Fisk began his career in Germany working in the American Embassy in Berlin between 1897 and 1900. He was later hired as a Professor of Commerce at Illinois in 1902 by David Kinley. Kinley, of course, deserves much greater attention than he has garnered to date from marketing historians for some of the reasons we have documented above – he was an important support for Ely at a difficult time in his career. Kinley was a student of Ely's at Wisconsin and had studied economics in Germany, later becoming head of the department of economics at Illinois, the director of courses in business instruction, and finally the President of the institution. Unusually, he visited Germany in 1900 *after* he completed his degree.

> [Kinley] was impressed with the extent of her [Germany's] commercial and industrial development and concomitant expansion of commercial education both on the high school and collegiate levels. 'The movement is in the air wherever I go', he wrote Draper [the University of Illinois President], and strongly urged the President to expand [course provision] in the direction of training for business and public service. The US consuls and diplomatic agents with whom Kinley talked agreed that such a program would be timely and useful.
>
> (Grisso, 1980, p. 85; cf. Kinley, 1949, p. 43)

Kinley's significance extends beyond the support of Ely. He was one of the clearest thinkers who was well versed in German literature to articulate the need for theory, stressing the core attributes that it should encompass. Specifically, he refers to the production of "general theory" in terms which resonate with the relativistic perspective of Karl Knies as well as his methodological stance regarding the historical structuring of the economy. There are genealogical affinities to the contributions of another GHSE pioneer – Ernst Engel – and his laws of consumption as well.

While Kinley's argument is generally a paragon of scientific method – as mentioned above, he praises the meticulous work of Engels on purchasing habits and elasticity – he also cites the importance of "bold imagination" in theory production. In other words, where GHSE advocates often reaffirm their commitment to induction, Kinley goes beyond it, mixing induction, deduction, and "what critics are likely to call guesses" (Kinley, 1914, p. 20). General theory, he writes, is not a theory of everything. It is merely a sketch of the economic world which has the potential "to show the general lines of probable truth" (Kinley, 1914, p. 18). Like the younger school, particularly Schmoller, he is in effect making the case that determining causality is fine, but stronger assertions of epistemological universality are not. The "truth" claims being made were limited to the context providing the empirical data, thereby underscoring the locational and temporal relativism that is a concomitant of the GHSE epistemology. In making this argument he refers to Engel's "laws" of consumption which reflected their Prussian context but, he believed, were probably not capable of wholesale extension without some modification to other countries, classes, and time periods (Kinley, 1914, p. 14).

Like Schmoller, Kinley held that economic statistics could uncover empirical "laws" that were regularities in sequences revealed within the appropriate data (cf. Streissler and Milford, 1993/1994). His references to "laws" reflected contingency. Their validity was not guaranteed in the future. They consequently avoided the problem of induction articulated by David Hume (1711–1776). In an unusual twist – especially given the apolitical claims made for contemporary positivism in marketing theory (cf. Tadajewski, 2010a) – Kinley self-associates with a politically oriented positivism (cf. Rutherford, 2010, pp. 64–65). He called for scholars to embrace statistics as a method of penetrating the social world. They provide us with insights that might otherwise elude scrutiny. In doing so, the politics of his positivism are apparent: "statistics enable us to present pictures of existing conditions showing wherein they are defective according to some accepted standard, and so enable us to make suggestions of remedies for the defects" (Kinley, 1914, p. 12). Mathematics and statistics are, therefore, essential inputs into social change; they are a means to inform political decision-making and reshape society. As he concludes, "carefully collected statistics will yet give us the ground on which we shall be able to formulate some of the general economic theories for which we are groping, and afford formulas wherewith to solve many problems of our industrial life" (Kinley, 1914, p. 20).

Although Fisk studied under Ely at Johns Hopkins, he was well connected to Wisconsin. He was known to pertinent figures in the institution when he worked at the American Embassy in Berlin and when ensconced at Illinois.

> Dr. Fisk had relations with the University of Wisconsin. . . . During the summer session of 1901 he was a member of that faculty [political economy], giving a course on European commerce, dealing especially with the history of commercial and diplomatic relations between the United States and Germany. In 1908 he also presented to the economic seminar of the University of Wisconsin a fine engraving of considerable size of Professor Gustav Schmoller of Berlin. It now hangs on the walls of the seminary room 122 in the historical library building and will always be a reminder of our friend, cut off, as it must seem to us, too early in a fruitful and promising career.
>
> (Ely, 1910a)

In 1908 Fisk resigned from Illinois and moved to Madison, Wisconsin. His wife was from Madison and they relocated to enter her family's business. That summer he died tragically from drowning. When Fisk quit, Kinley hired Simon Litman (see Figure 4.1) to replace him (Kinley, 1908). Litman had studied economics at

Figure 4.1 Simon Litman

Source: *Ray Frank Litman: A Memoir* (Litman, 1957).

Munich under Brentano (see Figure 2.1b). And so, marketing at Illinois became part of the legacy of the German Historical School. What distinguished the scholarship at Illinois was the extensive focus on international marketing. This was well informed and advanced, and our exploration of the topic adds considerable depth to the extant literature.

Simon Litman and the foundations of marketing thought

> The most pronounced influence upon the integrated and general development of marketing thought, however, centered not at Wisconsin or Harvard but at The Ohio State University, *the University of Illinois* [emphasis added] and Northwestern University – all Middle Western schools – whence flowed for a quarter of a century the writings and students of Maynard, Weidler, Beckman, Converse, and Clark.
>
> (Bartels, 1962, p. 35)

To continue this rollcall, he should have added "and Simon Litman", who, along with Jones and Fisk, taught one of the first marketing courses in America. It was offered and delivered by Litman, not at Illinois, but at the University of California, in 1902 – the semester following Jones's course at Michigan. This was only months before Fisk's offering ran at Illinois. Litman left California to accept Kinley's offer to join the faculty. This chapter documents his contributions.

Litman studied economics as an undergraduate in 1897 at the Ecole Libre des Sciences Politiques in Paris. One of his professors suggested that he pursue graduate work at the University of Munich (see Chapter 2, Figure 2.1b). He completed his PhD in 1902, returned to America, and settled in California. Litman was offered a position at Stanford University in the Department of Philosophy but felt unqualified to teach outside of economics. His only other option, as he later reflected, was to occupy the cutting edge of marketing pedagogy and research.

> My next step was to see Professor Adolph C. Miller at the University of California, Berkeley. He was organizing a new department, separate from that of history and kindred disciplines where economics was taught heretofore. Professor Miller was interested in establishing courses in commerce and industry. Could I undertake the work? Here my knowledge was also somewhat deficient, but I realized it was this or nothing. Nothing was out of the question, and so I decided to accept the offer. And so my academic career started in the second semester of 1902–03, when, as I learned later, I became one of the pioneers in teaching marketing and merchandising in the colleges of the United States.
>
> (Litman, 1957, p. 152)

University of California (1902–1908)

Litman taught three different courses during the second semester of the 1902–03 academic year: "Modern Industries", "Recent European Commercial Policies", and "Technique of Trade and Commerce". It seems that the idea for such a course may have come from Miller, but in any case, it was not Litman's. Nevertheless, he soon put his own stamp on it.

> When Simon Litman was asked to teach a course called "The Technique of Trade and Commerce", he had never heard of such a subject. Moreover, he was unfamiliar with American business, for he had lived and been educated in Russia, France, and Germany. . . . Thus Litman brought to the study of marketing a viewpoint probably unlike that of anyone else at that time.
>
> (Bartels, 1962, p. 30)

Bartels overplays the idiosyncrasy of Litman's education. His observation was more accurate when it came to Litman's international upbringing and personal experiences. Those did give him a rather unique perspective on trade and commerce, when compared with the backgrounds of other founding lecturers.

The "Technique of Trade and Commerce" course was described in the University Bulletin as "a study of the organization and institutions of commerce; commercial forms and practice" (1902–03). The next year, no doubt benefitting from Litman's increasing adeptness with marketing ideas, its Bulletin description was expanded.

> The system of weights, measures and moneys in different countries; the significance of price quotations and of the terms used in connection with sales in the different markets of the world; the meaning and determination of standards and grades as to quality; the forms and significance of invoices, bills of lading, warehouse receipts, consular certificates and other business documents relating to trade. The organization of trade and the devices used by governments and individuals to promote trade.
>
> (University of California, 1903–04, p. 17)

The references to different countries, various markets of the world, and consular certificates made it clear that this was not just a course in general marketing, but one that had a distinctive international focus.

The first couple of times he taught the material, Litman used German books on trade to help flesh out his lectures. As he later put it:

> There were no books, and trade and technical journals as well as governmental publications contained very little information which could be used either in the preparation of lectures or in the giving of reading assignments to the students. The works known to me covering the subject were mostly German treatises by Cohn, Grunzel, and van der Borght.
>
> (1950, pp. 220–221)

However, he soon developed his own content which better reflected and connected with the context his students would face:

> I abandoned it [the use of German texts] after two semesters and proceeded to deal directly with the status and characteristics of market distribution as it was organized by sellers of industrial raw materials, of agricultural commodities, and of semi-finished and finished goods. In order to gain information as to how the mercantile activities were specifically carried on in the United States, I interviewed wholesalers, retailers, managers of industrial concerns, brokers, advertising agents, exporters and importers. It took some time to make them admit the feasibility and desirability of having marketing courses in universities; their resistance was finally broken down and their rather hostile attitude changed to that of cooperation. The businessmen whom I approached thought that problems of merchandising could not be discussed effectively in the class room, that this had to be done in the field under the supervision of men of affairs. I pointed out that what they were favoring was a system of apprenticeship prevalent in many lines of endeavor in the past but discarded for more efficient methods with beneficial results to all.
>
> (1963, p. 28)

Like Jones at Michigan and later Taylor at Wisconsin, Litman recognized the value of hands-on learning (Litman, 1950). He took his cohort on field trips into Chicago where they visited the Board of Trade, Marshall Field's department store, Montgomery Ward, the Credit Clearing House, and other establishments (Litman, 1963, p. 41).

Litman included exporting and importing as an integral part of domestic marketing activities and was candid about the relationship between them.

> I acted on the assumption that marketing problems and methods do not differ in essentials from country to country, that fundamentals are the same irrespective of boundaries within which they are being applied. . . . The proximity of the port of San Francisco may have had something to do with the inclusion in my discussions of what has been termed foreign trade. I felt that this trade was not foreign to our national economy; the handling of outgoing and incoming products on docks and in piers, in warehouses and customs houses, in stores where importations were competing with domestic merchandise, seemed to me to present problems of salesmanship, advertising, and financing closely interwoven with national distributive activities. If this be heresy, I plead guilty to it.
>
> (1950, pp. 221–222)

This comment expressed his surprise that anyone would not consider international marketing a central part of the study of general marketing, especially for a country like the United States that was so deeply involved in global trade.

Litman has bequeathed us a detailed insight into his academic and non-work life. We have his reflections on teaching (1950) and an unpublished autobiography (1963). Usefully, a remarkable record of the course "Technique of Trade and Commerce" survives in the University of Illinois Archives (Litman, ca. 1902–08). Sometime during his tenure at California, he wrote a synopsis for a book he planned to write based on that course. A 23-page, handwritten manuscript survives, titled "Mechanism and Technique of Commerce" (a condensed outline is provided in Appendix 4.1). Litman referred to it as a "synopsis of a textbook which could be placed in the hands of students in our Colleges of Commerce", and as such it almost certainly represents the topics he covered at California as well.

Litman recognized that marketing had received little or no attention from American academics despite its "prime importance to students and business men" and called his proposed text "an analysis of the different institutions and organizations that have been established for the maintenance, protection and promotion of trade" (ca. 1902–08, p. 1). In fact, seven of the 22 chapters were to have dealt directly with institutions including retailers and wholesalers. His critiques of department stores anticipated related concerns voiced by Edward David Jones just a few years later: "[The department store] . . . reduces the number of independent small dealers, tends towards monopolizing trade, decreases the price of city real estate, offers sweat shop goods, reaches out where it should not, lowering standards (pictures, music), uses unfair methods in special sales, etc." (Litman, ca. 1902–08, pp. 20–21). As was remarked in Chapter 1, the institutional school later emerged as one of the three "traditional" schools of thought. This underscores Litman's prescience. The functional and commodity schools were also represented in his proposal, including chapters on the functions and methods of pricing and credit, advertising, and warehousing; and other material focused on commodities such as grain and cotton along with one on produce exchanges.

Within a few years, "Mechanism and Technique of Commerce" was published under the shortened title *Trade and Commerce* (1910) by the LaSalle Extension University, as part of a "course designed to meet the demand for efficient training in Commerce" (Litman, 1910, inside cover). It appeared in a collection of readings under the umbrella title of "Business Administration", combined with a six-chapter entry on "Government and Industry" and several other chapters, each written by different authors, all related to the overall theme of "Trade and Commerce". Thus, Litman's book is a book within a book. In *Trade and Commerce*, he defined the subject as a

> universal type of exchange . . . carried on by the modern merchant who is a necessary auxiliary to the agriculturer [*sic*] and the manufacturer of a country. It is he who . . . drives the wheels of industry, he who is responsible for the ceaseless activity in mines and in forests, in blast furnaces and in rolling mills; it is he who leads a nation to its position of industrial and commercial supremacy.
>
> (1910, p. 2)

It is evident throughout the book (and course) that Litman's use of the phrase "universal exchange" was a reference to what today is considered marketing. The content of the text parallels his 1902–08 outline, except for the addition of a section dealing with commercial geography and separate discussions of international trade organized by different commodities and countries as markets. The latter covers a wide selection of locations and details market size, consumption patterns, major industries, GNP, exports, and imports.

The most interesting and focused discussion of marketing is presented in a chapter titled "Competition in Trade". There Litman referred to what he called the "final struggle for the market". Every marketing activity is viewed through a lens of competition. Competition, he wrote, begins with the choice of location and the acquisition of goods. The means of retail competition are found in the personal characteristics of the merchant, such as innovativeness, friendliness, aggressiveness, and a precise knowledge of costs. Wholesale competition was presented as more specialized than retailing in its product range, but with wider geographic coverage and therefore more likely to face international market opportunities. Litman further distinguished between retail and wholesale practice by explaining the former as competition by "business unit" and the second as competition by "commodity". Techniques of promotion and pricing were indexed as "methods of competition".

In a critical move, he lamented the popularity of "underselling" (cost and price cutting) as a method of competition, blaming it for declining quality in many classes of goods, and the increasing use of bait-and-switch tactics. Although not calling it odd-even pricing, Litman unpacked the practice and ironically suggested (in 1910) that it had "lost a great deal of its value as a competitive scheme" (1910, p. 425). The use of rebates, trading stamps, and credit were all explicated as pricing "methods". And both the promotional as well as the protective functions of packaging were mentioned, with more emphasis on protection when goods were to be shipped to international markets.

Litman called attention to the greater importance of advertising for consumer rather than industrial marketing and remarked on the pros and cons of the newspaper as an advertising medium versus magazines for various product categories. Combined with brief discussions of personal selling and outdoor advertising, there is a detailed overview of direct mail, including the use of sampling and the construction of mailing lists. Indeed, it is remarkable how many of the practices explicated in these early texts and lecture materials are still relevant today.

Although published in 1910, *Trade and Commerce* is commensurate with the content of his earlier synopsis (i.e. "Mechanism and Technique of Commerce", ca. 1902–08) that was written while he taught at California. And, as we will see below, that material served as the basis of a course he taught for almost twenty years.

Litman's research during his tenure at California closely reflected his interest in foreign trade. He published multiple papers on the topic. Despite his productivity, he was concerned that advancement would be slow. To further enhance his output, generate industry-based insights for his teaching, and forge better connections to government – not to mention likely possibilities for promotion – he started looking for other opportunities. So, in 1908, when Kinley's offer came from Illinois, he accepted.

University of Illinois (1908–1948)

The University of Illinois was an enthusiastic proponent of collegiate business education. In 1870 it included in its nine departments a "School of Commerce" that offered courses in bookkeeping, commercial calculation, and correspondence (Scovill, 1952). It was discontinued in 1880 and, in any case, was not in the nature of the programs and schools opened at various other universities at the turn of the century. In 1902, perhaps sensing a rising tide, the university rejoined the movement by launching "Courses of Training for Business", with David Kinley as its Director. After graduating with the first PhD in Economics from Wisconsin in 1893, Kinley was hired as Assistant Professor at Illinois, promoted one year later to Professor (1894), and founded the Department of Economics in 1895.

After his return from Germany in 1901, Illinois President Draper approved of Kinley's proposition for business training, but like many experiments with commercial education, it lacked financial support from the administration. That changed in 1904 with the appointment of a new President, Edmund J. James, who had studied economics in Germany (see Figure 2.1a and 2.1b) and was the former Director of the Wharton School of Commerce. James had spent thirteen years at Wharton and was commissioned by the American Bankers' Association in 1891 to study continental schools offering education in commerce. The intended result was envisaged as a feasibility study regarding the possibility of establishing equivalent institutions on US soil. What he subsequently highlighted (1893) focused on the rising challenge of German trade to the British Empire and attributed its success to the superior preparation available to their students. As a response, fast-tracked development was desirable, with the establishment of college courses capable of inculcating the science of business and preparing students for management positions considered a priority.

James and Kinley's ruminations on the desirable future direction for business education were heading in a similar direction. Kinley envisioned economics, business, and marketing education firmly through the prism of ethics. Indeed, he could be highly critical of the existing political and business system. He referred to the corruption blighting the United States; the poor ethical standards exhibited by practitioners with respect to "public welfare" (Kinley, 1906, p. 378); and, like his mentor, Ely, sounded a cautionary note about the concentration of economic power. Even slightly more diffused power did not guarantee ethical probity.

To educate undergraduates well required them to be exposed to a variety of perspectives – again, this chimes with the ideal of social objectivity – and taught by people whose interest, knowledge, social responsibility, and ethics were given substantial room for growth. In his reflections on education, Kinley is effectively articulating a GHSE approach to pedagogy in which the core assumptions associated with the School are present. Education, he argued, was organic. It needed to change with society. As industry grew and expanded internationally, educational provision had to undergo transformation to ensure its relevance. This embodies his assumption about the "relativity, the changing character of economic institutions" (Kinley, 1910, p. 442). The university and school system, he submitted, must "promote the welfare of the pupils" (Kinley, 1906, p. 388). Economics education had to orient the student to the real world and foster critical thinking – "intelligent opinions" – regarding economic decision-making and institutions (Kinley, 1910, p. 441).

Kinley's educational philosophy resonated with the axiology and politics of the GHSE. It was relativistic whilst attuned to social need and welfare: "What things does the public wish the pupils to study? The answer would be different in Turkey from what it is in Illinois. . . . The schools should be close to the people and they should have local color; they should reflect in a measure the traditions, history, and character of the community" (Kinley, 1906, p. 390). Moreover, he expressed an interpretation of education that was consistent with Ely's "middle ground" attempt to defuse tensions between classes (i.e. mediating capitalism and socialism). His survey of educational requirements is sweeping, sensitive to political-economic requirements, and critical. It is worth citing in full.

> Today the successful pursuit of business is regarded by the community and country and the world as the test of a fully equipped man. Accordingly, our educational systems have been turning more and more to what is called practical training. Training for business . . . is the determining note of our educational course. The present demand that our schools shall train for economic success is particularly dangerous to the maintenance of our democratic ideals. The very test of excellence, economic success, tends to promote the formation of classes to the destruction of our democratic equality. . . . We need to remember that, after all, we are equal citizens of a free country, and that it should be our constant purpose to open the way for equal opportunity to all in all walks of life; that our schools, therefore, should afford training for all classes and all individuals to pursue any career for which they are particularly fitted. The establishment of trade schools for the children of people in particular trades is undemocratic; it tends to make and perpetuate classes.
>
> (Kinley, 1906, p. 394)

Education, for Kinley, had to enable social mobility (Kinley, 1949). It could defuse class conflict; and it was a means to foster one "general aim", namely, "social service" (Kinley, 1906, p. 395).

> Every pupil in the school should have the idea instilled in him that, while he is taking a course of study that will make him an economic success, and the school is maintained to let him achieve that economic success . . . [he is undergoing education with] the main purpose of serving society and promoting human progress.
>
> (Kinley, 1906, p. 395)

This perspective differs from what is discussed in Chapter 6 (i.e. in relation to Harvard Business School). Kinley's idealized education is optimistic, but he was not naïve. He did not assume that business would naturally pursue policies in line with community welfare without appropriate legislative rules of the game being set by an activist government. Harvard devoted considerably less – actually, very little – attention to the need for governmental intervention to ensure economic fair play. Kinley's students were not, in short, being trained to be business people first and foremost. They were being educated to act as informed citizens with commitments extending beyond pecuniary values (Kinley, 1910). Kinley's educational and administrative leadership, however, meant a loss to marketing thought; Simon Litman (1945) later reflected that his academic achievements were curtailed by his leadership activities. Still, his influence was felt, and as we have remarked above, Kinley is a significant figure in marketing for other reasons as well.

In 1902, the curriculum at Illinois included courses in trade, banking, transportation, journalism, and insurance. Content provision was revised for 1903–04 to include a much wider range of offerings in economics. As we have already discussed, one of the first professors Kinley hired to teach in the program was George Fisk. Litman replaced Fisk, taking over his role in 1908. The succession likely took place without the school missing a beat. Both men were very knowledgeable about marketing and devoted their considerable energies to covering relevant content. Nonetheless, there was a point of difference worthy of note. In contrast to Litman's beliefs about the interweaving of domestic with foreign marketing issues, Fisk taught them as separate, but related topics. The first was called "Foreign Commerce and Commercial Politics" and covered the following:

> Problems arising in connection with international trade relations, and various attempts to solve them; changes in theories and policies; economic systems (mercantile, free trade, and protective); classes of customs tariffs; commercial treaties; institutions for furthering export trade; commercial museums and bureaus of information, sample houses, consular reports, etc.
>
> (University of Illinois, 1908–09, p. 236)

"Domestic Commerce and Commercial Politics" focused more directly on marketing issues. As was explained, "The course deals with the principles and methods of buying and selling in internal trade" (University of Illinois, 1908–09, p. 236). Curiously, and in contrast to his own beliefs, Litman followed Fisk's example and continued to offer separate courses in domestic and foreign commerce. Perhaps, as a new member of the faculty, he was reluctant to promote his views. It might have been a matter of convenience or administrative expediency. Nevertheless, in 1911, Litman changed the title of the domestic course to "Mechanism and Technique of Domestic Commerce" which bore resemblance to his California course and was based on his (1910) book *Trade and Commerce*. "Mechanism" served as the introductory requirement (indeed, the only course) in marketing at Illinois until 1915. At that time, the business curriculum was reorganized under a "college" separate from the College of Liberal Arts and Sciences with several new modules, including "Salesmanship", "Advertising", and "Organization and Control of Mercantile Distribution" made available, none of which were taught by Litman. This said, he continued to deliver "Mechanism" until 1920.

Between 1912 and 1920, Litman was a frequent speaker outside the School on marketing subjects. In 1912, he provided lectures through the University YMCA on "Face to Face Salesmanship" and "Principles of Salesmanship". The School also offered non-credit, short business courses in which he gave lectures on "Credits and Collections", "General Aspects of Marketing", "Retail Distribution", and "Mercantile Credit", all during 1916. His pedagogic productivity continued in 1917, during which he gave several invited lectures on various aspects of "Retailing". Yet, by the cusp of the second decade, Litman redirected his attention towards graduate teaching and started to specialize in foreign trade.

> 1920 marks the end of my participation in business banquets as well as in short courses dealing with domestic commerce [marketing]. I started to devote full time to problems connected with international economic relations, with foreign trade in its various manifestations, with ocean shipping, and later with counselling graduate students and with the conduct of the seminar for doctoral candidates.
>
> (Litman, 1963, p. 44)

It is not surprising that he shifted his teaching from undergraduate and extension courses to graduate instruction. Then, as now, it reflected a pattern of career progression. Still, it is curious that he moved so completely out of marketing. There is no hint in his unpublished autobiography why this happened, but we can speculate about several reasons.

Following the war, in 1918–19, the School's enrolment and faculty doubled in size. This was the largest annual increase since 1902. At the same time, new majors were added to the undergraduate program and the number of graduate courses was expanded. A new department, "Business Organization and Operation", was formed under which all marketing courses were listed. Litman, at this point, was officially part of the "Economics" department within the School of Commerce. As a result of the organizational re-shuffling and change in the curriculum, 1920–21 was the last year he offered his course, "Mechanism and Technique of Commerce". By then, a new introductory offering, "Organization and Control of Mercantile Distribution", had taken its place and several new electives were available. The influx of faculty included marketing specialists such as Fred Russell in 1920 and Paul Converse in 1924. It was Converse who observed that Russell joined the faculty "to take over the marketing courses, allowing Litman to specialize in Foreign Trade" (1952, p. 65).

When he was hired, Russell was already a past President of the National Association of Teachers of Marketing and Advertising (NATMA, forerunner of the American Marketing Association) and author of two well-known textbooks on salesmanship. Converse later became President of the NATMA, and his distinguished career and contributions are well known (Huegy, 1958). With such high-profile specialists on faculty, Litman was no longer needed to teach courses outside of his current interests.

In 1919 he was promoted to Full Professor with an annual salary of $3,000. It might have been that he viewed this as a sign that his career had reached a stage of maturity requiring a different sort of contribution. Thus, by 1920 he had begun to do more research and writing than he had undertaken previously. Between 1917 and 1920 he was involved, under the auspices of the Carnegie Endowment for International Peace, in a series of studies on the economic effects of the World War. The opportunity for this work had come at the invitation of Kinley, who had been hired to edit the series and whom Litman admired and respected. That project led to his publication of a monograph, "Effects of War on Foreign Trade" (1919), and several articles including "Prices and Price Control in Great Britain and the United States During the World War" (1920), "Foreign Trade of the United States Since Armistice" (1921), and "Effects of World War on Trade" (1926). Of course, the effects were devastating. It brought to a dramatic halt the international economic integration triggered by the technological advances of the industrial revolution (Lindsey, 2002). It was ironic, then, that Litman would soon publish his most important contribution – a book about international marketing.

Essentials of International Trade (1923/1927) begins by stating its core premise: "There is fundamentally no difference between international, or what is termed foreign trade, and domestic trade. Both represent a private merchandising activity which is carried on for profit and consists of the purchase and sale of commodities" (Litman, 1927, p. 3). This statement was consistent with his synopsis of "Mechanism and Technique of Commerce" and his later (1950) arguments about the interweaving of domestic and foreign marketing. It does seem inconsistent with his practice during the twelve intervening years of teaching separate domestic and foreign marketing courses.

Essentials of International Trade is presented in two parts, the second of which deals extensively with market research, merchandising policies, channels of distribution and intermediaries, personal selling, advertising, credits and collections, and transportation. Once again scholars who believe that the marketing concept was invented by Robert Keith in 1960 would be shocked to read Litman's discussion of the desirability and difficulties of adapting products to market requirements and the profitability of such actions (*Essentials*, chapter 16). To improve the chances of successfully penetrating a foreign market, he recommends creating a separate department for export marketing, but advises that it be closely connected with other marketing activities taking place within the firm (*Essentials*, chapter 19). These issues – satisfaction of customers' needs at a profit and the requisite synergy between activities – are the central pillars of the marketing concept. As with other academic labor that followed an inductive approach, Litman's textbook writing *largely* eschewed theory and focused instead on the description of practice.

The *Essentials of International Trade* was relatively successful as measured by college adoptions. Between 1923 and 1932, approximately 66 different post-secondary institutions in North America adopted the book, including two Canadian universities (Eldridge, 1924; Litman, 1924–32). The Canadian usage is intriguing because of the obvious American positioning of the material. Its merit is underscored by the fact that it was translated into Japanese in 1929. The success of *Essentials* is anomalous and curious given the dramatic decline in international trade after World War I. Perhaps, even then, it was always best to be prepared for the unexpected.

Conclusion

Simon Litman was a pioneer at the University of California and Illinois. He published an important marketing textbook that has previously been neglected by our discipline. That book is most likely the best surviving description we have of the content of any collegiate marketing course of this period. As well, he authored what was undoubtedly one of the earliest textbooks to deal in any comprehensive way with the subject of international marketing.

Like other economists trained under the GHSE, Litman found that existing economic theory did not adequately explain the phenomena and problems associated with mass distribution. Consistent with the figures we have explored thus far, he used an historical, statistical, and descriptive approach that he hoped would inductively yield theory. He felt strongly, and at that time was distinctive in this belief, that the pedagogic experience must include the study of international marketing practices. In this he was one of very few surfers on the wave of international economic integration which came to a halt in 1914, not really returning until after World War II. This might be why Litman's work has passed unnoticed. His contributions appeared during that short window in time when the academic study of marketing was emerging and economic integration was stagnating.

How and why did Litman become a pioneer in marketing education? Being in the right place at the right time seems an apt description. At California, by his own admission, their course in the "technique of trade and commerce" was not his idea and initially he struggled with what the subject should cover. In order to develop his thinking, he drew from German books on trade, personal experience, and observations of business, as well as an extensive number of interviews with practitioners. The need to establish these connections was undoubtedly fostered by his graduate education, driven by necessity, and reinforced by the philosophy of education developed at Illinois by David Kinley and Edmund James.

Appendix 4.1

Outline of synopsis for proposed book (ca. 1902–08) "Mechanism & Technique of Commerce" by Simon Litman, University of California*

Preface

Scope & Purpose; an account of the complicated machinery of modern business; analysis of the different institutions and organizations that have been established for the maintenance, protection and promotion of trade.

Reasons for attitude taken: mechanism & technique of commerce has received little or no attention from English and American writers, although it offers a very broad field for investigation and is [of] prime importance to students and business men.

Part I. Institutions of commerce

Chapter 1. Caravans, Convoys and Factories

Historical and multinational (examples for Venice, Hamburg, Italian city republics, German Hausa, and English merchant adventurers, China, Japan, Africa).

Chapter 2. Consular Service

The judge for convoys and factories (examples – Turkey, Persia, Siam); organization of the consular service for the United States.

Chapter 3. Markets, Fairs and Auctions

Gathering places for buyers and sellers; examples of fairs – Leipzig, Novgorod; modern markets – Les Halls Centrales of Paris; auctions – London, Liverpool, Havres, Antwerp.

Chapter 4. Produce Exchanges

Origin, nature and significance; Classification; functions; methods of dealing.

Chapter 5. Stock Exchanges

Chapter 6. Chambers of Commerce

French type adopted by most European countries; chambers in England and the United States; New York chamber of commerce.

Chapter 7. Commercial Museums

Advantages in promoting foreign commerce; exhibiting producing and consuming capacities; testing new products; intelligence bureaus; examples – Philadelphia Commercial Museum, Imperial Institute of London, Museums of Brussels and Vienna.

Chapter 8. Ministries of Commerce

The state in its relation to trade; examples – Board of Trade in England, Department of Commerce and Labor.

Part II. Elements of commerce

Chapter 9. Labor in Commerce

Numbers and classifications of employees; salaries and working conditions for salespeople.

Chapter 10. Capital in Commerce

Chapter 11. Mercantile Credit

Extent and significance; various kinds of credit.

Chapter 12. The Credit Man

Duties and functions.

Chapter 13. Mercantile Agencies

Origin and growth of mercantile agencies; organization and management.

Chapter 14. Commercial Competition

Wholesale and retail; advertising mediums and methods, purpose and significance.

Part III. Organization of trade

Chapter 15. Single Trader and Partnerships

Suitability of single trader for commerce.

Chapter 16. Corporations

Advantages; economics of corporations.

Chapter 17. Agencies

Great value in the commercial life of today; universal, general and special agents; commission merchants, brokers, and commercial travellers.

Chapter 18. Wholesale Trade

Differences from retail; organization of wholesale trade in staple commodities; grain trade in the United States; cotton trade in England.

Chapter 19. Storage and Warehousing Industry

Significance; methods.

Chapter 20. Retail Trade

Growth and reasons for growth; effects of prices; peddlers and hucksters.

Chapter 21. Department Stores

Theories as to origins; business methods of the department store; advantages and disadvantages.

Chapter 22. Cooperative Distribution

Success in Europe, especially in England; growth in the United States; principles and methods of a cooperative store.

Note

* This is an outline of Litman's 23-page, handwritten synopsis of a proposed book on Mechanism and Technique of Commerce. The manuscript is undated but was written between 1902 and 1908 while Litman was at the University of California.

5 Foundations of marketing thought at the University of Birmingham, UK

Introduction

In this chapter, we chart the wider diffusion of the GHSE movement and its continued impact upon the earliest forms of marketing thinking and pedagogy. The scholar we examine had – until recently – been completely ignored by our discipline. And the institution he helped develop into an early bastion of marketing education was elided from historical research (e.g. Baker, 2013; Wensley, 2017; Wills, 1976).

Gordon Wills (1976) has sketched the contours of business education in the UK. This is an important account in the sense that it provides significant contextual background for the growth of business and marketing education in the post World War II period. He engages with institutional developments, government initiatives to forward business training, and his own involvement in helping create an institutional structure in which academics could flourish. With respect to the last point, he illuminates the establishment of a publishing company, a number of prominent journal outlets (e.g. *Management Decision*, *British Journal of Marketing* – subsequently the *European Journal of Marketing*), and the trials and tribulations of negotiating academic politics in a major growth period for our subject.

Baker (2013), likewise, has provided a thorough overview of his personal intellectual development and role in building marketing education in Scotland. Like Wills, Baker was an academic-entrepreneur, starting his own publishing company and a series of journals all carefully positioned to appeal to different segments of the marketplace of ideas (e.g. the *Journal of Marketing Management*, *Marketing Review*, *Social Business*). Baker was notably prominent in academic and practitioner associations (e.g. Academy of Marketing, Chartered Institute of Marketing) using his influence to help speed the development and professionalization of the discipline. His role in the UK has been equated to that of Philip Kotler in the US, courtesy of his prolific textbook output.

While these people and their institution building have been important, they were not necessarily breaking completely new ground. That distinction belongs to another individual, in another period entirely. In this chapter, we turn back the genealogical clock beyond the period that has received attention from Wills, Baker, and Wensley. We have to head to a different institution – the University of

Birmingham – and a pioneer advocate of commercial education whose name will be unfamiliar to even well-read marketing historians, William Ashley.

In this chapter we go beyond the narratives provided by Baker, Wensley, and Wills. What this account underlines is that the influence of those trained under the paradigmatic values of the GHSE was profound. This is true of the United States and it appears to have equally strong warrant in the case of the United Kingdom as well. To state the obvious, the former is an historical terrain that has been mined much more heavily than the latter – hence the weight of the content in this book being biased in favor of the US – but this also indicates an area for further investigation. One of the take-aways from this chapter is that those wishing to pursue research in the history of marketing thought would do well to consider exploring the UK as well as other countries to see what connections can be unearthed.

In terms of the content we cover, this chapter describes William James Ashley's early study and teaching of marketing in the Commerce Program at Birmingham. We offer a brief history of business education in Britain to provide appropriate context. Delving into the background of our focal figure, we explore Ashley's training and career leading up to the founding of the Commerce program in 1902. Most of the chapter explicates the structure and curriculum of that program, including the role of "business economics", within which marketing formed a topical component. He kept careful records of his teaching and students' research. This provides a mountain of archival materials that document coursework and assignments. These include lecture notes and the minute books of Ashley's Commerce seminar, course syllabi and exams, and one student's complete set of notes for Ashley's course on Business Policy.

William James Ashley (1860–1927)

The first British university degree program in business was offered by the Faculty of Commerce founded in 1901 at the University of Birmingham under the direction of William James Ashley, who served as Dean and Professor of Commerce until 1925 (Ashley, 1938; Fauri, 1998; Redlich, 1957; Usher, 1938). The impetus for the program came from the Birmingham Chamber of Commerce in 1898 (Neal, 1902; Sanderson, 1972). In 1900, after visiting "similar institutions in the United States and Canada", an advisory committee on commercial education recommended to the board of the University of Birmingham the formation of a Faculty of Commerce (Adamson, 1901). Smith (1974, p. 12) notes that the institutions visited by the committee included the University of Wisconsin, where their Course in Commerce was formally established in 1900, as well as the Wharton School at the University of Pennsylvania, and the University of California.

We presented Wisconsin as a wellspring for the value system associated with the GHSE. Likewise, California was at the cutting edge of marketing pedagogy. The University of Birmingham advertisement inviting applications for the Faculty's first dean signaled that "the Council does not wish to limit its choice by specifying in what department the first Professor shall be a specialist, but assumes that it will probably be in one or more of the following subjects: Economics,

Industrial Organization and Administration, Finance and Statistics, Commercial Law, or Commercial History" (Adamson, 1901, p. 51). They needed someone who could clarify the content of what should be taught in commerce, then teach the curriculum and sell the program to potential students as well as to employers in the British Midlands. They got all that in economic historian Ashley (see Figure 5.1). Notably, for our purposes, his application for the Dean's position was supported by Lujo Brentano and Gustav Schmoller (Kadish, 1991).

Ashley had been a student in history – with a strong interest in economics – under Arnold Toynbee at Oxford University. He also studied in Germany no less than three times (1880, 1883–84 under Knies at the University of Heidelberg, and 1902), acknowledging the influence of the German Historical School, especially Brentano and Schmoller, on his thinking. Later considered to be the leader of the British Historical School of Economics (Koot, 1987; Scott, 1928), Ashley has been compared with Schmoller, to whom he dedicated his (1900) *Surveys Historic and Economic*. In that dedication, he wrote: "[F]or a dozen years I have received more stimulus and encouragement from your writings than from those of any other" (Ashley, 1900, p. vi). In 1910 Ashley received an honorary doctorate from the University of Berlin. Of all the English economic historians, "perhaps only Ashley

Figure 5.1 William James Ashley, ca. 1923

Source: National Portrait Gallery, London, with permission.

was fully in sympathy with the German historicist aim of laying a foundation for a new and historical economic theory to be derived inductively from patient historical research" (Koot, 1980, p. 202). Those were precisely the characteristics of Ashley's approach to the study and teaching of business in general and of marketing, or "commercial policy" as he described it, in particular.

As the Dean, he designed a program that included marketing as an integral part of its curriculum. As Professor of Commerce, he used an historical, inductive approach to study and teach marketing as part of what he called "business economics". Beginning in 1903, Ashley taught his charges about the kinds of decisions they might face when undertaking various facets of marketing strategy (obviously, he did not use this terminology). His focus was primarily on channels of distribution and the functions performed by intermediaries. His teaching and the research by his cohort shared much in common with the commodity, institutional, and functional approaches.

Business education in Britain

At the turn of the twentieth century, England had one of the largest, most developed economies in the world, and an advanced system of postsecondary education including Oxford University, Cambridge, and the London School of Economics. The British economy was the fourth largest in the world behind only China, America, and Germany (Maddison, 2007). Despite a lower rate of industrial growth than her foreign competitors, America and Germany, growth in commercial occupations dramatically outstripped that of the other professions in Britain (Sanderson, 1972). At a time when the study and teaching of marketing was emerging in America, one would think that related developments were occurring in the UK.

Nonetheless, when compared with its sister countries, Britain was slow to develop a formal system of business education, likely due in part to a traditional anti-vocational, anti-technical bias in its pedagogic system (Engwall and Zamagni, 1998; Sanderson, 1972; Vincent and Hinton, 1947). The purpose of a British university at that juncture was generally considered to be the provision of a liberal education. Commercial education was, by contrast, viewed as "cheap and nasty" (Bryce, 1899, p. 696).

As early as the eighteenth century there was a relatively well-known proposal for formal business education in England (Norwood, 1961; Redlich, 1957). Among the eight subject areas in Postlethwayt's (1774) proposed British Mercantile College was "A General Survey of Trade and Commerce", including marketing-related material such as the importance of trading port to port, knowing how and where to "buy cheap and sell dear", and skill in freighting and hiring out ships. Redlich (1957) considered Postlethwayt's proposal as one of the earliest for the instruction and training of merchants in Europe (cf. Spender, 2005), but it never came to fruition. The idea of collegiate training lay dormant for about 100 years until a proposal was submitted in support of commercial courses in 1852 at King's College, London, but nothing came of that plan either (Redlich, 1957, p. 73).

When the London School of Economics was founded in 1895 it was the first in England to provide training in economics and was to have included preparation for business, but instead became more a school for civil servants and politicians (Engwall and Zamagni, 1998). A degree program in commerce was not instituted until 1919 (Smith, 1928). At Cambridge University, Alfred Marshall's Economic Tripos was approved in 1903. It was an attempt to link the study of economics more closely to industry (Sanderson, 1972). The curriculum included economic history, law, the structure and problems of modern industry, wages and conditions of employment, banking, and international trade (Nishizawa, 2002). While Marshall may have succeeded in making the study of economics slightly more relevant to business, it was not really intended as a commerce program in the tradition of those in America or Germany (Smith, 1928; Sanderson, 1972). Tribe described the claim that the Economic Tripos was training the practitioners of the future as "fanciful" (2003, p. 688).

The Manchester Faculty of Commerce and Bachelor of Commerce degree program, established in 1903, was developed by Sydney Chapman, whose strategy was quite different from Ashley's. What we mean is that he focused more on economic principles and theory, less on economic history, was more influenced by Marshallian economics than by German Historical Economics, and did not share with the Birmingham program the same emphasis on practical and descriptive analysis of the subjects at hand (Tribe, 2003). The University of Liverpool was also among this first generation of commerce programs and, not unlike Manchester, pursued an approach focused more on economic theory (Tribe, 1993).

What marks out the course of instruction at Birmingham is that it was the first university-level business program. It shared genetic origins with Wisconsin and Harvard Business School (HBS) – the GHSE. That led to an emphasis on marketing threading through the subject matter being delivered.

Ashley – economic historian and business educator

In 1888 at the age of 28, Ashley was appointed as the first Professor of Political Economy at the University of Toronto. In his first full-time academic position, he developed and taught courses on the elements of political economy, the history of political economy, and on current economic issues. For most of his teaching he used the conventional lecture method. But he supplemented these with an Economics Seminar, "at the weekly meetings of which students took turns in reading a paper, acting as reporter, and acting as critic" (Ashley, 1938, p. 40). In its pedagogical method, it borrowed from the GHSE and foreshadowed an important course he provided at Birmingham.

Because his position was a new one at Toronto, Ashley wanted his inaugural lecture to explain the terrain covered by his subject.

> [T]he great achievement of German thought in the last fifty years – the discovery and application of the Historical Method, had already transformed the study of Law when it passed to Political Economy. . . . It is asked what light

> is thrown upon the difficulties of today by merely antiquarian research into the gilds of the fourteenth century. Much more, perhaps, than the critic supposes. But the method I mean is the method of direct observation and generalization from facts, whether past or present; a method you can call 'inductive' if you wish to be polite, or 'empirical' if you wish to indicate scorn. . . . It seems to me that the economist could examine, for instance, the position of the agricultural interest in Ontario by just the same sort of method. . . . So the economist will not aim at ending with a 'law of rent' or a 'law of production' based on Ontario facts, but with a picture of Ontarian agriculture and of the influences that will affect it.
>
> (Ashley, W.J., quoted in Ashley, A., 1932, pp. 50–51)

The value he saw in the historical method was that an understanding of economic *history* was the foundation for grasping *current* economic problems or conditions. He consistently advocated an inductive, historical method of study for economics and business (Ashley, 1900, 1902, 1903a, 1903b, 1906, 1908) and believed that the exploration of economic history must have a practical purpose (1902, 1906, 1908): "I have never been ashamed to be frankly and nakedly utilitarian in the curriculum I have recommended" (Ashley, W.J., quoted in Ashley, A., 1932, p. 96).

In 1892 Ashley left Toronto to accept a position as the first Professor of Economic History at Harvard, where he spent the next nine years teaching economic history and applied economics and serving as associate editor of the *Quarterly Journal of Economics*. One of his colleagues was Professor Frank W. Taussig, the editor of the *QJE* and later one of the founders of HBS. During this period Ashley published extensively on English economic history (e.g. Ashley, 1887, 1888, 1900) and he was aware that business education was being developed across the country. Although Harvard Business School did not open its doors until 1908, it had been in the planning process for ten years. Moreover, towards the end of Ashley's tenure, there was increasing discussion of the possibility of offering training for executives, with Ashley's "work at Harvard . . . being developed to meet these new needs" (Usher, 1938, p. 151).

Moving to Birmingham

Ashley longed to return to England, and the opportunity to develop a new faculty of commerce at Birmingham seemed a good fit with his views of economics and business training. He was hired as the Dean of the new faculty in July 1901 and courses were first offered in the autumn of 1902. From the inception of the program until 1909, Ashley was "responsible for the entire arrangement of lectures – in that year [1909] he passed responsibility to individual lecturers for their own classes" (Smith, 1974, p. 43; Ashley, 1907, p. 15). This is important because it foregrounds the central role that Ashley played in developing the curriculum and the content for most of the courses over the formative period of the Commerce program. The intellectual energy required for this massive undertaking must have been significant. But it did mean that the structure of the Birmingham program was literally putty to be shaped and formed as Ashley – in conjunction with input from relevant gatekeepers and external groups (i.e. local business people) – deemed desirable.

During the year between his hiring and the actual start of courses in 1902, Ashley visited Germany to investigate the business schools at Cologne, Leipzig, Aachen, and Frankfurt. He later related these "educational experiments" in an article published in *The Times* and it is here we see an inflexion of the ideas that would later dominate the HBS, its managerial emphasis, and more conservative gestures to the importance of "service" which differentiate it from the socially progressive Wisconsin school.

Ashley sought to develop a curriculum that responded to the needs of business people. This was a highly salient move to legitimate Birmingham and its course offerings amongst influential community members that he did seek to bring into his orbit (this is evident in his "manifesto", which communicated the philosophy and instrumental utility of the program for prospective students and local business people respectively; discussed below). And this was important for someone with credibility to build. After all, the early cohort(s) when they eventually displayed their knowledge and skills could substantiate or undermine the value of the commerce course in the eyes of their employers and other influential groups. As Ashley explained what he had witnessed during his tour on the continent:

> [W]ith regard to economics, which in some form or other furnishes the backbone of every curriculum . . . in Germany that term includes a far wider range of topics treated in large measure descriptively, statistically, and historically, than is the case in England. . . . It may, however, be also urged that in training future men of business, the economist should not all the time occupy the standpoint of national production and distribution [as German Historical Economics did]; that he would do well to put himself in the position of the individual man of business and that he should try to obtain from economic literature and from current experience some light upon the way to tackle these general questions of policy which from time to time confront every merchant and manufacturer. . . . Here is the field for a true, industrial 'Betriebswirtschaftslehre' [business economics], which shall be more than that collection of coffee rules which is sometimes dignified in Germany by the name.
>
> (Ashley, 1903a)

Ashley asserted that the study of business was essentially one of applied economics and that the historical method was best suited to developing knowledge of the subject and practice. What is equally apparent is that while the GHSE provided a model of *how* to study and teach business, he felt that its focus on macroeconomics was not particularly useful to businessmen (Locke, 1984; Meyer, 1998). The *Handelshochschulen* had recognized that problem but, in 1902 their curriculum seemed inadequate to Ashley, too narrowly focused on accounting, production, and engineering. He would have to develop his own educational strategy. This was a herculean task.

When he returned to England, Ashley produced his manifesto for the new Program: "The Faculty of Commerce in the University of Birmingham – Its Purpose and Programme" (1902). He acknowledged that business schools in Germany and America had provided the "motivation" for the faculty and was impressed by the commerce programs at Wisconsin and Cologne (1903c). Illuminating his audience, the Birmingham program would address the concerns "not of the rank and file, but of the officers [of business firms], those who, as principals, directors, managers, secretaries, heads of departments, etc., will ultimately guide the business activity of the country" (1902, p. 1). In that way, Ashley was distinguishing his program from most German business schools, which he believed provided lower-level training. He was also setting an example followed later by the HBS, by focusing on senior management. Since his manifesto was targeted at potential students and employers, it did not go into detail about the use of the historical method, but he connected the expansive vision enabled by induction to teaching.

> It is not pretended for a moment that text books exist on 'Commerce' so understood. . . . The world has now had a long enough experience of modern means of production and modern means of communication for the accumulation of a large fund of experience . . . [to allow] a body of principles of policy deduced from current practice. The place of the academic teacher is not to elaborate some a priori theory, but to gather, arrange, and present lessons of practical experience. . . . [A] good deal more material in the shape of recorded experience exists than is commonly supposed. . . . [It] must first be got together and codified; and supplemented by constant references to the current experience of the leaders of commerce in the neighborhood.
>
> (Ashley, 1902, pp. 2 and 13)

There was a clear connection between Ashley's epistemology and pedagogy. Just a few years later he added,

> His [the teacher's] function is rather to collect examples as a naturalist collects specimens, of the way in which they have actually been dealt with, successfully or unsuccessfully, in real instances. These he will classify and arrange; he will bring to bear upon them all the knowledge of industrial history. . . . The materials lie all around us in the reported proceedings of companies; and American economists are already showing us how to use them.
>
> (Ashley, 1906, p. 10)

In place of "as a naturalist collects specimens", Ashley could have written "as an economic historian gathers evidence".

During the inaugural semester, Ashley arranged for ten lectures to be given by various businessmen from the British Midlands, "all of them authorities in their respective fields", and later they were published under his editorship as a "modest contribution to the preliminary survey and description of English business life" (Ashley, 1907, p. 3). These lectures delivered on his promise to gather, arrange, and present lessons based on practical experience, and they serve as an example of what would follow in Ashley's courses. The industries elucidated included the British cotton industry, woolen and worsted industries, linen and flax, railways, British shipping, the trust movement in Britain, and a lecture on the iron and steel industry by the Secretary of the British Iron Trade Association, who included in his notes a discussion of the "marketing and distribution" of steel (Ashley, 1907). By "marketing", the author meant selling and distribution through various channels using a variety of middlemen. He included a clear answer to the question regarding the value-added contribution of intermediaries. Keep in mind that this was being taught in 1902.

> We all know that the suppression of the middleman has been a popular cry with manufacturers and economists, as well as with buyers, for generations; but he will not be suppressed. The merchant usually has a better knowledge of the conditions affecting different markets than the producer. He comes more directly in contact with the buyer; he knows better to whom credit can safely be given, and is prepared to risk credits that the manufacturer would often refuse; he is well posted in railway and shipping rates and conditions, understands the peculiarities, practices, and requirements of particular markets, and has all other necessary commercial information, including freights and tariff duties, at his fingers' ends. On the whole, therefore, it is probable that the merchant will continue as hitherto to play a leading part in the principal industries of this country, the iron trade included.
>
> (Jeans, 1902, in Ashley, 1907, pp. 21–22)

In other words, intermediaries are essential to exchange. You can eliminate the middleman, but not his functions. What we have here is an example of historical evidence being used to generate the basic functions of middlemen. Whether he knew it or not, this business person manifested an appreciation of locational relativism. He refers to the specificities of the "particular markets" that form the object of their attention. The first concept – the functions of middlemen – are still taught today; the second point about relativism continued to be the subject of intellectual wrangles well into the late twentieth century. Issues of product, advertising, and other forms of adaptation on a country-by-country basis are core components of any international marketing course being delivered today.

Much of Ashley's manifesto for the Commerce program was devoted to outlining the curriculum. This consisted of four main categories: (1) languages and history (European and American), (2) accounting, (3) applied science and business technique (including economic history), and (4) commerce. "The courses on commerce", he wrote, "will give their colour to the whole scheme of instruction. . . . [T]hey are intended to be the most characteristic feature of the Birmingham plan" (1902, pp. 7 and 12). There were four of these courses required of all enrollees, one each in the first (Commerce I) and second year (Commerce II) of the program, another (Commerce III, also known as "Business Policy") in the third and final year, and finally the "Commerce Seminar", which, in the early years of the program, had to be taken by all students. Ashley delivered Commerce I, which was basically a history of British industry and trade. Commerce II was a mirror of Commerce I but covered the United States, Germany, and other European countries, and was offered by another instructor, although likely designed by Ashley. Most importantly, he taught Commerce III–Business Policy, and led the Commerce Seminar, and it is in these two courses that we find the most direct evidence of marketing ideas in the curriculum. One of the reasons Ashley taught these was because he "had experience of the successful working of courses of this character in Harvard University" (1902, p. 12), which suggests that he had been involved in the planning discussions about their potential business school.

Ashley was the only instructor for the Business Policy course for several years and he chaired the Commerce Seminar with other faculty members. Other than Accounting and Finance (in the form of the course on "Technique of Trade", later renamed "Business Technique"), the program did not separately treat what we consider today as the various sub-disciplines of business (including marketing) as was typically done in US schools, even then. It covered production, management, and commercial policy (marketing) together as related parts of one course called Commerce III–Business Policy. To put this into perspective, we need to understand Ashley's concept of business economics, of which business policy was a central part and under which we find commercial policy or marketing (see Figure 5.2).

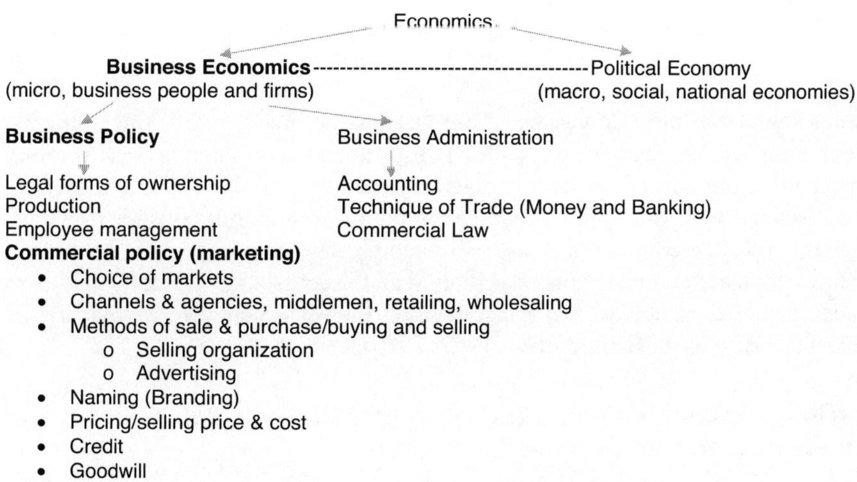

Figure 5.2 William Ashley's business economics and commercial policy (marketing)

Source: Adapted from Ashley (1902; 1908; 1926a; 1926b).

Business economics and marketing

Of course, Ashley held the view that "the really constitutive and most characteristic part of a commercial curriculum at the university must be found in Economics" (1906, p. 8), not Political Economy (it was too abstract and theoretical), or the *Volkswirtschaftslehre* (the social and national economics of peoples) that was taught in German universities, and not even the *Betriebswirtschaftslehre* (business economics) or *Privatwirtschaftslehre* (private economics) currently being developed. He envisioned the enlargement of economics to encompass the perspective of the individual business man or organization (1908, 1926a). This was parsed from what he had seen in Europe, which, in his opinion, devoted too much attention to accounting. To give students the necessary viewpoint, it must be based on economic history, which would provide the background for detailed studies of the present-day questions and conditions of any trade. Those individuals taking this course were going to be exploring business problems involving the "series of judgments one after the other on matters of policy" (1908, p. 190).

> Business policy comes to be considered under two heads of 'commercial' and 'manufacturing'. Of the two sides, it is, of course, the commercial that must control; it is of no use in business to make a thing, however, beautiful, unless it can be sold. Commercial policy is simply a matter of buying and selling – and of these processes as mutually determining one another; for buying of material and of services depends largely upon the price at which we can sell finished goods, and selling price depends largely on the cost of what one has to buy, the time and terms of purchase and sale, of the amount and length of credit to be accepted and granted, and the like . . . the agencies and channels for sale in the home and foreign markets, the relations to wholesale merchants and other middlemen, to agents or to branches, and the question of the purpose and methods of advertising.
>
> (1908, pp. 195 and 197; see also Ashley, 1903c)

Ashley registered the importance of production and marketing as the core of a relevant curriculum. He goes further than this, stating that marketing was the more important of the two. That view was later shared by the new Dean at Harvard, Edwin Francis Gay. For Ashley, commercial policy or marketing was the driver of business policy. We get some sense of the emphasis being placed on marketing when we look at the final exams associated with the course. They usually included ten essay questions, at least two and sometimes four of which were devoted to the subject (University of Birmingham, 1902–1910).

Teaching commercial policy (marketing): "Business Policy" and the "Commerce Seminar"

Ashley's Commerce III–Business Policy course was lecture based, but there was synergy between it and the Commerce Seminar that relied on historical case studies and a Socratic method of teaching. It is highly likely that the field trips and student research presentations in the Seminar provided some of the examples used by Ashley in his Business Policy lectures.

Commercial policy included most of the elements of marketing strategy we think of today: choice of markets, channels and their various agencies or middlemen, methods of buying and selling, including personal selling and advertising, naming or branding products, the establishment of selling price, credit, and building goodwill. Much of what we know about this course is based on detailed notes taken by a student in 1905, some of it from Ashley's lectures published in 1926, which were developments upon "the lines of a course [Business Policy] I have been giving for years at the University of Birmingham" (1926a, p. vi). The assigned readings included, among others, selections from his works on economic history as well as a volume of "Lectures on Commerce" published by the University of Chicago in 1904, including "The Commercial Value of Advertising", "At Wholesale", and "The Credit Department of Modern Business" (Hatfield, 1904).

The topic "choice of markets" was important enough to be listed in the University Calendar description of "Business Policy" and this signals Ashley's appreciation of market segmentation and the notion of using various policies or strategies for different markets. His views of marketing were consistently influenced by costs, efficiency, and the maximization of profits (1926a). For instance, he justified targeting multiple markets with differentiated prices as a means of achieving efficiencies in production. A related justification was invoked for diversifying the number of products offered by one firm as well as the number of markets targeted, since these policies would spread fixed costs over a broader base of sales. In other words, companies targeted multiple markets because it was more efficient and profitable to do so. More interesting was his reasoning for diversification. This was related to addressing the seasonality of demand; it is effectively a risk-reduction strategy. As examples, he cited an organization in the greeting card business that moved into printing books, and a motor car company that added "public service cars" (taxi cabs) to its main line of "ordinary traveling cars".

Channels of distribution warranted much attention, including a relatively sophisticated understanding of the reasons for and against the use of intermediaries, a theme that Ashley wove throughout most of his lectures on marketing. He pointed out that channels tended to be longer (i.e. there were more middlemen) when handling perishable items, when transporting longer distances, and when a wider variety of products and markets were being served. Shorter channels tended to characterize the marketing of products with high selling prices or that required detailed technical knowledge (Ashley, 1926a). As the reader can no doubt appreciate, these are basic principles that are still featured in general intro-level courses through to more specialized business-to-business options available today.

Middlemen were useful, he averred, as long as they resulted in satisfactory prices and regularity and timeliness in delivery, combined with a decent range of choice, all in a location that facilitated consumer access and purchase (1926a, p. 58). He also recognized that advertising was changing the role of, and need for, retailers.

> The function of the retailer has been profoundly modified by modern advertising. . . . Today the manufacturer or the merchant supplying the goods seeks by advertisement so to impress a name upon the general public that the retailer will be compelled to keep his particular goods. . . . There is a particular brand, we will say, of tea, with a rememberable [*sic*] name, which extensive advertising seems to have successfully printed on the public mind.
>
> (1926a, p. 61)

In his lectures on "commercial middlemen", Ashley used examples from the furniture industry, bicycle trade, automobile industry, textiles, and the steel industry of the region to emphasize the value of intermediaries and the functions they performed (Tasaki, 1905). He "ensured that his course kept in touch with the realities of business life in the Midlands through his own and his staff's close contacts with local industrialists" (Sanderson, 1972, p. 197). We also know from the minutes of the Commerce Seminar that those connections were further developed by undergraduates via their visits to companies, first-hand observations, and research into the workings of nearby firms. In that way, again, there was a symbiotic relationship between Ashley's two courses, with these excursions redolent of the influence of the GHSE.

Other examples of industries assigned for study in the Commerce Seminar and which functioned as cases in Ashley's Business Policy course included London furniture retailers who attempted to integrate backward into manufacturing and Birmingham furniture producers who integrated forward into retailing. Both were used to demonstrate the advantages and disadvantages (or requirements) of adding channel functions such as retailing and advertising. He taught about the pros and cons of granting geographic monopolies to wholesale agents in the bicycle industry and the experiences of one cycle manufacturer that decided to circumvent agents altogether by selling direct to consumers in their own retail shops. But the increased cost of advertising and retailing, of course, more than offset the cost of agents' commissions, illustrating the earlier cited point that you can eliminate the middleman, but not their functions.

Next to channels, more attention was devoted to selling price than any other marketing topic in the Business Policy course. Ashley presented price as the "fundamental question or phenomenon of business" (Tasaki, 1905). He made a point of distinguishing between the theory of price in economics and the way pricing decisions were made in reality. For example, economists differentiated between price and value; business people did not. Price was not simply determined by supply and demand, but by the "intensity of desire" that customers registered towards an object or service.

In one of his lectures Ashley proposed that manufacturers adapt their costs of production to price rather than the other way around. Most notably he unpacked how merchants try to "secure a quasi-monopoly, some sort of special hold [that is, control] of the market . . . by using trademarks [brands]" in order to influence price (Tasaki, 1905). The well-known British brand, Pears Soap, was used as an example. Being at the forefront of scholarly practice, Ashley even tied the concept of branding to price elasticity.

Another marketing topic listed in the University Calendar description for Business Policy was "buying and selling". Quoting the adage that "goods well bought are half sold", Ashley explained what "well bought" meant and, not surprisingly, his rationale was largely consistent with what later came to be known as the marketing concept. Where his account differs is that he focused on the role of managerial intuition in divining what products people would desire. However, we are nitpicking a little here, and the practice that he proposes was fairly common, and often called "putting yourself into your customer's shoes" (Tadajewski and Saren, 2009). Furthermore, he was talking about local merchants in many cases, and local producers were closer to their market. They would, therefore, be more likely to have an accurate grasp of the needs of their customers. As Ashley explained,

> As a buyer of merchandise, he [the retailer] must be governed in his purchases, not by styles and qualities which manufacturers produce for the country at large, but by his own personal judgment as to the wants of his own particular customers. . . . [H]e has to think of only one side – his customers. . . . [The retailer needs to consider] the relation of the commodity to the desires of the customers.
>
> (Tasaki, 1905)

Ashley went on to distinguish between the commercial strategy of designing (for instance, the quality of) products from what he called the "moral strategy". From a marketing point of view, a product's "quality should be related, not to the thing itself, but rather to the purpose to which it is desired". In other words, product quality should be designed to meet customers' expectations, not some morally determined level. In this way, he differed in opinion from E.D. Jones and H.C. Taylor. According to Ashley, it was a "mistake to provide quality in goods beyond [that] likely to be needed" (Tasaki, 1905). Explaining this issue, he suggested that one of the reasons the Germans and Americans were invading the British market for machinery and tools was because the products of English manufacturers were better finished, "finished for the finish's sake, simply wasted", and customers were not willing to pay for it.

Of course, Ashley's coverage of "selling" included both personal selling (peddlers and commercial travelers were discussed) and advertising. Saying this, given the relatively limited amount of information available on advertising at that time, there was less discussion of this topic. He did lecture on the history of advertising and how technology had reduced the cost of paper, thereby touching upon print advertising, which had enabled the production of more visually appealing marketing communications (Tasaki, 1905). In fact, he sounded a critical note about the profusion of advertising in public spaces, a topic that was starting to get some coverage in the presses. He bemoans the "bewildering multiplicity of advertisements". The primary objective of advertising, Ashley opined, was not to provide information, but rather to create familiarity with the name of the company. The example he used was Cadbury's Chocolate, which was known for the outstanding artwork in its print advertisements but rarely included substantive information. Even so, for products sold to the general public, in large quantities, with greater effective demand, characterized by a range of wants and "owing to the spread of education", advertising was essential. On the other hand, he registered that for some businesses, especially those in markets with small numbers of buyers which required a high degree of technical knowledge (i.e. the ship building trade and its clientele), there was no need for advertising. The same logic applied to firms that did not deal with the general public but, rather, with other manufacturers (so, he dealt with business-to-business marketing) or the government (and business-to-government). This evaluation of advertising was the focus of a question posed on the final exam in 1908.

> Can any general principles be laid down with regard to Advertising from the point of view of business policy? Take some trade with which you are acquainted, and compare Advertising with other possible means of bringing about an increase in sales.
>
> (University of Birmingham, 1902–1910)

Despite the fact that he may not have used the term "principles" in his lectures, Ashley used generalizations based on the inductive method. He looked at what practitioners were doing in their everyday lives and developed general statements as a result. For example, he taught that advertising works best with products sold to the general public in large numbers, whereas commercial travelers (personal selling) works better in markets with small numbers of customers requiring a high degree of technical knowledge. And channels tended to be longer when handling perishable items and when transported long distances, whereas channels tended to be shorter where selling prices were relatively high or products required technical knowledge.

Ashley's policy course borrowed from and reinforced his Commerce Seminar, which was quite unique for undergraduate education at that time. As one of his students observed, "as a teacher he could apply the Socratic method with great skill" (Heaton, 1927, p. 683). The Commerce Seminar obviously borrowed from the seminar method of teaching and field trips used in German economics courses and foreshadowed the case method later developed by Harvard Business School. The purpose of the Commerce Seminar was

> to train students in independent investigation and reasoning. . . . A subject is assigned some weeks beforehand to each member of the Seminar. He consults the literature of the subject and makes such inquiries as the Professor [Ashley] may suggest; and then prepares a paper which is read at the Seminar.
>
> (University of Birmingham Calendar, 1903/04, p. 347)

At each meeting, one or more attendees would present their research findings followed by questions from Ashley and Adam Kirkaldy, the faculty member who also taught Commerce II. A general discussion then commenced. One student served as secretary and produced a two- or three-page summary of what transpired in the meeting. These notes were gathered and saved as the "Minutebooks of William Ashley's Commerce Seminar" and provide a record of research and seminar discussions from 1903 until 1919 (Ashley, 1907–1912; 1913–1920). Since the seminar met weekly through the academic calendar, there were approximately 20 sessions and therefore 20 or more presentations made each year.

Table 5.1 lists a sample of topics that were assigned during the earlier years, subjects that included much discussion of marketing, and the source materials

Table 5.1 Commerce seminar marketing topics assigned and source materials

Topic Assigned (date)	*Readings and Source Materials*
The Organization of Retail Trade (1903)	
Branch Offices, Agencies, Their Organization (1904)	
The Markets of Birmingham (1904) [agricultural]	Guide books, and people actually engaged in the markets
Carpet Industry (1905)	Actual specimens of carpet
Lancashire & Some of Its Industries (1905) [cotton, lumber, woolens, flannels, glass, flax, iron foundries]	Board of Agriculture Report; Baine's History of Lancashire; The History of the Port of Manchester
Birmingham Jewelry Trade Past and Present (1905)	*The Industrial History of Birmingham; The Birmingham Hardware District;* Interviews with local companies
The German Toy Trade (1906)	
The French Toy Trade (1906)	London agent of a French firm; *Dictionnaire du Commerce*
Birmingham Exhibition [Motor Trade] (1906)	Visit to the exhibition
Commercial Methods [wholesale vs retail] (1906)	
Motor Industry (1907)	Visit to the Humber Motor Works in Nottingham
Olympian Motor Show (1908)	Visit to show as well as to Daimler Motor Works and BSA Motor Works; photographs
American Consumers' League (1908)	Guest speaker: John Graham Brooks, first president of the National Consumers' League
Business Organization and Marketing of the Carpet Industry (1910)	
Corn Merchants (1910)	Internship at Messrs. Dreyfus Merchants
The Merchanting of Hardware (1911)	First-hand information; trade papers

Sources: Ashley, W.J. (1902–12; 1917–18).

used in preparing some of the papers which were delivered. There was an approach shared by most of the undergraduate papers. They were case studies which started with an historical sketch of the company or industry assigned, followed by a description of then-current practices, sometimes a comparison with different industries or other countries. The business practices were often marketing related, usually dealt with various aspects of distribution, and could varyingly be defined as reflecting functional, institutional, or commodity approaches.

Some examples of the channel-specific seminars reviewing the various institutions and their roles include "Organization of Retail Trade", "Classes of Business Through Which Goods Went Before Reaching Customers", "Merchanting Hardware", and "Branch Offices and Agencies". Commodity studies included "The Agricultural Markets of Birmingham", "The German Toy Trade", and "Flour Milling". Reflecting their more descriptively oriented training, the presenters seldom attempted to define or conceptualize their topics. One exception was "The Merchanting of Hardware", where the novice made a point of defining his use of the terms "merchant", "merchanting", "factors", and "jobber" – drawing a distinction between the use of the term "factor" in Britain and "jobber" in the United States. In this seminar, merchants (wholesalers) in Britain were presented as being "assailed" by commission agents and, in America, by manufacturers using catalogs to sell direct to consumers. "Merchanting" included all the processes of distribution carried on in wholesale quantities, but excluded the direct trade of manufacturers and retail shop-keeping. Those processes (functions) entailed assembling an assortment of goods, sorting into small quantities, extending credit, storing goods, shipping, and providing information to manufacturers and retailers. The presenter delivering this paper concluded: "the manufacturer and retailer would suffer if the middleman was eliminated".

One of the earliest Commerce Seminar sessions dealt with the "Organization of Retail Trade" (1903) and emphasized the importance of location, the use of vans for delivery, and the critically important selling role filled by "shop assistants". One gets the reassuring impression that the student making this presentation believed that selling was the most important work carried out in a retail establishment. According to the seminar minutes, in answer to a question from Ashley about the methods used by [clothing] retailers for buying, the student noted that "trade was frequently put out by the fickleness of the lady customers who were never certain of what they would wear in the near future" (Austin, 1903, in Ashley, 1902–12).

This perspective highlights the positive tenor of Ashley's overall approach regarding the value of marketing, its affiliations with what would become Harvard-style approaches to management pedagogy, connections to industry, and the more conservative positioning of this course when contrasted against the activist approach that we saw in some institutions in the United States.

Ashley's decisive call for a broadening of economic theory to encompass research that would generate managerial utility necessitated a shift in perspective. It is here we see the kernel of the managerial orientation prior to its articulation at HBS, which continues to dominate marketing today. Consistent with this micro-orientation, marketing functions and strategic decision-making were featured in many of these presentations. Sometimes a paper would focus on one or more areas of marketing strategy as in "Commercial Methods" (see Table 5.1). This reviewed the use of trade shows such as the Birmingham Motor Exhibition as a form of advertising, and explicated what is known today as a price skimming approach.

Fittingly, given the references that Ashley had made to corporations and firms trying to secure quasi-monopoly controls over their targeted markets, the seminar notes referred to the ability of larger firms to control channels and set prices in order to "skim the cream" and increase profits. That is the first use of the idea of price skimming of which we are aware and may not have appeared in publication until half a century later when Dean (1951) wrote: "the strategic decision in pricing a new product is the choice between (1) high initial prices that skim the cream of demand and (2) a policy of low prices from the outset . . . for market penetration" (p. 419). It is uncanny that Dean used the exact same phrase – "skim the cream".

Conclusion

William James Ashley retired as Dean in 1925 at the age of 65 and died just two years later. His legacy as a scholar, administrator, and teacher includes significant contributions to the study of marketing in Britain. As the first Professor of Economics at the University of Toronto and first Professor of Economic History at Harvard, he was a pioneer in the study of economic history. As the Dean of the first university commerce program in the Commonwealth, he continued to operate at the cutting edge by being among the first to teach marketing in the UK. This appears to have had personal repercussions that were a function of his multifaceted position at Birmingham. One of Ashley's American (University of Wisconsin) colleagues, William A. Scott, wrote that Ashley "suffered from being a pioneer" (1928, p. 319), a reference to him spreading himself so thinly that he fettered his own contributions to knowledge.

Ashley was strongly influenced by the GHSE, especially in epistemology, research method, and pedagogy. But his views did not necessarily echo those of the other scholars we have explored in the rest of this book. Ashley's position was more conservative when compared with his activist colleagues. This should not really be a surprise. Intellectual inquiry attracts people of various political persuasions. Some seek to demand large-scale social change, wanting to reform the market without compromise. Others tread a more cautious path. Those located at Wisconsin were fortunate to be situated within environmental circumstances which permitted, even encouraged, a greater degree of radicalism than others. Ashley did not have the privilege of these conditions. Nor was his background, despite its GHSE inflexion, likely to foster a politically activist approach. He grew as an academic in the environs of Harvard, then found himself having to help develop, promote, justify, and legitimize business education in a climate that had not previously been hospitable to this offering. To do so successfully required him to be the consummate politician, adeptly engaging with the local practitioner community, and helping produce students who would reflect well on the newly established program. The graduates who left Birmingham were encouraged to engage in critical thinking. It is just that their critical reflection ran along trammeled lines – those that were pro-marketing, underscored the value added by its associated practices, and sought to advance business needs for profit. To expect anything else in this context would be unrealistic.

Ashley's contributions to scholarship, while modest in number, placed him at the forefront of the English Historical School of Economics (Koot, 1987; Scott, 1928). He brought the same approach to the study of marketing. Although never a mainline focus of his research and writing, he recognized that marketing was an axis of business practice and, as an administrator, he gave the subject a central role in the curriculum he designed and implemented. He gathered examples of appropriate practice from industrial history and local businessmen to use in his teaching. It might be because the Birmingham Commerce Program was intended as a vehicle for training senior managers that marketing was imparted as part of business policy, rather than a separate discipline as was the case in America.

Ashley's business economics was taught using the same approach as the seminars in Germany and the case method later popularized at Harvard Business School. The resulting historical, descriptive accounts of market selection, design of distribution channels, methods of attracting demand, setting prices including the use of credit, branding products, and selling and advertising were used as the foundation for many of his lectures as well as topics for undergraduate research. If we look beyond our twenty-first century marketing terminology to the ideas behind the concepts, it is not difficult to find evidence of their existence in early twentieth century university education, including Britain's. Admittedly, Ashley was not a specialist. In spite of this, the range of topics covered in his courses was considerable, and he placed a clear emphasis on channels of distribution. In that way, his pioneering efforts were in line with those in the US.

6 Foundations of marketing thought at Harvard and beyond

Introduction

In this chapter, we explore the contributions to marketing thought made by academics aligned with the Harvard Business School (HBS). We begin by illuminating the personal influences that impacted the formation of the HBS. Their connections with the GHSE are differentiated from those exhibited at institutions like Wisconsin. We then engage with Scientific Management, which shared – to some extent – certain epistemological assumptions with German Historicism. This parallelism was not true with respect to political values. Subsequent sections of this chapter focus on the philosophical and conceptual contributions made in Cambridge, Massachusetts, devoting particular attention to the role of Arch W. Shaw.

Cambridge, Massachusetts

Along with the University of Wisconsin, Harvard University was another center of influence on the development of marketing thought. Founded in 1908, the Graduate School was based on a vision of business as a profession, an art, and a science. As such, it became one of the first academic, professional business schools in the world.

> Harvard not only was influential during the early years but, unlike Wisconsin, continued as a center of influence in the development of marketing thought and practice. To Harvard went such students as Cherington, Shaw, Copeland, Tosdal, Weidler, Maynard, McNair, Borden, and Vaile. Their contributions . . . have included methodology for the analysis of problems of market distribution, methodology for teaching marketing by the use of problems, major works on advertising, merchandising, sales management, retailing, and general marketing.
>
> (Bartels, 1962, p. 35)

The “methodology for the analysis of problems” was, of course, an inductive, historical approach. Harvard became (and still is) famous for the case method, which is consistent with the seminar method of teaching delivered in Germany that

Figure 6.1 Edwin Francis Gay, ca. 1908

Source: Wikimedia. https://upload.wikimedia.org/wikipedia/commons/1/18/Edwin_Francis_Gay_in_1908.jpg.

was familiar to the founders of HBS. Nonetheless, the contributions developed at Harvard were manifested in different ways from the research and teaching at Wisconsin. There was not the same emphasis at Harvard on social reform and the role of government in the economy, and less attention was directed to the dark side of business practice.

The seeds of teaching and research in marketing were planted by the Economics department. Of the economists at Harvard who studied under the GHSE (see Figure 2.1a), only Edwin Francis Gay, Frank Taussig, and Harry Tosdal were involved with the business school and credited by Bartels for their contributions to marketing. Taussig and Gay were instrumental in the planning of the HBS, and Gay became the School's first Dean (see Figure 6.1).

Formative influences on the Harvard Business School

In 1898 the innovative and progressive-minded President of Harvard, Charles W. Eliot, considered the possibility of founding a school for diplomacy and government service. During the next decade, his plan evolved through various stages to include public service and administration and public and private business, and ultimately focused on the latter. The Business School was Eliot's final innovation as President before retiring in 1909.

He endorsed the ideals of nineteenth century German professional education, which included vocational preparation and obliged faculty members to engage in teaching and research. During Eliot's presidency (1869–1909) the seminar method was introduced by Henry Adams in history, by Archibald C. Coolidge in government studies, and by Taussig in economics. The *Quarterly Journal of Economics*, launched in 1886, was the first of its kind to produce content for a community of scholars, rather than the general public. This was followed by the publication of *Harvard Economic Studies* in 1906.

During 1907, when Eliot had settled on starting a school of business, he exchanged views on professional and graduate training in business with Frederick W. Taylor of Scientific Management fame. Taylor had addressed the audience attending the opening of a new engineering building at the University of Pennsylvania (Taylor, F.W., 1906), making a plea for bringing students into early and close contact with the working world. In a letter to Taylor, Eliot supported that strategy.

> I heartily agree with you that laboratory and shop work in an university do not serve the same purpose as work in real shops and factories among men working for a living and that this actual contact with men working for a living is a necessary part of preparation for any one of the scientific professions, including business.
>
> (Eliot, 1907)

If this exchange did not come to the attention of Gay, the soon-to-be-appointed Dean, it prophesized his use of the term "laboratory method" to describe the School's unique approach to teaching. We will discuss this point more fully below. But before turning to Gay's role in planning for the School, we must briefly reflect upon the contributions of Frank Taussig.

It was noted in Chapter 2 that Taussig was a student of the GHSE (see Figure 2.1a). As the reader will recall, he was less enthusiastic than others about the ideas of his continental teachers, claiming greater influence on his thinking by Alfred Marshall, the famous English economist. That was no serious disclaimer against the GHSE. While best known for his mathematical reasoning and theoretical results, Marshall praised the work of the GHSE and considered it an important source of inspiration for his own insights. He was fluent in German and studied under GHSE scholars in Berlin (1870–71), absorbing their ideas like a sponge (Hammond, 1991). Most notably, he was influenced by their metaphor of the social organism and held that historical facts were necessary (but not sufficient) to unravel the market and that both inductive and deductive approaches were valuable. In assessing the contributions of this group, Marshall reflected,

> It would be difficult to overrate the importance of the work that has been done by the great leaders of this school in tracing the history of economic habits

> and institutions. It is one of the chief achievements of our age, and is an addition of the highest value to the wealth of the world. It has done more than almost anything else to broaden our ideas, to increase our knowledge of ourselves, and to help us to understand the central plan, as it were, of the Divine government of the world.
>
> (quoted in Pigou, 1956, p. 165)

It seems likely, therefore, that Marshall's influence on Taussig might have actually reinforced his training in Germany, even if he failed to appreciate it.

Taussig was also a friend and colleague of Ignaz Jastrow, who became the first Rector of the business school established at Berlin in 1906. The *Handelshochschule*, under Jastrow, shared an educational philosophy with Harvard that "focused on the real world of business and at the same time was truly academic in nature" (Redlich, 1957, p. 35). In a refrain that could have been uttered by Ashley, Jastrow had realized that the

> transmittal of knowledge was less important than training in the application of knowledge. . . . [H]is answer was an increase in the use of seminars at the expense of lectures. Moreover, in his own seminar Jastrow deviated from established university seminar methods and developed his own. He used source books which he had compiled, distributing topics based on the selected sources to each two students, one of whom had to report in a ten minute speech.
>
> (Redlich, 1957, pp. 64, 87)

Taussig had worked with Eliot since 1898 on the plans for a business school. In 1901, when Ashley left Harvard for Birmingham, Gay joined the faculty as his replacement. Both Taussig and Gay were members of a committee formed in 1906 to formalize plans for the HBS. Writing to Gay, Taussig singled out the German business schools as exemplars.

> The movement for advanced instruction of this kind is active throughout the world, most so in Germany and in the U.S. In Germany it has resulted in at least two large institutions of high grade, liberally supported at Berlin and Cologne. In this country, the Universities of Pennsylvania, Michigan, Wisconsin, Illinois, California and Dartmouth College [are worthy of praise and attention]. . . . [However] no one of the American schools is unequivocally graduate [in orientation].
>
> (Taussig, 1907)

Gay was not President Eliot's first choice for Dean of the new school. That distinction belonged to Mackenzie King, who had lectured in political economy at Harvard in 1900–01. When Eliot was considering King for the Deanship, the latter was actually Deputy Minister for Labor in the Canadian government. He ultimately became Prime Minister of Canada. In fact, it was King's citizenship status which generated Taussig's disapproval of him for the role (Heaton, 1952, p. 67). Taussig favored E.R. Johnson (see Figure 2.1b) of New York University, whom Eliot felt was too old (Gay, n.d.a). Eventually, Eliot and Taussig compromised on Gay (Gay, n.d.a). Together, they laid the philosophical and operational foundations of HBS.

Edwin Francis Gay

Gay joined the Harvard faculty as an instructor in economic history in 1901 after studying in Germany for over four years (see Figure 2.1a). He commenced graduate work in history (although he attended lectures on economics from Roscher) at Leipzig in 1890 and moved to Berlin the following year, where he studied economics under Sering, Wagner, and Schmoller. Traveling around Europe, he moved to Zurich, spent several years doing research at the British Museum, and returned to Berlin to complete his PhD dissertation under Schmoller's supervision in early 1901. Gay was much more appreciative of the experience he accumulated while negotiating the system of higher education in Germany, especially under Schmoller, than was Taussig.

> It was Schmoller . . . who really fired Gay's attentive interest and enthusiasm. In the first place because he believed that economics could be brought into close interrelation with psychology, ethics, history, and political science to produce a real science of society; that its field was the relations, not merely between man and material goods, but also between men; that the economic order must be regarded as only one integral part of the entire social life and as such was to be evaluated from an ethical point of view. In the second place, Schmoller was the last notable representative of the German historical economists. . . . Schmoller and his students were expending great energy when Gay joined them. Here were the things he [Gay] believed in: devotion to history as the key that might unlock many doors; the attempt to see 'the interaction of all manifestations of the human spirit, economic, legal, political, social, and intellectual'; all rigorous criticism of evidence; and the hope that from it all would emerge a science of economics which would serve as a sure guide for policies of social betterment.
>
> (Heaton, 1952, p. 38)

Ideologically, Gay was sympathetic with the social democratic values of the GHSE.

> He went to Europe an economic romanticist, critical of modern industry with its machines and division of labor, and enamored of the spirit of artist craftsmen. . . . On landing he was impressed by the attention being given to social problems, the rising tide of socialism, and the paternalistic policies central governments were adopting. His German professors had certainly not extoled individualism as an all-sufficing creed. . . . Much had already been

> accomplished by voluntary groups and by the state, but much more remained to be done. They should be based [Gay felt] on ceaseless study, on insight into the historical development of social classes and institutions, into economic and technical necessities, and on careful experiment. . . . That in essence was Gay's attitude toward economic and social change throughout the rest of his life.
>
> (Heaton, 1952, p. 49)

When Gay moved to Harvard he replaced William Ashley. Both men shared views derived from their common training, and the two schools, Birmingham and Harvard, were built on a relatively similar ideological podium, namely that business education had to offer a valuable service to their core stakeholder, industry. Their orientation did not necessarily imply ethical vacuity. Rather, to ensure the security of the marketplace for their educational offerings, the pragmatic focus of the curriculum continued to be foregrounded and woven into the training of prospective business leaders. Ethics and social responsibility were hailed as important, but there was a much more instrumentally oriented ethics in play at Harvard.

In terms of their assumptions and approaches, both Gay and Ashley defined the essence of business to be production (making things) and marketing (selling them). They used and encouraged the application of inductive, historical methods of study, fostering processes of reflection on strategy via seminars and the case method. Not surprisingly, Gay's lectures included nineteenth century German economic thought and English economic history. Quickly earning a reputation as a demanding teacher, he later commented, "If I could only transfer some of Schmoller's qualities into my work as a teacher I would be happy" (quoted in Heaton, 1949, pp. 12–13). One of Gay's students also later observed, "he was not given to vague theorizing. . . . [H]e hardly ever paused to generalize" (Cole, 1970, p. 34).

By 1905, Gay was attracting numerous graduate supervisees. When asked about suitable topics for theses, his suggestions often reflected his belief that

> commerce was the plastic element in economic development . . . and that it would be more revealing to trace changes in the methods of distribution and the widening of the market area than to concentrate so much on the way production was organized. . . . Hence he urged the need for research in this important neglected area.
>
> (Heaton, 1952, p. 62)

By "methods of distribution and widening of the market area", he meant marketing. Later, as Dean, Gay would settle on marketing and production as the two pillars of instruction, but with greater emphasis on the former (Heaton, 1952, p. 76), thereby creating an echo chamber between the educational programs being offered on both sides of the Atlantic. Taking this point slightly further, Gay could almost be paraphrasing Ashley's vision about marketing's centrality to the increasingly competitive business system.

Together with Taussig, Gay was a major force in the foundational years of the HBS, recognizing the "claim of modern business to be regarded as a profession, equally with the applied sciences, medicine, law and divinity" (Gay, 1908, p. 7). As such, Gay averred that commerce required professional training and this involved crafting a sense of group solidarity, fealty to a code of ethics, a motive of "service" to the community, technical training, a test of fitness, and a free and open imparting of new knowledge to the profession (Gay, 1926). An essential part of the planning Gay was involved in turned upon the determination of the subject matter for course work.

What to teach?

Taussig had noticed that there was an intermediate group of courses in economics offered at Harvard after 1891 that were "in the nature of business courses . . . offering instruction in money and banking, railroads, industrial organization, accounting and statistics" (Taussig, quoted in Morison, 1930, p. 199). Importantly his statement was nuanced and he realized that since these were taught by economists, the point of view was different from a teacher of a profession who had to offer advice that reflected the reality of the marketplace and was capable of application in some respect.

During this time, Frederick W. Taylor and his associates were developing a body of knowledge about industrial management and Gay adopted it enthusiastically for the HBS. Put slightly differently, HBS would be a vehicle for helping create the "mental revolutions" that Taylor (1911/1998) wanted to disseminate across management and workers. Within these institutional walls, the ideas that management should structure work routines, attempt to obtain and codify employee knowledge (so that their skills would not be lost should they leave the organization), and stress the cooperation of labor and management were inculcated. This was a training ground for the prolongation of the political-economic status quo. The promotion of Taylorism – to those learning about production or marketing – offered a veneer of scientific objectivity and credibility that university education and Taylorism struggled to obtain within the business environment and wider society.

The popular account of Gay's introduction to Taylor's work credits Wallace C. Sabine, Dean of Applied Science at Harvard, for taking Gay to visit the Taylor estate in North Philadelphia in 1908. Already, by then, Gay was familiar with Taylor's work. In his personal diaries for March 1907 there are references to Taylor and his writings on the "Art of Cutting Metals" (1907) and "Shop Management" (1903) (Gay, 1907–08). Apparently, as a member of the committee drafting the curriculum for the new business school, Gay was identifying materials for their courses. F.W. Taylor's papers were among the first to be listed in this connection. Other materials Gay included were Sparling's (1906) *Introduction to Business Organization* and W.D. Scott's (1903) *The Theory of Advertising.*

Whilst Taylor's principles of Scientific Management were used to teach industrial organization, it was his basic approach, his method and scientific ideals (i.e.

empirical investigations replacing rules of thumb), rather than the principles *per se*, that Dean Gay found most interesting. At a superficial level, it could be argued that the compatibility of Scientific Management and German Historicism was amply demonstrated by Gay's acceptance of it as an essential part of the instruction material for HBS. This is underscored by the fact that at the end of the first year after opening its doors, Taylor delivered lectures at HBS on "Workmen and Their Management" and "The Organization of a Manufacturing Establishment under Modern Scientific or Task Management" (Taylor, F.W., 1909). He continued to do so right up until his death.

Moves to introduce the philosophy of Scientific Management – especially its conception of scientific inquiry – would be forwarded by the development of the marketing curriculum. When the School opened in 1908 there were three required courses: "Principles of Accounting", "Commercial Contracts", and "Economic Resources of the United States". According to Copeland, the general idea for the latter course was developed by Gay, based on his background in economic history and in marketing (Copeland, 1958, p. 3). That course was first taught by Paul T. Cherington, who joined the faculty in 1908. It subsequently (in 1914) evolved into what was rather succinctly called "Marketing". This early version of the marketing course was required for all students, whereas a course in "Industrial Organization" was offered, but only as an elective. Marketing was consequently one of the few required courses at HBS. How it was taught is considered an important part of Harvard's legacy in the development of marketing thought. We discuss that "methodology for teaching marketing" later in this chapter. Before doing so, the links between Taylorism and German Historicism deserve some attention.

Scientific Management and German Historicism

Taylor's research involved closely monitoring the time it took specific workers to undertake a designated activity (e.g. shoveling). He timed them and worked out what extraneous movements could be eliminated. By doing so, he was fleshing out his core principles of Scientific Management. These revolved around the idea that business could and should be made scientific (principle 1). This is where he was suggesting – for quite political reasons, since Taylor (1911/1998, p. 1, 3) was concerned about the rise of socialism, (Tadajewski and Jones, 2012) as were many other groups (Tadajewski and Jones, 2016) – that employees, their selection, and the determination of their workload could be subject to careful analysis and measurement (principle 2). This would help ensure that staff could undertake their tasks in the most productive fashion, maximize their income level, and facilitate the achievement of output and profit goals set by management.

Taylor made a plea for management and workers to unite in the interests of productivity (principle 3), so that all earned appropriate rewards for their work and investments (principle 4). By highlighting the "scientific" nature of his system, he was effectively arguing that it was "class neutral" (Khurana, 2007; Nyland *et al.*, 2014). This was a politically apposite stance in a period of tense labor relations

(Jacques, 1996), providing "an aura of objectivity" (Khurana, 2007, p. 49) and "the halo of the disinterested expert" for management (Khurana, 2007, p. 93).

What we see here is a bounded version of social change. There is no serious questioning of the distribution of the economic surplus, past or present – just an imagined and hoped for future where labor strife could be eliminated. The picture Taylor presented was meant to be appealing to management as well as workers (notwithstanding his occasional racist and xenophobic references to certain groups of employees). Despite the fact that the language he used will make modern readers wince, it was very much a "happy families" account of otherwise turbulent management–labor relations. Taylor had his rose-tinted glasses firmly emplaced when he wrote the following.

> These men [employees] . . . looked upon the men who were over them, their bosses and their teachers, as their very best friends; not as nigger drivers, forcing them to work extra hard for ordinary wages, but as friends who were teaching them and helping them earn much higher wages than they had ever earned before. It would have been absolutely impossible for anyone to have stirred up strife between these men and their employers.
>
> (Taylor, 1911/1998, p. 35)

Needless to say, this was extremely idealistic. His science was not just about the generation of abstract principles, but involved shaping worker subjectivity. Increasing their remuneration, aside from defusing calls for socialist change, was envisaged as helping elevate the lifestyle of the worker in ways most amenable to capital reproduction: "this increase in wages tends to make them not only more thrifty but better men in every way; that they live rather better . . . become more sober, and work more steadily" (Taylor, 1911/1998, p. 37).

It is reasonable to suggest that it was the last item on this list that most interested Taylor. The items that preceded it were the conditions of possibility for greater control over and productivity by the worker, not just inside the factory gates, but outside. Taylor's "mental revolution" was literally that – a way to change the character of the employee while maintaining the external political-economic landscape in its capitalist form. With the efficiency gains that were promised by his system, Taylor – and Henry Ford – helped to cement a circuit of capital reproduction where consumption could be expanded to almost unimagined levels.

We have, however, made the point that commensurability between Scientific Management and GHSE values is a much more complex question than it appears at face value. There are links between Richard Ely, John Commons, and Frederick Taylor (Nyland, 1996). Recent historical revisions of Taylor's work have clarified his value system and referred to his concern for the scientific improvement of business practice and interest in enabling distributive justice. Taylor applauded the Wisconsin Idea, maintaining that he anticipated the day it became a generally accepted axiology (Nyland, 1996).

Taylor's ideas developed over time, shifting perspective, often becoming more critically directed, and this needs to be registered. His followers in the Taylor

Society – including Edwin Gay (Bruce and Nyland, 2001), Arch Shaw (Usui, 2008), and various other influential actors (Tadajewski and Jones, 2012) – made explicit connections between Taylor's interest in macro-economic stabilization, marketing, and advertising. They outlined how distributive practices had a central role in demand creation (Shaw, 1915) *and* demand management (White, 1927), helping "mitigate the effects of [economic] depression" (Bruce and Nyland, 2001, p. 972).

At its core, the idea that marketing had a role to play in demand stimulation (Shaw, 1915) or consumer "education" (White, 1927) is consistent with the GHSE focus on the central importance of key institutions in directing and shaping economic life. An institutional orientation was meant to focus attention upon the fact that the economic and distribution system was not a naturally occurring phenomenon (Rutherford, 1997). There were no natural laws guiding the development of all marketplaces without human intervention. When viewed through the lens provided by institutional economics, "marketing" is the enabling practice used by various groups to shape the economic and social world. But while GHSE advocates tended to view the market through a darker prism than managerially oriented marketing contributors, both groups wanted to foster a commitment to realism and the experiential world. This, in turn, leads to slightly different discussions of the nature of relevant research – a topic we will unpack below.

What we must realize is that the two strands of thought are not commensurable in the Kuhnian (1962) sense. They do not map on to each other on an exactly point-by-point basis. At best, this is a partial "melding" of GHSE influences and Scientific Management (Bruce and Nyland, 2001). This issue becomes even more complicated as we follow the path of the mobilization of Taylor's ideas in marketing via the publications of Arch Shaw and Percival White.

While the latter's publications take us outside of the orbit of HBS, we focus upon them in this chapter as the logical culmination of Taylor's perspective. White's work contains one of the earliest and most detailed expressions of the marketing management approach (Tadajewski and Jones, 2016) – an approach developed at Birmingham and more extensively at HBS and whose genealogical threads feed through to the present day (Tadajewski and Jones, 2012). Effectively, as marketing becomes more managerially oriented, it moves further away from the GHSE axiology, interest in social objectivity, and interest group pluralism. Despite these differences, there are some areas of overlap between White's work and that of the institutional economists writing at the time he was publishing, particularly with respect to the invocation and application of the language and tools of science, combined with the issue of "relevance" (Rutherford, 2010).

To understand the similarities and differences between these bodies of thought, we need to move beyond surface-level scrutiny to position these discourses against the cultural, religious, and scientific climate. Reading both against the context highlights that we have two different perspectives that are interlinked in terms of their operationalization of progressivist political and scientific ideals. But, at base level, they diverge axiologically and politically.

Ely and his colleagues at Wisconsin had been immersed in the Social Gospel and articulated firm ethical commitments (cf. Bateman, 2003; Herzberg, 2001). F.W. Taylor's work falls under the rubric of "scientific" progressivism (Bateman, 1998), gaining attention and momentum due to its commitment to efficiency, productivity increases, and incremental improvement to worker salaries. As such, while Ely, Gay, Shaw, and F.W. Taylor all stressed their interest in ameliorating social ills, as we move across the listing of authors above, we see a decrease in attention to the "social good" and more emphasis upon securing profit for business owners and managers (Goodwin, 1998). Gay, Shaw, and Taylor, for example, held that Scientific Management had the potential to ease the economic turbulence that negatively affected all involved in the market (Fourcade and Khurana, 2013). This is an instrumental justification for Frederick Taylor's ideas that inflect it with a sense of ethical responsibility. But, thinking through these references to the attempts being made to stabilize the economy (Fourcade and Khurana, 2013), with the university and business school being positioned as "order-creating" institutions (Khurana, 2007), highlights the plurality of ethical and political values in circulation.

Ely and those educated in the tradition of the GHSE at Wisconsin generally directed their attention to the creation of a just social order. They were interested in playing a role in ensuring that society retained functionally useful institutions, cultural mores, and values, whilst rethinking taken-for-granted assumptions, practices, and legal frameworks that were not advancing public welfare. And they reminded us – as we noted in previous chapters – that efficiency and large corporations were not always forces for good in the world. This is not to claim that the authors or practitioners most closely associated with Scientific Management were uninterested in the views of the public; they had to take them seriously; and they appreciated the need for the business community to present a reasonably pro-social image. After all, the state was "increasingly interventionist" (Cuff, 1996, p. 16). Ignoring the latter was likely to restrict the field for industrial practice in the future.

So, there are links between Scientific Management and the communities of intellectual practice we have explored in this book. In 1915, for instance, Richard Ely tried to convince Frank Gilbreth, a well-known proponent of a version of Scientific Management, to co-consult on efficiency for a large department store. At about the same point in time Ely inquired to Taussig about having Arch Shaw, who used some of the insights of Scientific Management to refine thinking about marketing and sales, lecture at Wisconsin (Ely, 1915). He saw that Scientific Management had the potential to improve the efficiency of the economy and the quality of life experienced by labor. Taylor's views were, however, managerial, conservative, and economically expansionist. The real limitation embedded in his work is that he assumes that ideals of scientific objectivity, commitment to debate and evidence-based decision-making would remedy any points of contention between managers and labor (Nyland, 1996). This was too optimistic and Taylor gradually came to appreciate that there was an important role for unions in Scientific Management. Sometimes, he registered, the ultimate basis of decision-making had to be located above the firm level – that is, in a government commission – if consensus could not be obtained between owners, management, workers, and union officials.

By improving the management of a firm, by studying worker movements and practices, revising and codifying the most effective ways of undertaking a task, Taylor articulates his interest in informing managerial rationality. We have already pointed out that Taylor's views eventually gravitated towards greater inclusiveness regarding firm governance – a perspective taken even further by the left-leaning Taylor Society (Bruce, 2007; Nyland, 1996), whose *Bulletin of the Taylor Society* functioned as an important outlet for advanced marketing ideas during the period 1914 to 1934 (Tadajewski and Jones, 2012). This said, his 1911 book (and the articles that constituted it) was the primary touchstone for marketing scholars who drew upon his ideas. In the book, he presents a managerial objectivity (Schachter, 2016). This does diverge from the social objectivity that underwrote Ely's thinking (cf. Usui, 2008, p. 50), even if GHSE and Taylorite ideas would converge later. When Taylor's ideas were drawn into our discipline, they contributed to an emergent managerial orientation. As one of the key figures in the foundation of marketing thought at the HBS, Arch Shaw's interpretation of Taylor's work is important.

Arch W. Shaw on Frederick Taylor

Shaw is explicit in his writing that he is not simply repeating Taylor's core ideas, presenting them to a marketing audience. He is rethinking and reinterpreting them. What, in effect, we get from Shaw is an argument that has a family resemblance to Taylor's philosophy, but is not an identical twin. His reading, perhaps expectedly, avoids engagement with the potential dark side of Taylor's "science".

He rehearses typical Taylorite themes such as the importance of the scientific study of worker activities and the need for careful data collection and for managers to structure employee activities to ensure the appropriate flow of materials and goods within the factory, and emphasizes the financial benefits of efficient working practices. In doing so, he bypasses the less salubrious aspects of systems of routing worker activities. Efficiency and exceeding performance expectations are praised for increasing incomes. No attention is paid to the potential longevity of the speeded-up processes or the fact that workers are being trained to undertake a limited range of tasks, which had implications for job mobility and employee power. Shaw (1911) moves from Taylor's ideas to practices divorced from his recommendations, focusing on the National Cash Register Company and its methods of training salesmen and controlling their activities. This firm was famous for various reasons, but the structured nature of the interaction between employees and the public was one of them. Interaction routines were highly standardized. This standardization of process provides Shaw with the genealogical, family resemblance he requires to embed an otherwise non-Taylorite example within a promotional piece for Scientific Management applied to salesmanship.

Employees at NCR had to memorize sales talks and refutations of common counterpoints, and they were subject to the disciplinary pressures of a demanding quota system. The final point here is an example of the enactment of disciplinary power beyond the factory (Foucault, 1977/1991). Not only was marketing and sales management still based largely on rules of thumb, the nature of sales activities placed the employee beyond the direct gaze of the owner or management of a company. They could not be as closely monitored as their factory-based brethren. "Useful" control mechanisms were discussed in more detail in the body of literature that was devoted to "scientific sales management" (Hoyt, 1913) and "scientific marketing management" (White, 1927), outgrowths of Shaw's initial reflections.

As the literature shifted in emphasis from the former to the latter, it increased in sophistication. The core theme was that firms had to rethink their relationship to the market (White, 1927). Contra Say's law, marketing was about "demand creation" (Shaw, 1915), but this was not the same as manipulation. Neither Shaw nor White are naïve enough to present marketing as a manipulative science, interested in defining the field of consumer action in ways that do not add value for the person concerned. They go out of their way to specify how marketing can and should add value to the individual, to the firm, shareholders, and wider society.

The logic in use by Shaw (1911; 1915) and White (1927) reversed the idea that companies should produce products and then try to identify markets for what they had to offer. A more efficient approach to marketing management hinged on determining the needs of the customer through appropriate forms of marketing research (this was the scientific part). Historians have made a case that this literature reflects early marketing concept ideas, combined with an ethical orientation. It was ethical in the sense that business people were expected to elevate how they dealt with the customer. Hard-selling was out. This tended to be viewed as exploitative, inefficient, and likely to harm long-term business success. In this respect, White offers a lite version of the criticism that emanated from J.M. Clark (an institutional economist). Clark went into much more detail regarding the various types of manipulations the consumer might face in the marketplace (Rutherford, 1997). To rectify these, he sketched multiple approaches to rebalance the playing field for less powerful actors like single, cognitively limited, buyers. Stated simply, Clark saw the marketplace as needing various forms of intervention from the state (Rutherford, 2010).

White (1927) and Shaw (1911; 1915) do appreciate that the government can shape and limit firm and managerial activities, but they do not conceptualize it as the major influence helping "reform" the market. Rather, they view reform in micro-managerial terms. Reform is not so much a function of government, but of management and specifically of companies tailoring their business activities around customer needs (Tadajewski and Jones, 2012). They were encouraged to provide what was requested or genuine advances on what was currently available (these themes fall under what was called the "objectivity of demand"). White (1927) goes further in distancing marketing from any manipulative associations which were potentially implicit in Shaw's writing when he references "demand creation" by explicitly arguing that marketing does not create demand, it serves customer needs. To be sure, this is a tenuous and problematic position in a climate where supply has outpaced demand and Say's law has been jettisoned. This point is made more ambiguous because White does leave room for practitioners to "educate" the public about products and services that would improve their quality of life. Even so, according to White, an ethically oriented practitioner should not produce me-too products that merely clutter the market, making decision-making more difficult and the market less efficient. This was likely to delegitimize the business community in the face of public concerns about rising prices for distribution, marketing, and advertising.

Advertising, like other facets of marketing management practice, had to be subject to scientific analysis. In making this argument, these authors are presenting a more complex picture of advertising's influence over the consumer than is found in historical studies of this period (Shaw, 1911). Advertising, on their reading, is not a deterministic force, shaping consumer reaction (Shaw, 1911; White, 1927). The fact that marketing communications were amenable to testing and should be the subject of scientific analysis indicates that not all advertisements were equally successful at demand creation (Jones, 1997). It was the task of the scientifically minded business person to find out what variant of communication worked (e.g. in what medium, in what page location, in the best aesthetic arrangement) in terms of attracting and educating the consumer. Efficiency and effectiveness were central here.

The justification, explanation, and operational guidance provided within this literature was often remarkably well informed. Practitioners like Percival White (1927) called for the use of multiple disciplinary perspectives in gathering data (e.g. economics, psychology, sociology, use of statistics). Much like Ely, this paradigmatically pluralistic approach enables him to deflate taken-for-granted arguments about the consumer, that is, as exhibiting the characteristics of economic man. White, for example, frames the individual in nuanced terms, stressing his/her "abilities, disabilities, prejudices, and finances" (Tadajewski and Jones, 2012, p. 49, footnote 4). This perspective brings him quite close to the views of both Ely and Commons. There are other areas of conjunction between institutional economics and White's managerialism, notably around the issue of relevance.

As we might expect, "relevance" had a more macro-structural emphasis in institutional economics (Rutherford, 2010). It was linked to the necessity for all theories and arguments to exhibit realism. They had to be founded upon an empirical basis and be directed towards ameliorating some social problem. Relevant research, moreover, had to be realistic in another sense. It must reflect the best insights available from multiple academic traditions. Schmoller and Ely's importation of ideas from psychology to conceptualize aspects of their economic theorizing are exemplars of this interdisciplinary strategy.

White exhibits a commitment to realism and relevance in that he tells practitioners to use the insights available from – usually – four academic disciplines. Tadajewski and Jones (2012) describe this as a version of critical pluralism. This entailed the deployment of disciplinary-level approaches (e.g. sociology, psychology) being used to sensitize business people to various facets of the marketplace and consumer behavior, combined with multiple methodological options (e.g. questionnaires, interviews, ethnography) and a mixture of induction and deduction to generate managerially usable insights.

Making marketing realistic and relevant in this way was political in at least two senses. Firstly, it helped legitimate marketing practice in society, demonstrating the commitment of management to help improve standards of living in an efficient and effective manner whilst reducing any wastes to an absolute minimum. Secondly, research-derived insights into consumer needs, combined with appropriate control mechanisms like budgets, were the vehicles to attain customer satisfaction at a profit (Tadajewski and Jones, 2012; Tadajewski and Jones, 2016). Using the lexicon of science, citing Taylor, and enveloping marketing theory and practice in a vocabulary associated with "positivism" (aka logical empiricism) shifted power relations within the firm. White (1927) is aware of the managerial politics of the scientific method. By emphasizing the objective nature of research, by aligning marketing with the ability to articulate the voice of the customer within the boardroom, he is providing disciplinary specialists with the intellectual and argumentative resources necessary to shape the internal decision-making processes in their organization.

In his writing, data gathering was undertaken iteratively as a major part of organizational planning, monitoring, control, and policy modification (White, 1927). White, most explicitly, sketched out a vision of organizational structure, stressing inter- and intradepartmental cooperation and coordination. The consumer and their needs were the axes around which the company should operate. Consumption, in other words, led production. Adam Smith's long repeated statement had now acquired suitable managerial specificity in terms of guidance (White, 1927). By focusing on customer needs, solutions to consumer problems could be determined. This was more efficient than trying to push items and services via hard-selling in the short, medium, or long term. "Supersalesmanship" was expensive and likely to destroy micro- and macro-level goodwill for the firm (White, 1927).

Overall, then, Shaw (1911), like White (1927), explains the importance of correct systems – managerial directives, financial controls, sales records – and the need to continually gather information about the changing nature of the marketplace. Organizational cooperation, control via scientific research (Shaw was a fan of new sampling approaches), product differentiation within certain bounds, appropriate (often integrated) marketing communications, and pertinent incentives for personnel were the vehicles to facilitate cost reduction and grow the market. This "scientific" approach to managerial decision-making and employee practice was the "mental revolution" that F.W. Taylor stimulated in Shaw (1911) and White (1927). It was not, of course, wholly a function of reading Taylor; Shaw had long been interested in systems for office management, his firm had sold them, and he published a popular business periodical called *System* (Litterer, 1961; Usui, 2008). To disseminate this scientific, somewhat progressivist orientation, Shaw (1911) was ready to finance a research organization (discussed below) which would provide practitioners with operating benchmarks. More importantly, he wanted to foster a new "mental attitude" amongst them. Basically, this involved them undertaking their own market and marketing research.

We can say, then, that Shaw's (1911; 1915) analysis is treading the middle ground. It engages with themes and methodological injunctions that were common to German Historical scholarship. He stresses the importance of having knowledge about the historical development of a given society, the market within it, as well as its present organization and likely future directions. He recognizes a degree of ontological instability and epistemological relativism, and his writing is managerially centered. It speaks to the leaders of the companies and those tasked with ensuring that corporate objectives are met (Shaw, 1911). Managers seem to be the linchpin for ontological stabilization (i.e. preventing boom–bust cycles of disturbance), whereas government control does not loom as large in his attention (Cuff, 1996). Reaffirming what we wrote above, even academic-practitioners like Shaw (1911), whose devotion – much like HBS itself – was transfixed on one core interest group, were not able to ignore the reality that business was embedded in a wider social system, hence the discussions of ethics becoming more overt (but still less central than witnessed at Wisconsin) as the literature on scientific marketing management developed (White, 1927). This system could influence – positively or negatively – what practitioners were doing. Reflecting this, Shaw (1911) extends his argument to stress the social desirability of his vision of Scientific Management and its implications for sales and business practice.

At first, he realized, the firm able to implement it would be at an advantage. Efficiency reduced costs, thereby increasing profits (Shaw, 1911). GHSE pioneers would have taken this analysis in more critical directions, referring to the problems that this might entail for power relations in the marketplace (i.e. decreasing competition and fostering oligopoly). Efficiency gains, they would have said, might create the conditions for market concentration; with concentration skewing the already asymmetric power dynamics between producer, retailer, and consumer. Their remedy was government intervention. Shaw's (1911) entailed sharing scientific approaches to the market as widely as possible, with governmental action being limited to collecting information and supporting the efficiency gains of the business community (Usui, 2008). Over time, as it was applied by greater numbers of companies and industries, "the economies will be shared by the industry generally and thus become external. The inevitable result will be a lowering of prices to the customer" (Shaw, 1911, p. 332). This statement chimed with public sentiment and was part of a concerted effort to foster a revaluation of marketing practice.

When Shaw was writing, there was a great deal of attention being devoted to the increasing cost of living. Prices were rising and hard choices had to be made about consumption. Distribution, marketing and advertising figured prominently in these debates. As Edward David Jones had pondered, the costs of marketing constituted a large and rising proportion of the prices being paid by the ultimate customer. This caused consternation. It led to serious political investigations into the topic and the founding of consumer organizations and required a response if capitalism was to retain legitimacy (Usui, 2008). Shaw (1911) and like-minded commentators attempted to provide the discursive, analytical, and research tools to buttress the status quo.

While he does not signal his appreciation of it, the notion that companies would share the benefits of efficiency is a strong assumption. Shaw seems to believe that retaining the good will of their customer base and wider society is the motive force to engage in acts of distributive justice (Jones, 1997). There was, of course, nothing "inevitable" about this. Micro-level firm practices did not causally translate into public good and welfare gains. This assumes a psychological egotism that the pursuit of profit often undermines (Crane and Desmond, 2002). Some of the more critical voices within Taylorite circles, like Mary van Kleeck, were acutely aware of the problems presented by the uncontrolled pursuit of profit. She indicated that vested interests would pursue their own self-interest at the expense of wider society (Nyland *et al.*, 2014).

Here, in addition, Shaw differs from those more closely aligned with the Social Gospel–inflected GHSE. Firms could engage in potentially illegal restraint of trade, delimit competition, and generate supernormal profits without necessarily benefitting the customer. Alternatively, they may pursue non-price competition, thereby complicating consumer decision-making and extending their reach in quasi-monopolistic terms. Shaw's (1911) perspective thus sits uncomfortably with the nature of marketplace competition at the time. Conflict, in other words, is largely excised from his view of the machine-like marketing system (Jones, 1997). The politically fractious ontology that GHSE advocates fed into their analyses is displaced by an ontological posture that links "efficiency" with "social harmony" (Scully, 1996).

Outside of the university, the darker side of Taylorism (something Taylor did contest) was gaining public traction. Many people wrote to the periodical outlets that published his work expressing their concern over the accuracy of his reporting, the dehumanization and exploitation of workers, and the fact that the profit being generated was not being shared equally (Dean, 1997). Taylor's ideas have undergone a substantial rethinking by contemporary historians. They read them against the context of the time, stressing that compared with other commentators and practitioners, he was a progressive advocate for the employee and unions alike (Dean, 1997; Nyland *et al.*, 2014).

Scientific Management has, more recently, been conceptualized as helping replace power as the key variable structuring organizational policy-making and employee opportunities for advancement with knowledge and skill. This is hailed as an advance over nepotism or managerial perfidy. Connected to this, the charges that Taylor sought to deskill the worker have been questioned. Nyland argues that he took relatively unskilled individuals and upskilled them, giving them training and knowledge, and improved their performance, thereby enhancing their life opportunities (Nyland, 1996).

As Taylor made clear, he wanted to foster better relationships between capital, management, and labor. This is where he runs into trouble. Like Arch Shaw, he was too optimistic about management, their abilities, and willingness to work with labor. Wagner-Tsukamoto (2007) sees this as a major limitation. There was room for conflict on both sides. Owners and management could be as opportunistic as employees (Wagner-Tsukamoto, 2007). And, despite the value of these kinds of re-readings, the positive account that is provided is not consistent with the views of those reading his writings at the time of publication.

Even so, as Shaw (1911) registered, marketing was still largely virgin territory for scientifically derived efficiency gains. Taylor, extending the logic of Adam Smith, had signaled the importance of marketing and especially the consumer in his 1911 book – a vein of his thought that has been mostly ignored to date. He conjured the consumer when trying to defuse labor claims to a greater share of the economic benefits of industrial production by asserting that management and workers had to consider the needs of the marketplace because consumer spending was the condition of possibility for employment. Labor and management needed to work together to satisfy the market. In doing so, they would expand the economic "pie" available, rather than having to split a smaller quantity of returns. This largely reinforces the position of management, continues remunerative flows to the owners of companies, their shareholders, and bankers, and stabilizes workforce routines and appeases employee demands to some extent. Within the literature developing out of the Scientific Management movement, therefore, the ultimate buyer was used to deposition management – the actual bosses of the firm – as the stick that beats the worker to greater levels of efficiency (Tadajewski and Jones, 2016). In their place, the customer was rhetorically presented as the "real" power, the actual "boss". Effectively, management tried to claim the status of a conduit passing on the requests of the marketplace, rather than the disciplinary vehicle they represented in actuality.

So, through Gay and Shaw the philosophy of Scientific Management became part of the foundation of the marketing curriculum. How that curriculum was taught is considered a central contribution to the development of marketing thought.

Methodology for teaching marketing

The case method is often cited as a distinctive contribution of Harvard to business education. Converse reported that it was voted one of the most important techniques in marketing (Converse, 1945b, p. 20). Although Gay is generally credited with promoting the case approach, its unique development has never been explicated. Its genealogy is clouded by the variety of terms used during its evolution, including "discussion method", "problem method", and "laboratory method". Much of the kudos for the case method has been attributed to the Harvard Law School (Copeland, 1958). Copeland cited Professor Williston's use of cases in the Law School as influential when Arch Shaw first tried to bring businessmen into his course on Business Policy in 1911 to discuss the problems they faced in their day-to-day activities (Copeland, 1958, p. 26). Shaw's own account to Gay of this development is similar.

> My recollection of the origin of the problem method is something like this: One day I was making some criticisms of the lecture method for a school of the type we both were interested in and you told me to sit in on Professor Williston's course on contracts. This I did and together we hammered out the problem method idea.
>
> (Shaw, 1944)

Professor Taussig's influence has also been mentioned. This was a function of his training which had exposed him to the use of cases in legal inquiry (Cole, 1970). Dean Gay's affirmation of, and ongoing support for, the case method helped ensure its legitimacy. However, there is a slight problem with the existing interpretation of the origins of the approach. Taussig used the seminar method in his economics teaching. His appreciation of it was derived from his German education. It seems reasonable to suggest that there was probably a connection to the GHSE training he received and his support for this approach. Likewise, for Gay. Additional evidence can be found in the comparison of the development of the Berlin *Handelshochschule* and the Harvard Business School that Redlich conducted. He concluded that the seminar method, extensively employed in Berlin, was a "rudimentary [example of the] case method" (Redlich, 1957, p. 42).

Consistent with his vision of business as a profession, a science, and an art, Gay recognized from the outset the need for a unique means of pedagogic delivery.

> The teacher of business . . . must discover the fundamental principles of business system, and then, in a scientific spirit, teach not only these principles, but the art of applying them after investigation, to any given enterprise. This means, then, that new courses of study must be organized and that a laboratory-system of instruction must, as far as possible, be introduced . . . The laboratory method of instruction, for one thing, will permit that closer personal relation between teacher and student so essential to the best work of both. And as far as possible, students will be brought into touch not only with the professional spirit of an advanced technical training, but with business men and actual business conditions.
>
> (Gay, 1908, p. 161)

Gay also recognized the inductive nature of his laboratory method of teaching. In describing to F.W. Taylor the approach they were adopting towards teaching, he wrote the following.

> Our experience leads us to believe that it is advisable to commence with the facts and concrete methods of organization, working up through them [students] to the understanding of general principles. But in doing this we give the students at the outset a preliminary view, so that they usually realize what the study of the facts in detail is leading toward. In other words, the method is inductive rather than deductive.
>
> (Gay, 1914)

In a 1926 speech about the founding of the Business School, Gay further described this conception of the laboratory method as an "experimental laboratory studying genetically and theoretically the institutions and processes of our economic organization and practically [applying] the new insights for the continued betterment of our business practice" (Gay, 1926, p. 400). So, his conception of a "laboratory method" was evident from the beginning of his involvement with the Business School.

Another closely related theme in Gay's reflection revolved around historical study. In his personal journal (1908), just after the School first opened, he jotted the following.

> For most business men do not know enough history to make analogies, those who do, know enough to make analogies. . . . Some influence of the historical method in spirit. Gaining of perspective, realization of [the] changing character of institutions apparently stable. . . . Sense of proportion . . . relation to principles. . . . Realization of complexity and interrelations and their modification of too rigid and simple standards of judgement.
>
> (Gay, 1907, p. 1014)

We will not belabor the point that this ascription of value to history obviously ties his thinking to the GHSE. As it was originally formulated by Gay, the laboratory method was intended to follow the historical method and the use of seminars by the GHSE. Alfred Chandler puts this very well when he alerts us to the fact that "the heart of this school's curriculum has always been the case study, and the case study is precisely what a historian does, what a historian is trained to do" (1986, p. 82).

It is not clear whether the case method was influenced by Pragmatism in the philosophical sense associated with William James (who was based at Harvard) in which historically contingent laws could be developed when scholarly views cohered around a topic or practice (James, 1909). The younger GHSE agreed with such sentiment. Historical investigation on a case-by-case basis could – with a sufficient accumulation of data – generate temporally and contextually restricted laws. Ultimately, it is difficult to come to any definite position on this point. So, somewhat expeditiously, let us distinguish between the philosophy of Pragmatism (big P) and a principle of pragmatism (small p) which we might view as a watered-down version of the Jamesian position emphasizing the importance of experience and solutions to real-world problems. The teaching of any applied science or profession, then, that followed the philosophy of either the GHSE or Pragmatism would be based on this principle of pragmatism. At Harvard, marketing was considered to have the potential of being developed into such an "applied science".

Pragmatism (small p) in teaching was evident in the pedagogic practice used at HBS – when they took students on field trips. In the *Harvard Annual Reports* for 1908, approximately twenty companies are listed as having been visited by postgraduates who took the courses on "Railroad Operation", "Industrial Organization", and "Commercial Organization", the latter being an earlier version of the marketing course (*Harvard Annual Reports*, 1906–09, p. 152). The following year, an additional twenty firms supplemented the tally. Consistent with the prior exchange between Eliot and Taylor, a related agreement was struck between Gay and Taylor.

> I heartily agree with you that it is advisable for young men who plan to go into business to have an opportunity of working before their graduation. We are

> doing what we can in the Business School to bring about this contact with the work-a-day world. Our students are expected between the first and second years to work in shops and offices, and the experiment as tried last summer proved successful.
>
> (Gay, 1909a)

Thus, whether in the form of seminars, a laboratory approach, field trips, historical study, or teaching with cases, the underlying epistemology and pedagogy were based on an inductive logic. Long before Copeland's first book of marketing cases was published in 1920, and prior to Shaw's experiment with the discussion of business problems in class during 1911, subscription to pedagogical realism was embedded in the planning exercises for the HBS.

Research in marketing at Harvard – a simple scientific endeavor

Gay followed Eliot's ideal, and the practice in German universities, of combining research with teaching by including the former as a necessary part of the profession and science of business. As mentioned above, marketing remained relatively underexplored in the empirical terms being made famous by Taylor in industrial organization (Tadajewski and Jones, 2012). Marketing, therefore, became the research focus of Dean Gay's "simple scientific endeavor".

Gay's training as an economic historian influenced his views on methodology even more than those on pedagogy. He singled out the contributions of Wilhelm Roscher, Knies's principle of historical relativity, and the use of a comparative method as important (Gay, 1941). He also recognized the intense struggle of the German Historical economists, especially Schmoller, with knowledge production; notably with respect to the question of how generalizations could be formulated from the mass of economic facts being collected, summarized, and synthesized. The reason for this struggle was the inherent complexity of economic events: "The longer I live, the more inclined I am to agree with the late Professor Schmoller of Berlin that the world of political, social-psychological, and economic phenomena is a terribly complicated business – 'Es ist alles so unendlich compliciert'" (Gay, 1923, p. 2).

Not to be put off by this task, Gay maintained as the younger school had, that the *ultimate* objective of inductive research was to produce generalizations and principles. Extensive research, observation, and induction were conduits to the practical wisdom that HBS lecturers could articulate and managers utilize. The first step towards this objective came in 1911, when the Bureau of Business Research was established with the financial assistance and intellectual stimulus of Arch Shaw (see Figure 6.2). As was briefly gestured to earlier in this chapter, Shaw had published a highly popular business magazine called *System*. In a letter to Dean Gay, he expressed his philosophy.

> [T]he *System* idea [was that] every business man has a body of principles or opinions which represents generalizations of experience. . . . [These]

> principles [are] not vital and effective until verified. . . . So, at this particular stage in the development of the science of business it seems to me it is the function of *System*, at least, to distribute as widely as possible the concrete, or as we call it, the 'how' information of business.
>
> (Gay, 1909b)

What Shaw meant was that there was a need for the institutionalized collection of facts about business and marketing, the "how" information of business. And he was eager to see that "data" informed the development of principles and generalizations which could be delivered to practitioners.

In 1911 Gay remarked to Shaw, "What is needed is a quantitative measurement for the marketing side of distribution" (Gay, quoted in Cruikshank, 1987, p. 59) to which Shaw replied, "I wish to give for use in this School a fund which shall be applied for the purpose of [the] investigation of business problems, primarily for the problem of [the] distribution of products" (Shaw, quoted in Cruikshank, 1987, p. 59). The result of his initiative was the establishment of the Bureau of Business Research under the direction of staff members of the Business School, and the first studies carried out by the Bureau were marketing related. Gay later explained the rationale for the Bureau as follows.

Figure 6.2 Arch W. Shaw, ca. 1917

Source: Wikimedia: https://upload.wikimedia.org/wikipedia/commons/thumb/6/67/Arch_Wilkinson_Shaw_in_1917.jpg/220px-Arch_Wilkinson_Shaw_in_1917.jpg.

> There are laboratories for the natural sciences both pure and applied; there are agricultural experiment stations for the farmer; why not a laboratory for business? The primary object of this research is the development of instruction in the school. But it should also give to the business man a partial basis for judgement in meeting his particular problems. . . . A scientific study means the collection of the facts in a painstaking and impartial spirit, the ascertaining of the true and the elimination of the irrelevant facts, the classification and correlation of this sifted material, and finally the statement and publication of significant and useful conclusions.
>
> (Gay, 1912a, pp. 1215–1217)

The director was Seldin O. Martin, and initial studies explored the retail shoe industry, wholesale shoe trade, and the grocery trade among others (Khurana, 2007). Martin explained their focus.

> The field of marketing . . . had apparently received less scientific attention than production. . . . The concrete fact that from one-fourth to one-half of the retail selling price of an article is consumed in getting the article from the producer to the consumer seemed of itself worthy of study without prejudice for or against the existing order.
>
> (1916, p. 266)

The final sentence hints at the conception of objectivity being employed by those working under the auspices of the Bureau. The present organization of the market was not the subject of *a priori* critique – there was enough of that around – rather, they sought to explore what was happening (the "how") in the distribution system. Simply because prices reflected large marketing costs did not necessarily mean that distribution practices or the activities of middlemen were wasteful.

What was necessary was better distribution of information. This was particularly the case with smaller retailers whose cost structures and incomes limited their access to marketplace intelligence. The Bureau assisted in this regard (Goodwin, 1998). Substantively, it was meant to help inform practitioners by providing benchmarks against which they could evaluate their performance (Cuff, 1996); ideologically, contributing to the overall efficiency of the distribution and marketing system was a means to defuse criticism of the wastes of marketing. But, any attempt at resolving the criticism of the marketing system was something that could only move towards settlement (recalling William James's conception of truth as consensus and the GHSE focus on the accumulation of data and induction) with a combination of primary and secondary research, not just across one industry, but many.

The more industrialized economy of the eastern United States resulted in a different class of marketing problems being studied from that of the Midwest. Whereas agriculture had provided most of the subject matter for research into marketing problems at Wisconsin and Illinois, retailing and manufacturing structured investigative work at Harvard. As a result, classroom discussion often focused on topics such as "The Department Store", "Retailers Work and Methods", and "Marketing Problems as Factors in Industrial Development" (Harvard

Business School, 1910–21). Not everyone thought that the material developed in this way was useful.

It had been collected by relative neophytes with little practical experience and underdeveloped academic skills, and the resulting cases were liable to contain errors. Cutting to the core of a divide between theory and practice that persists today, it was alleged that Bureau-collected case material was less valuable than equivalent material produced by actual practitioners (Schachter, 2016). Far from providing a bridge between the academic community and practitioners, the relationship appears to have become almost parasitic. The Bureau harvested managerial insights which informed its teaching. It did not firmly connect staff with the business community, exposing academics to the empirical realism of the marketplace in quite the way Shaw had in mind (Usui, 2008). Nor did the case materials being produced reflect the ethical values and commitment to service and social responsibility that HBS liked to publicly profess (Khurana, 2007, p. 128).

The Bureau did undertake a variety of research projects and these had utility for certain groups. But the sheer volume of the research required to help improve operational efficiency across many varied industries was far beyond the resources of Harvard. Other business schools did pursue more firm-centered research, engaging in consultancy activities, and this seems to have yielded managerially usable insights. Harvard, though, remained somewhat aloof from the specific needs of practice, and this was compounded after Gay had stepped down as Dean, when Bureau attention was devoted to defining "rules and principles applying to all situations" that might face practitioners (Khurana, 2007, p. 173) – an epistemological universalism that could not be further removed from GHSE influences. Anticipating resource constraints, Shaw had already stressed the need for government to undertake the types of research needed by business people. This was achieved in the 1920s, as a function of the actions of Shaw, among others (e.g. Usui, 2008, pp. 52–53).

The use of an inductive and historical method went beyond the activities of the Bureau. It was evident in early theses, such as "Sales Methods in The American Automobile Industry" completed in 1910 (*Harvard Annual Reports*, 1906–1909). One of the first student research papers that applied the historical approach resulted in a now well-known piece of the literature – the characterization of the basic functions of marketing.

Arch W. Shaw – the functions of marketing

The concept of marketing functions or functional analysis has been compared by historians – without irony – to the discovery of atomic theory (Converse, 1945b, p. 19). The work of Edward David Jones and Henry C. Taylor on this topic was underlined in Chapter 3. Those are certainly among the earliest discussions of marketing functions. That said, Shaw's (1912) article is usually credited as the first and deserves recognition. He used the term "functions" to refer to acts or services performed by middlemen and highlighted a number of core functions: sharing the risk, transporting the goods, financing the operations, selling (communication of ideas about the goods), and assembling, assorting, and re-shipping (Shaw, 1915, p. 76).

In his 1912 article he did not explain the genesis of his ideas. However, in his 1915 book of the same title, an introductory chapter is included where he outlines his views on the epistemology and methodology of business science. A "body of scientific business principles" or "common factors" could be developed, in Shaw's view, by observing, discovering, and verifying the nature of business activities. This would be achieved by gathering, classifying, and interpreting facts, as it turns out in Shaw's case – historical facts about marketing intermediaries and the work they undertook.

Harvard University Press in their promotion of his book stated that it did for distribution the work that Scientific Management had achieved for manufacturing. The notice that was published is interesting because it signals the legitimacy of distribution and marketing, along with Shaw's general approach. As he puts it:

> The most pressing problem of the business man today . . . is systematically to study distribution, as production is being studied. In this great task he must enlist the trained minds of the economist and the psychologist. He must apply to his problems the methods of investigation that have proven of use in the more highly developed fields of knowledge. He must introduce the laboratory point of view.
>
> (Shaw, 1915, p. 44)

Shaw's reference to the "laboratory point of view" was more than a chance restatement of Dean Gay's own words. The compatibility of their positions had resulted in the formation of the Bureau as one of the first collegiate business "laboratories". He also used that laboratory approach in conducting his historical case study of the development of distribution. This had been proposed to him by Gay. Their shared fascination with British economic history led to this path-breaking research assignment which resulted in the article and book we have already mentioned.

> Dean Gay of Harvard had the knack of challenging the energies of students. In one of his lectures . . . he put special emphasis on the contribution of the merchant in the extension of the British economy both at home and around the world. The emphasis to me was, in effect, a challenge to trace the development of distribution stage by stage starting with the role of the British merchant as the handicraft period came to a close. Of course I found that no problem of demand creation of consequence existed in the handicraft period. Much trade was conducted by barter and there appeared to be a market for whatever was produced. The British merchant, however, under the putting out system, began laying part of the groundwork for the development of the factory system in England in the eighteenth century of which, of course, market distribution was an essential. So it seemed of significance also to trace through the functions supplementing those of the merchant, which together with his

> functions made up the compound of the British economy and then to search for some simple concept by means of which these functions would fall naturally into definite classifications and their interdependence [be] disclosed. The objective was to give order and usability to the knowledge of market distribution accumulated as of that time.
>
> (Shaw, 1950)

Shaw's article was an historically grounded "theory" of marketing. The GHSE pioneers would have applauded this attempt at producing "historical theory". And the importance of marketing at Harvard was truly gaining ground at this point.

> One of the most interesting problems which the historian of domestic trade will face is that of the organization of the domestic market, and with this goes the study of the middleman, the morphology of the merchant. The generation now living is assisting in a movement which looks toward the elimination of the middleman. With large scale production, with the growth of independent agencies of functions formerly exercised by the merchant and now available for the producer – I refer, of course, to forwarding and transportation, credit and insurance agencies; – above all with the growth of advertising and its wide and direct appeal to the consumer which formerly could be made only through a chain of middlemen, the old system of market distribution seems today to be breaking down. Selling agent, wholesaler, local jobber, retailer – all find themselves engaged in a struggle to maintain the old organization of trade against enemies from within and from without . . . It is of importance to know how this orthodox system of market distribution came into existence, what needs it met, how far and in what industries those needs have persisted. We ought to know more definitely what has been the evolution of the merchant and his various functions.
>
> (Gay, 1912b)

The term "morphology" reflects a tendency to anthropomorphize the phenomena of economics, a move characteristic of the GHSE. In his lecture notes on the GHSE, Gay frequently referenced their "organic conception of society" (Gay, n.d.b). In doing so, he is conjuring the spirit of Roscher and his desire to understand the physiology of the market. Business and marketing thought thus evinces the evolutionary standpoint tied to the German Historical School.

The extent to which Shaw may have consciously used the biological metaphor is uncertain. It is plausible, at least, that his focus on the functions of marketing agencies reflected an analogy between institutions and living organisms.

Conclusion

Harvard President Charles W. Eliot established a hospitable intellectual environment for German Historicism. He hired German-trained economists Frank W. Taussig and Edwin Francis Gay, both of whom were instrumental in designing the

HBS curriculum, pedagogic practice, and research activities. Via Gay, and to a lesser extent Taussig, there was considerable potential for the GHSE to shape the epistemology, methodology, and pedagogy of marketing at Harvard.

Gay essentially defined business as making and selling things. Taylor's Scientific Management provided a foundation for teaching, explaining, and indicating ways of fostering efficiency gains for the "making" side of business. As we have pointed out, we must be cautious about assuming philosophical and political consistency between Scientific Management, the GHSE training that people like Gay received, and how it was eventually enrolled in the circuits of pedagogic practice at HBS and beyond. The picture is complicated and Taylor's publications were not simply consumed wholesale by those citing them.

Arch Shaw made it clear that he was taking inspiration from Taylor's work. At best, the former's ideas and publications bear only a family resemblance to the latter's. When reading Shaw's publications – especially his 1911 paper – it becomes apparent that he had already been mining a field of related activity before he chanced upon Taylor's work. Shaw was interested in system, with structuring business routines, in order to make organizational practice more efficient. He had been a very successful practitioner selling office equipment that enabled the streamlining of data management. Taylor's scientific approach enabled Shaw to more rigorously express his own views and flesh them out for a wider audience via his periodical and activities at HBS.

Taylor provided marketing scholars and practitioners with a lexicon of science which was culturally valorized at the time. It enabled them to legitimate their practice in a societal context which was concerned about the wastes of distribution and rising prices and generally suspicious of the motives of business people. It had an ideological function in other words. Not only did it legitimate the discipline, but as Taylor's ideas were developed and refined via the emerging literature on marketing management – the tradition that Harvard promoted via its educational offerings – it helped proselytize the value of marketing within the firm. Science in marketing entailed the use of objective market and customer research and this was a token in organizational politics. Certainly, this managerial inflexion of the importance of science and scientific method did not envisage itself playing the kind of direct role as an input into government decision-making to help ameliorate social problems that was a calling card of GHSE approaches.

Nevertheless, those aligned with managerially oriented marketing did express their optimistic view that increasing the efficiency of micro-level firm activities could have macro-economic reverberations that would be felt far and wide. Reduced costs, it was assumed, would be passed on to the ultimate consumer. The consumer would therefore be the recipient of the efficiency gains enabled by Scientific Management. This optimism is obviously far removed from the stance adopted by GHSE pioneers who were more critical of the efficiency of the marketplace, its ability to deal with distributive injustices, and the ongoing prevalence of customer manipulation and exploitation (Rutherford, 1997, 2010). Depending on the focus of our attention, then, the arguments offered by Arch Shaw or Percival White sometimes reflect similar themes to GHSE ideas or classical economics.

The most obvious point of difference between the GHSE – whether we are referring to the younger school, Ely, or those trained under him – is the decreasing pluralism of stakeholders considered by those fleshing out the marketing management approach. This is not to suggest that the managerial contingent expressed only a rapacious concern with profit at the expense of social welfare (cf. Ely, 1938, p. 171); this would be far removed from the truth, as White's reflections on "supersalesmanship" serve to underline (see also Tadajewski, 2011) – merely that the managerial approach did focus on business interests and efficiency first and foremost, using the prisms of cost accounting, "the sales dollar" (Tadajewski and Jones, 2016), and other disciplinary mechanisms to ensure that their profit objectives were met.

Ethics was salient to the extent that it impacted upon instrumental interests in the short, medium, and long term and provided additional buffering against social criticism. While we have no reason to doubt the commitment to ethics expressed by White (1927), it must be registered that his ethics had a more instrumental, individual company focus, than the type of interest in distributive justice characteristic of Wisconsin. Furthermore, Wisconsin placed more emphasis on the embeddedness of business practice within the orbit of society. The interests of society had to come above individual practitioners, and students were expected to register that group welfare voided claims to profit when they conflicted (Ely, 1938).

Notwithstanding this, Arch Shaw (1911) and Percival White (1927) both expressed an interest in reforming marketing practice, albeit at the micro-managerial level. Reform could be enabled by an increased customer focus and the provision of goods and services that were needed and wanted and represented an advance on what was already available. Such "reform" was going to be enabled by the greater use of the scientific method, by applying the resources and insights offered by multiple academic disciplines, and various methodological toolkits that could unravel the nuances of the market and consumer desire.

In the hands of Percival White, broadly "positivistic" approaches could be used to improve the effectiveness of all marketing functions. In this respect, his approach calls to mind the work of Kinley, especially his reflections on theory production and the necessity for inductive and deductive insights alike to be juxtaposed against the relevant empirics. Kinley's approach – although labeled "positivistic" – was a politically motivated positivism that sought to ameliorate social problems. Where people like Shaw and White differ is that their positivism is focused upon improving and legitimating marketing practice, rather than asking more fundamental questions about the existing organization of the economic system.

In developing the "selling" elements of the pedagogic vision he wanted to promote at HBS, Gay leaned heavily on Shaw. Shaw was the first to apply the case method of teaching; he was the benefactor and intellectual supporter of the Bureau of Business Research, and is credited – albeit this is contested – with originating the functional analysis of marketing. He receives much of the credit for the development of marketing at Harvard. Nonetheless, he owes much to the foresight of Dean Gay. Shaw was a student of Gay's and eventually his colleague. They formed a close and enduring friendship, with parallel intellectual interests that helped maintain their comradeship. Together, they made significant contributions to the foundations of marketing, helping position HBS as an early generator of intellectual locomotion in the managerial orientation that has come to dominate the discipline, and which was extended by Percival White and forwarded by "progressive" members of the banking industry like Fred Warner Shibley (Tadajewski and Jones, 2012; 2016).

As we have shown in this chapter and those that preceded it, the insights that were "absorbed" (Rutherford, 2006) from the GHSE were manifold and complex. The absorption process was contingent upon a variety of political, social, economic, and technological changes, as well as the university environment and the interests of the scholarly contributor, among many others. The lines of genealogical influence are more clearly cut in some places than others and certainly the patterns of diffusion involve both consistency and change. What is uncontestable is that the GHSE have directly and indirectly shaped marketing theory, thought, and practice in a host of ways. In this chapter, we highlighted the connections and disconnections between the GHSE and the more managerial approach at HBS.

7 Conclusions

Introduction

Our discipline has started to take research in the history of marketing thought and practice with greater levels of seriousness. However, there is still a discernible level of anti-intellectualism which requires that the production of knowledge always serve some interest above and beyond the elucidation of our paradigmatic, conceptual, theoretical, and empirical origins. This is a real shame. We need more research that investigates the missing links in the development of our discipline, theory, and thought. Whether this is the study of a school of thought, like the GHSE, a theory that was significant but remains largely underappreciated, or perhaps a concept that connects currently disparate threads, or helps us rethink taken-for-granted arguments, our community needs to be more welcoming of these contributions. We fall far behind our sister disciplines in appreciating historical research and embracing it within our curricula. We need to register what it is: capable of illuminating the core of our subject, the people who worked hard to develop it, and provided the conditions of possibility for our current practices.

In this chapter, we review the major arguments and contributions of this book, beginning with our findings about the influence of the GHSE on marketing thought. Curiously, though, the links we have excavated regarding German Historicism and the emergence of our discipline have been largely neglected. This amnesia is, at least partly, a function of the First World War. We follow this chapter with an epilogue that reveals the inconsistent nature of progressivism, the racist and eugenicist assumptions threading throughout this vein of research, and indicate ways forward for studying marketing theory, thought, and practice.

Rewriting marketing history

Marketing, broadly defined, has been practiced since the time of the ancient Greeks, and scholars from Aristotle and Plato to medieval churchmen and eighteenth century economists have contemplated marketing and its role in the economy. However, following the industrial revolution, driven by improvements in transportation and communications technology, marketing evolved to a more sophisticated level practiced by larger business organizations that increasingly needed professionally trained managers. As marketing came to play a more visible role in the economy, concerns emerged about the costs of distribution and the ethics of marketing behavior. Those needs and concerns led economists to study and teach marketing at universities in America and Britain around the turn of the twentieth century.

The first generation of marketing historians writing during the 1930s and 1940s published chronological lists of textbooks and university course catalog descriptions dated to the early 1900s. They wrote short biographical sketches of pioneer marketing scholars, essays that did not probe very deeply the backgrounds, motivations, assumptions, and influences on those pioneer scholars. Nevertheless, this work was important because it identified the individuals and institutions – at least those in America – that were instrumental in developing this new field of applied economics called marketing. The archives of those institutions that gave birth to the marketing mind proved to be rich sources of material for the story told herein.

Conventional wisdom among marketing historians was that early marketing scholars were most heavily influenced by classical and neoclassical economics. If one carefully reads what is widely recognized as the first published literature about marketing, books such as Ralph Starr Butler's (1910) *Marketing Methods*, Henry Erdman's (1921) *The Marketing of Whole Milk*, A.W. Shaw's (1915) *Some Problems in Market Distribution*, and Paul Nystrom's (1915a) *Economics of Retailing*, as well the periodical literature such as the *Annals of the American Academy of Political and Social Science*, the *American Economic Review*, and the *Journal of Political Economy* in which economists published the first academic studies of marketing, we find historical, descriptive accounts of marketing practice sometimes motivated by surprisingly (compared with today) high ethical ideals of economists-turned-marketing scholars who wanted to understand the problems associated with market distribution. Similarly, the earliest case books written by Harvard Business School marketing professors, such as Melvin Copeland's (1920) *Marketing Problems*, were simply descriptions of actual marketing problems to be used for teaching based on an inductive approach. Again, as Harvard business historian Alfred Chandler observed, "the case study is precisely what a historian does, what a historian is trained to do" (1986, p. 82). If we read and think about the published catalog descriptions of the first university courses in marketing offered in America and Britain, we find pragmatic approaches to teaching that engaged students in various ways to solve the marketing problems of that era. These teachers and students were not grappling with the intellectual challenges of classical and neoclassical economic theory. They were gathering simple, descriptive, historical accounts of the activities or functions carried out in the marketing process by institutions ranging from producers to consumers, commodity by commodity, hoping to eventually develop principles and theories of marketing.

We know now that there is a clear and compelling explanation for that distinctive approach used by early marketing scholars. Even a cursory examination of the backgrounds and training of those economists who are widely recognized as the pioneers of the marketing discipline leads us to consider institutional economics and, by extension, German historical economics as key influences on those pioneers. Beyond the circumstantial historical evidence of those influences, we have documented herein written acknowledgements by many early marketing scholars. They studied in Germany under leading figures in the German Historical School of Economics, or under other American economists who were so trained and who repeatedly acknowledged the influence of the GHSE (see again Figures 2.1a and 2.1b).

As Wittgenstein reminds us: "One keeps forgetting to go down to the foundations. One doesn't put the question marks *deep* enough down" (Wittgenstein, 1998, p. 71e; emphasis in original). The first generation of marketing historians did not place the question marks deep enough. They did not probe the backgrounds, motivations, assumptions, and influences that shaped the individuals that were the subject of their attention. To identify earlier precursors to the content explored by Bartels, we had to move the question marks, and look at the methods of socialization that formatted the approaches taken by the earliest academics in our discipline. We had to look beyond our traditional intellectual horizons. Taking this perspective entailed studying economics. But it was not the version of economics that Bartels stressed was influential in the development of marketing thought. Orthodox economics was not the spring that provided intellectual sustenance, underpinning everything that was written. Our pioneers registered the unrealistic nature of the assumptions that undergirded it, combined with its failure to offer meaningful solutions to the problems facing either continental Europe or the US at the time.

We have presented clear evidence that the GHSE influenced the foundations of marketing in America and Britain. Before us, there had been limited engagement with these ideas. These had explored the philosophical basis of the GHSE and its links to marketing (Jones and Monieson, 1990; Jones and Tadajewski, 2015). Reference was made to differences between the two American centers of influence – Wisconsin and Harvard. This material was analyzed succinctly, with much of the philosophical and methodological complexity given short shrift. The reasons for this were simple and straightforward. It appeared in the *Journal of Marketing* (among others) and space was circumscribed. Connections had to be made quickly, which elided many of the aspects of the discussions that we brought to the foreground in this book.

For example, Jones and Monieson (1990) and Jones and Tadajewski (2015) gave us some insight into the GHSE and how it shaped our scholarly identity. They tended to focus on the methodological implications of this school for our discipline. We wanted to do something more in this text. Of course, we needed to traverse related topics. But we sought to go beyond them, making connections between the macro-factors that formatted the institutional environment and the intellectual vistas that these early pioneers constructed. To do so, we had to ratchet up our analytical lens to include the context that orients the lifeworld and experiences of the individuals whose influence has been so profound. We needed to understand the political-economic and cultural context that these people navigated. This demanded sensitivity to national points of difference, political-economic nuance, and the various factors that affected those involved in the formative development of marketing.

In doing so, we needed to cut through a thicket of misunderstanding and misrepresentation. We are not saying that everything that had been written on this subject – the history of marketing thought and marketing practice – previously was mistaken, but there were several omissions we had to correct and over-simplifications we had to avoid. Where other publications focused on homogeneity, we sought to unpick the diversity of intellectual commitments. Initially this meant parsing the transmission of economic values into orthodox economics and its close sibling, neoclassical economics, apart from the paradigmatic assemblage that was being communicated by the GHSE.

We have taken the history provided by Bartels and revealed threads that he – and many others – had missed. We have knotted these together to create a compelling picture of the emergence of a discipline which was shaped by external as well as internal factors. Not only did Bartels miss core influences on our discipline – namely the GHSE – he completely failed to make connections between some of the titans of economics and the people he labeled as significant in the development of marketing thought. By bringing in issues of axiology, epistemology, and – highly unusually for marketing theory – politics, we unraveled the multitude of factors that impacted upon the conditions of possibility for our subject.

Underwriting our narrative is a concern that multiple groups have had regarding the stability of society. Like a specter haunting the genealogy of economics and marketing, the perceived threat and opportunities presented by socialism have been an ever-present theme. Yet, this has remained largely unacknowledged (Tadajewski, 2006a). It followed the German Historical School and was a factor that motivated the formation of the *Verein für Socialpolitik* (Fourcade-Gourinchas, 2001). We engaged with the emergence of this institution and traced their interest in ensuring ontological stability via the greater intervention of the state in economic affairs.

Their humanitarian impulse was something their students, especially the young Americans who trained at their feet, found deeply attractive. They brought this back with them to their home country, using the knowledge, skills and insights their continental education provided to help improve the functioning of the economic and political system. As we argued, their position effectively mediated a mid-point between socialism and laissez-faire (Gilbert and Baker, 1997). By the time we arrived at Chapter 6, the issue of socialism and potential overthrow of the existing economic system and the distribution of benefits this entailed was a factor that worried Frederick Taylor and he engaged with this topic in his famous work on Scientific Management (Tadajewski and Jones, 2012; Tadajewski and Jones, 2016) – ideas that were incorporated into marketing by groups seeking to buttress their financial muscle, organizational power, and the status quo. Marketing, consumption, and Scientific Management were linked in the battle to defuse the appeal of socialism (Tadajewski and Jones, 2016).

We have added generational links between major figures in economics, their role in training the first cadre of marketing academics, and have delved into the philosophy of marketing thought to an extent beyond that undertaken previously. Where Rutherford (1998) wondered about what was being transmitted between GHSE oriented scholars and their students, we not only traced intergenerational pedagogic structuring, but narrated the links between economics and marketing.

We excavated the philosophical assumptions being passed from pioneers to neophytes, combined with the methodological injunctions they adopted with aplomb, and explored the politics generating their labors. Our story extends the heritage of the field. Highlighting the important roles played by Richard Ely, Edward Jones, Henry Taylor, David Kinley, Simon Litman, William Ashley, Edwin Gay, and Arch Shaw in the emergence of marketing thought is among our contributions. Looking back, all the elements were there, they just needed to be pieced together.

The topics, methodologies, and ethical commitments of the first academics associated with our specialism were not consistent with the type of deductive thinking and abstract representations that classical and neoclassical economics usually produced. German Historical Economics was a much more commensurate source of influence. Circumstantial evidence buttressed our initial speculations, speculations which were substantiated with extensive archival research. Even if they did not travel to Germany directly, they received this instruction indirectly via American economists who were exposed to the rigors of the German education system (Figures 2.1a and 2.1b).

The influence of the German Historical School

Broadly speaking, the GHSE was motivated to solve the economic problems facing Germany in the nineteenth century, problems that could not be solved with orthodox economic theory. Those solutions required an understanding of the issues. So, the GHSE began by studying the history of the German economy. Their approach was historical, descriptive, and *largely* inductive. This does not, by any stretch of the imagination, make the GHSE or those they educated atheoretical or uninterested in the development of theory. They simply had a very different view of what theory encompassed compared with their orthodox or neoclassical brethren.

They were interested in developing what was called "historical theory", theory that was specific to the time and context in which it was produced. This reflected their dynamic concept of society and the economy (Kinley, 1899). Neither was static. They changed. GHSE scholars dealt with this in a variety of ways: historical, institutional analysis was one; they collected large amounts of data (Clark *et al.*, 1906), using this to develop, refine, and overhaul existing theories, concepts, and lines of argumentation, including Say's law among many others. Methodological rigor was notable in their empirical research. Attempts were made to undermine taken-for-granted arguments about empirical phenomena to present more realistic depictions of marketplace activities.

Reading this material closely presses home the point that these academics were cautious in terms of the way they evaluated the data being gathered and the statements they made. In methodological terms, research was not viewed as a one-shot practice. More positivistically minded GHSE scholars (cf. Rutherford, 2010, p. 65) were interested in the replication of studies for comparative purposes: "A single investigation is of little value. The value of the investigation, whatever it is, depends upon the continuance or repetition of such inquiries in order that comparisons may be made from time to time, and the trend of the phenomena be more clearly set forth" (Kinley, 1899, p. 244). The theory that was produced was considered "good" when it had practical value, that is, when it helped better administer organizations and the economy (Clark *et al.*, 1906). Connected to this was their realism. This was discussed in Chapters 3, 4, 5, and 6.

By contrast to a more managerial literature which emphasized social harmony and downplayed conflict (Jones, 1997; Scully, 1996), they were highly attentive to the conflictual nature of the social world (Balabkins, 1993/1994; Commons, 1964), especially where industry was concerned (cf. Kinley, 1925, p. 236). Attention was directed to the fractious nature of capital and labor relations, with attempts made to engage with these issues in a realistic manner, that is, fully cognizant of the unequal nature of power relations in many different exchange situations (e.g. Kinley *et al.*, 1902). In other places, the economic and distributive injustices that were faced by the farming community were revealed in vivid terms (e.g. Jones, 1912d; Kinley, 1895; Taylor, 1941). There might have been progress in relation to economic growth and the standard of living, but not all benefitted equally and this posed problems for social stability. Political realism and epistemological relativism, thus, underpinned the ideas of the GHSE and the advice they provided to multiple stakeholders. Their relativism was temporal and locational in nature (Kinley, 1895; 1899).

The historical sensitivity of the GHSE, their awareness that English classical economics did not transfer to the continent or US in an unproblematic fashion, or help them solve salient economic and social problems, led them away from this tradition. We are understating their critique of universalism. They could not stress strongly enough the problems associated with abstract systems of deductive thought which were *sometimes* far removed from the empirical realism of the marketplace. Early marketing academics immersed in the GHSE value system wanted to reconnect economics with the market.

The strongest examples of this approach were found at Wisconsin. By the late nineteenth century, Ely's students were examining marketing-related topics as part of their assessment program. At more advanced levels, Wisconsin was a veritable factory for PhD graduates and these were often steeped in the GHSE (cf. Commons, 1964). Their socialization occurred in multiple ways. Ely was obviously a conduit. Equally, he never lost an opportunity to encourage his students to study on the continent.

Edward D. Jones, Samuel Sparling, James Hagerty, Henry Taylor, and Benjamin Hibbard, among many others, all studied under Ely. Above all else, they were instructed to "picture the marketing process clearly in order that the true character of the problems of marketing might be discovered" (Taylor, 1941, p. 22). Reflecting this, Ely's apprentices sought to develop solutions to economic problems such as inequity and inefficiency in the marketing process. They did so by studying the contributions made by institutions such as agricultural cooperatives. Such an ethical and activist approach is found in Taylor's and Hibbard's work in agricultural marketing as well as in Jones's studies on the merchandising of manufactured goods.

Simon Litman had no direct connection to Wisconsin, but he was part of that Midwestern group recognized as pioneers who had indirect affiliations with the GHSE. While Litman's status as the delivery mechanism for the first marketing course at California is well known, we brought new material to light that enhanced our understanding of what he taught. Previously our knowledge on this front was cursory to say the least. Most notably, we cited an undocumented version of a text published for the LaSalle Extension University, which described course content (see Litman, 1910). Litman deserves much more attention. His contributions to international marketing have been seriously neglected to date.

For our purposes here, perhaps the most significant untold story about the foundations of academic marketing is that of William Ashley and the University of Birmingham. The complete lack of awareness on the part of marketing historians about the early study and teaching of marketing in Britain as well as the influential role played by the GHSE both there as well as in America is likely due to insularity on the part of earlier generations of marketing historians, all of whom were American. Given Ashley's earlier employment at Harvard and therefore his likely awareness of the planning of the Harvard Business School, it is remarkable that no marketing historians (with the exception of Jones and Tadajewski, 2015) have investigated Ashley's Commerce Program founded in 1902 at Birmingham. In his "Commerce III–Business Policy" course, Ashley anticipated the later emphasis on strategy for which the Harvard Business School became well known. And just as Gay later did at Harvard, Ashley believed that production (manufacturing) and marketing (commercial policy) were the pillars of business instruction, and that marketing was the more important of the two. He covered a wide range of marketing topics in his Business Policy course, but his emphasis was on channels of distribution and the role of "commercial middlemen". As was later the practice at Harvard, Ashley made extensive use of connections with local businesses both as a source for lecturers and as sites for his students to visit and study. The results of those field trips often served as the basis for student research and discussion in his Commerce Seminar. Neither Ashley nor his students ever published the students' descriptions of the marketing problems of local businesses, but they were nonetheless case studies, as surely as the collections later published by professors at Harvard. His extensive use of the seminar method of teaching followed the example he learned in Germany and anticipated the case method later used at Harvard. Ashley was clearly influenced by the GHSE in his epistemology, research approach, and pedagogy. However, like his former colleagues at Harvard, he was more conservative than either the GHSE or the early Wisconsin school of marketing thought. While he adapted the philosophy of German Historicism to the study of marketing, Ashley felt that the *Volkswirtschaftslehre* of the GHSE did not adequately deal with the perspective of individual private businesses and senior management.

In focusing our attention on the HBS, we were initially guided by Bartels (1962). He proposed that the chief contributions emerging from this school were its methodology of analysis and pedagogic practice. Harvard President Charles Eliot together with GHSE-trained economists Frank Taussig and Edwin Gay envisioned a business school based on pedagogical pragmatism and the goal of creating an inductive science of business; the latter reflecting the influence of Schmoller on Gay's thought. As an administrator, Gay managed the careers of others, originating decisions which directed the development of marketing in Cambridge, Massachusetts.

His faith in induction was the driving force behind the formation of the Harvard Bureau of Business Research. It was also the basis for Gay's advocacy of a "laboratory method" of teaching, that is, the case method. Arch Shaw, who was initially a student, and subsequently colleague, of Gay's, shared his fascination in English economic history. This cross-fertilization of interests and ideas led to Shaw's well-known publication on marketing functions (Shaw, 1912). Where Gay's debt to the GHSE was direct, Shaw's was via Dean Gay.

Together with Shaw, Gay institutionalized research in marketing courtesy of the Bureau of Business Research. The investigations conducted by this organization were undertaken to provide teachers with material to use in the classroom. It was a means to inject empirical realism into the lecture and seminar; to bring the specimens of the business world into the university "laboratory". Research and the insights that flow from it were not meant to be confined to the ivory tower; however, it had to be disseminated to people who could use it to facilitate a more efficient and customer-centered marketplace.

The orientation of Birmingham and Harvard differed from Wisconsin. The first two institutions focused on the problems of retailing and industry, especially those occupying marketing managers; the latter on agriculture. This reflected contextual and locational needs. In Arch Shaw's words, at HBS they were concerned with the "how to" of marketing. Ashley, likewise, designed a "nakedly utilitarian curriculum" (1932, p. 96). This was targeted at the "principals, directors, managers [who] will ultimately guide the business activity of the country" (Ashley, 1902, p. 1). In other words, there was not the same level of concern with the general welfare of society at Harvard or Birmingham compared with Wisconsin. Nor was there the same degree of involvement in active reform through engagement with legislators and the state government.

Having now surveyed some of the themes presented in this book, we are left with a slightly perplexing question. The influences of the GHSE were profound and enduring, and should have been obvious to the first generation of marketing historians. Why did they ignore this evidence? This becomes even more odd when we realize that some of them "forgot" these influences in the published accounts of their own contributions. We say this was odd because they had privately signaled the significance of their educational exposure to the GHSE (e.g. Hagerty, 1906; Litman, 1963). Moving into more speculative territory, we submit that directing our attention to the context in which they were writing might reveal plausible reasons why they neglected certain aspects of their socialization; a neglect that shaped the representation of the genealogy of marketing thought subsequently. What we are suggesting is not necessarily unsurprising or unrealistic. After all, they were writing between World War I and WWII. Major events like this do have a habit of affecting the trajectory of academic inquiry and we believe they performed a similar role here. This is a very complex thread which needs a large amount of further research. Nevertheless, let us make a few tentative steps in this regard.

Being perceived as unorthodox in a time of social pressure

Institutions like Wisconsin were known for their tolerance of unorthodox positions. This brought both the people employed there and the university itself under the gaze of those looking for un-American values. Ely faced academic trials because of unwanted attention. Kinley had to protect him and this enabled Ely to continue his career, albeit adopting a more cautious stance regarding his public statements. Reflecting on Kinley's death in the pages of the *American Economic Review*, Litman recalled:

> Dr. Kinley . . . was a determined fighter for what he considered just. On one of my last visits at the hospital, just a few weeks before Kinley's death, I found him reading Professor Ely's autobiography. Feeble as he was, sitting slumped in a large chair, too large for his emaciated body, he showed me certain passages in Ely's book. With pride and with some of the fire which often illuminated his face in his former years he spoke of the way he carried on to successful conclusion the defense of Ely, who was ill at the time, against the attacks of the Wisconsin Superintendent of Education who accused Ely of radicalism, of economic "heresy", of encouraging strikes and practicing boycotts.
>
> (Litman, 1945, p. 1043)

As we signaled, some of the economics teachers who helped cultivate the subjectivities of our ancestors held unorthodox views; views that got them into trouble and which they sought to shroud by calling them a variant of conservatism. We must not be misled by this discursive cloaking. Richard Ely's writing before his academic trials and after does differ in terms of the way he framed his work, but many of the themes and content remain commensurate. He was interested in social change. He wanted to make the world a better place. He wanted to help those with less power in the marketplace and distribution system secure a better deal. At the same time, he was not espousing a commitment to radical social change. He was very clear about not aligning with extreme groups like the anarchists, but his writing comes close to positions that some would have found uncomfortable. To us, he often communicates ideas that are similar to the socialist labor movement, and this, combined with his sometimes pretty caustic comments about industrial and business leaders, made him a target, courtesy of his deviation from social mores. Ely's writing was easily understandable and his public position placed him on dangerous territory.

But, he survived. For this, marketing academics should be appreciative. He brought his "ethical economics" and "warm humanitarianism" to our discipline. Ely's ethical orientation helped to mold an axiology which some of our pioneers adopted and applied in their own social change efforts. His "progressive conservatism" entailed looking at the world – the "look and see" method – and determining what was good about it, what demanded rectification, and encouraging appropriate groups to enact change efforts through pertinent channels. His was a cautious optimism about social change. He did not commit himself to the idea that the world could be modified so dramatically that all would experience it as a land of milk and honey. Nor was he a Hobbes. Life did not have to be nasty, brutish, and short. It would not be easy, but legislative change could make the experiences of the masses more bearable than they might otherwise have been. H.C. Taylor's efforts at improving the existence of those toiling on the farm, helping elevate their knowledge, training, and skill in producing what the market would clear – at a profit – at the same time as enhancing their ability to secure more value in marketing processes, typify GHSE change efforts. They were piecemeal forms of change, but helped reduce information asymmetries and disrupted power relationships that favored some groups over others.

This political ethics permeates the educational values that were communicated. These issues have not been unpacked previously. David Kinley was the best exponent of the implications of the GHSE axiology, epistemology, methodology, and politics in relation to education. We touched upon this in Chapters 3 and 4. Social mobility was a key issue for him. He wanted to enable students to transcend their class and reach their potential. As he grew older, this agenda took on a greater status quo orientation (e.g. Kinley, 1925; cf. Kinley, 1949). So, even a progressive mind like Kinley shied away from the potential for radical change to take hold in American society. In his case, he called for universities to avoid encouraging excessive intellectual specialization. The danger inherent in this was that it "fostered the movement towards class consciousness"[1] (Kinley, 1925, p. 232). Change was welcome; but only within certain bounds.

We know from Chapter 3 that Ely subscribed to social objectivity. All sources of information about the social world were potentially useful inputs into his research, reflections, writing, and political engagement. Reading Ely's publications, which were written when access to information was much harder than it is today, it is apparent that he engaged with an extensive range of material. He read across the paradigmatic and political spectrum, marshalling it into compelling narratives that elucidated some of the most contentious issues of the day.

In an astute maneuver, he wrote that he welcomed proposals for rethinking elements of the economic system, but placed the onus for social change on the representatives advancing it. They had to prove the merits of their suggestions. They had to be willing to debate them. In what seems quite Habermasian in intent, Ely averred that he hoped the population of the United States would not replicate mistakes of other, less progressive societies, by failing to permit dialogue on these issues. Such an approach only makes the taboo more attractive. It was better to reflect openly, critically, and constructively on ideas for change. Even though Ely was cautious, this was not enough. But he was attuned to the needs of the environment in which he operated. The mistakes of his youth were not going to be replicated in his later life. Like other university lecturers active in the run-up to

World War I, Ely responded to the waves of sentiment that called for patriotic contributions which delegitimized the German war machine whilst supporting the Allies (Herzberg, 2001). Did these patriotic demands exacerbate the amnesia surrounding the GHSE and its connections to marketing? Maybe. There are various possible reasons why the GHSE influence was forgotten or excised. The ascension of marketing management perspectives was important in this regard. We traced the rise to prominence of this body of scholarship in Chapters 5 and 6, differentiating the core assumptions that underwrote this tradition from the values associated with the GHSE. Where efficiency was questioned by the GHSE, it was valorized by the managerial contingent, helping support their claims to be undertaking "science", and this chimed with the social climate of the 1920s and 1930s (Jones, 1997; Scully, 1996) – a period of time when marketing management professionals rose to prominence in the ranks of corporate capitalism (Tadajewski and Jones, 2016).

As the marketing management approach became more widely accepted between the 1920s and 1950s, the focus on social welfare and ethics was sidelined by greater attention being devoted to profit (cf. Abend, 2013; Tadajewski, 2017). Kinley (1925) was clear about this matter in his discussions of the university curriculum (see also Commons, 1964). He suggested that the rise of business education had led to declines in socially oriented leadership. Specialization and a focus on efficiency, profit, and the occasional gesture to "service" fostered "limited" understandings of the role of business in society. The narrowness of the education that these groups received made them largely useless when it came to policy-making. They were unable to look beyond their own corporate and personal needs. This is a marked contrast to the repeated claims being proffered in support of its version of business education coming from the HBS at the same time.

Marketing professionals were not proclaiming the virtues of laissez-faire. There was no massive reversal on this front. Instead, they continued White's (1927) reformist agenda by presenting themselves as the conduit for the consumer within the organization, often positioning their contributions as helping ameliorate the class conflict that was a dangerous concomitant of the Great Depression (Nyland *et al.*, 2014). Marketing practitioners could understand, interpret, and provide what the customer wanted, at the right place, at the right time, in an appropriate quantity. The state did not figure prominently in this worldview. They theoretically joined Shaw (1911; 1915) and White (1927) in talking about the importance of conducting market research, focusing on the customer, and engaging in processes of demand management to achieve profit requirements. They were the masters of the marketing universe – within certain anti-trust bounds (Tadajewski, 2010b) – and their writings, monographs, and textbooks were increasingly specific in their operational guidance. This was all ably supported by official organizations like the American Marketing Association and related groups who provided a standardized lexicon to unite professionals in the field (Cochoy, 1998, 2014; Witkowski, 2010).

But we suspect that a need to distance marketing scholarship and research from any perceived associations with Germany was a motivator in the refusal to acknowledge the influence of the GHSE.[2] Certainly, looking at the turn against Germans and the negative citation of figures associated with the younger school, notably Schmoller, indicate that there are other factors involved here. He was a willing participant in propagandistic efforts; and willing to express his nationalism in uncompromising terms.[3] Senn (1993/1994, p. 304) posits that this did "hurt his influence among many in the English speaking world".

Nevertheless, this narrative is almost byzantine. GHSE-trained scholars were working against the mainline of what conventionally constituted the role of the academic in the nineteenth century. This was often depicted as presenting what was currently known; intellectuals were discouraged from making original or critically oriented investigations of their own (Commons, 1964; Tyler and Cheyney, 1938). Economics, particularly the GHSE, undermined this value system. They were well known for making important and influential "theoretical contributions" (Streissler and Milford, 1993/1994, p. 60). It already had one mark against it. This constituted it as a radical science (Coats, 1985). The second was its German origins which were heralded, but slighted at the same time.

Working in the social sciences made the position of the individual even more precarious. As Tyler and Cheyney (1938, p. 11) remark, "In the social sciences . . . evidence of any deviation by the professor from the straight and narrow of conservatism will not be far to seek. Watchful critics surround and beset him". Those associated with the GHSE were walking on thin ice. With the above in mind, it is not surprising that Ely framed his approach as a form of conservatism. As a report produced under the auspices of the American Sociological Society revealed, there were two "special dangers" for those involved with social science teaching and research.

The social sciences were epistemologically immature. They were studying the social world, the system of production, distribution, and exchange, collecting "specimens", producing books, articles, and periodical matter, and taking students into the field to visit practitioners, speak to the laboring classes, and so forth. The socially minded economist or marketer could not easily avoid making statements about the economic and business system that sometimes placed him at odds with powerful figures, especially the industrialists who occupied positions as trustees on university boards (Commons, 1964). Wisconsin offered more support than most. Ely was protected and his commitment to social objectivity meant that even when he was introducing "controversial" ideas that made economics seem provocative, he and his colleagues argued that this rendered them more effectively non-partisan than those who communicated one perspective, whether that was laissez-faire or something else. Even so, protections only hold for so long.

By the start of the First World War, preachers were making scathing statements about Germany and engaging in concerted and frequently horrific "anti-German war propaganda" (Bateman, 1998, p. 42). The Social Gospel values that had steered progressives like Ely and Commons were in freefall. The idea that progress could be attained through "enlightened social control" was undermined by the mass "slaughter and uncontrolled irrationality" of the cataclysmic confrontation taking place between 1914 and 1918 (Leonard, 2016, p. 15). The discourse had fundamentally shifted. While references to humanism, cooperation, and industrial peace would continue to be articulated (Simha and Lemak, 2010), social tensions (Dean, 1997), nativism, anti-individualism, and high levels of patriotism took center stage (Leonard, 2005, 2016).

When the social climate shifts in this way, institutional protections may not always be enough. Hugo Münsterberg, the Harvard polymath who studied advertising among many other facets of industrial research, ran into trouble for his continued support of his home country (Germany) in the period leading up to World War I. Harvard, to their credit, refused to bow to pressure (on a number of occasions) to remove him from faculty, rejecting Münsterberg's own resignation at one point. German faculty members located elsewhere were not so lucky (Tyler and Cheyney, 1938). Academics who had experience of the political climate, like Ely, were attentive to shifting social currents. Apart from personal exposure to the dangers of politicized charges, they had witnessed their friends, colleagues, and more distant members of the university community suffer from discrimination and persecution. In the period before and during World War I, these dangers became more acute.

Herzberg (2001) traces the impact of the war on a number of people, including Ely and John Commons. He registers their heterodox orientation prior to the confrontation but stresses that the pressure for expressions of patriotic sentiment, commitment to the war effort, and a willingness to denunciate Germany shaped their statements and activities. Like other historians, Herzberg points out that Ely had been politically lucky and fairly astute in negotiating what were "career-threatening controversies" (Herzberg, 2001, p. 125). As the war approached, Wisconsin found itself surrounded by a political community aligned with the Republican Party, rather than the progressivist values proclaimed by Robert LaFollette. The response by the university was predictable (cf. Commons, 1964).

> [O]wing to a series of highly public incidents that had cast doubt upon the university's loyalty, officials and professors at Madison had more reason than most to flaunt their patriotism. . . . Instances of 'questionable' loyalty were accordingly viewed with the utmost gravity. . . . The pro-war fervor provided more than sufficient reasons for Ely, Commons [and others] . . . to join the patriotic parade. . . . [E]xperience had taught each of them the importance of presenting themselves carefully before suspicious trustees and a volatile public.
>
> (Herzberg, 2001, p. 127)

Herzberg highlights that this was not simply a cynical ploy to deflect attention. They did feel obligated to help articulate reasons why Germany had to be confronted and beaten. To do so, they applied their formidable intellects to help propagandize Allied war efforts. For Herzberg (2001, p. 127), "one would search in vain for a member of the Wisconsin faculty more passionately committed to the patriotic cause than Richard T. Ely".

Ely's critiques were varied, some directed internally at LaFollette, others focused on Germany and how it was being poorly led by elites in ways antithetical to social progression and growth. For less sophisticated observers, the mistakes of then-current continental leaders were conflated with the ideas produced by academics publishing from within the country. This is one of the reasons "anti-laissez faire" perspectives, that is, exactly those types of ideas communicated by Ely and his students, were tainted with the slur of un-American doctrines (Tyler and Cheyney, 1938).

Ely argued that the kind of social engineering that was taking place in Germanic society was a form of devolution, a return to tribalism that presented grave dangers for world peace (Herzberg, 2001). Better leadership was his cure for German devolution. Only this could reconnect it to a progressive path. This theme of the necessity of social evolution being controlled by those most knowledgeable, informed, and able to direct change in beneficent directions was an extension of ideas that were present earlier in Ely's career. The war provided the opportunity for his technocratic bent to be more forcefully expressed.

We believe that the influence of social pressure that was a concomitant of the First World War played an important role in discouraging our scholars from expressing the German influence on the foundations of marketing thought. We explore how strong this reaction to Germany and its system of ideas was in the final chapter.

Conclusion

This chapter has called for greater historical research. While the receptivity of marketing journals to this type of scholarship has markedly improved in the past decade, publishing this content is made more difficult by the latent positivism that underwrites most reviewer comments, even those adopting ostensibly unorthodox positions. Demands are made of historical scholarship that it demonstrate its utility above and beyond the elucidation, critique, and rethinking of received wisdom that is usually accomplished by some of the best material in this tradition. Such rethinking projects achieve what most published content in Consumer Culture Theory or related approaches are praised for – taking an object of attention and changing the way we understand it, accompanying this with a narrative that clarifies the claims being made. This is the production of a narrative; otherwise known as a "theory" in such a paradigmatic orbit (Maclaran *et al.*, 2009). Those seeking to publish historical research would do well to mirror these types of claims for theoretical contribution if they wish to further the agenda we are trying to advance in this book and which we articulate in more detail in the epilogue.

As part of our project to encourage more attention to the historical record, we have demonstrated the various ways this book has contributed to rethinking the foundations of our discipline, tracing the set of values and assumptions associated with the German Historical School. We pinpointed the locations on the continent where many American students went to study at the feet of some of the most well-respected economists of the nineteenth century. They were exposed to a rigorous education. It was scholarly, presented the importance of connecting economics with the market, and expressed a commitment to ethics as a foundational factor shaping the problem-solving projects that researchers were required to undertake.

We unpacked the ways these ideas were communicated through influential institutions, tracing the patterns of diffusion from teacher to neophyte, which were revitalized in the process and disseminated further afield as these newly minted PhD's taught the next generation. The influence of the GHSE is undeniable. Yet, what has always perplexed us is why this was elided by those reflecting on the discipline in the 1930s and 1940s. This, as we pointed out, was odd for a very specific reason. These authors had noted the influence privately, but were unwilling to do so in print. To account for this, we proposed that attention to the wider cultural context might offer us some insight. In this case, focusing on the social climate in the run-up to World War I indicated that performing patriotic sentiment by criticizing Germany and its desire for world domination was important.

In the next chapter, we continue the exploration of these issues. In doing so, we reveal the dark side of progressivism. The bright side that has been presented thus far in this book is only part of the story. As we will document, progressivist values could be used to legitimate seriously problematic solutions to perceived social problems. This account will take us into the realm of racism and eugenics – areas that require much more historical exploration than they have received to date.

Notes

1 This obviously did not happen, as specialization has continued to be a feature of university education.

2 In response to a letter from the first author, Robert Bartels responded to a question about the lack of recognition of German influence on marketing thought by writing, "Inasmuch as early marketing thought was a product of this country [America], I could attribute no influence to German writers. Simon Litman did say that in planning his first course on trade and commerce he relied upon material obtained from three German writers. I assure you that that was the last that was heard of them in marketing circles" (Bartels, 1985).

3 There is an interesting point made by Senn that requires further research. It suggests that while Schmoller's influence declined in the leadup to and following World War I, the emigration of scholars to avoid Nazi persecution led to a reengagement with his ideas (e.g. Senn, 1993/1994, p. 315). This is something the historian of the future may wish to follow up.

8 Epilogue

The contradictions of progressivism and future research

Introduction

In the last chapter, we reviewed the contents of this book. This was undertaken partly to set up the narrative we wish to present in this chapter about various ways forward for studying early marketing thought. We proposed that the nodal point for the distancing project, that is, the forgetting of the GHSE, can be traced to the First World War. Where previously we focused on Ely's espousal of patriotic sympathies, we now explore the more vociferous political denunciations of Germany and its value system by Kinley. He provides some of the most scathing critiques of Germany, its leadership, and the philosophical assumptions guiding the nation.

We then call attention to the need to study the dark side of progressive economic and marketing theory and practice. After this, we suggest that the progressive and managerial traditions – the perspectives that we examined in Chapters 3, 5, and 6 in most detail – were fused by Kinley possibly for reasons of appearing congruent with the social climate and to avoid the problematic gaze of powerful gatekeepers. For those seeking the application of progressive values, like Bateman (2003), who bemoans the fact that progressive economists were not as progressive as he expected, we recommend that they look to marketing scholars and practice. It is within our discipline that progressive ideas and values were translated into operational guidance for business people.

Central to the literature we explore is the idea that practitioners should focus on meeting the needs of the customer. This, of course, is a core part of the marketing concept. It differs from all current interpretations of this notion in that it goes beyond White's (1927) ethical orientation to present marketing practice as a method to deflate prejudice. In the hands of Kinley, our discipline channels progressive values and managerial instrumentalism at the same time.

From accusations of socialism to patriotism

As was indicated in multiple places in this text, highlighting the roles performed by people like Gustav Schmoller, Richard Ely, and David Kinley and the threading of the theme of socialism throughout the emergence of marketing thought are major contributions of this account. This political-economic perspective suffuses this book. From our engagement with the *Verein*, most notably Schmoller, there was an obvious interest in integrating the working classes into the social system with the minimum of friction (Balabkins, 1993/1994). The same can be said of H.C. Taylor and Frederick Taylor. Eliding many points of difference, their common response was to preemptively defuse the appeal of radical social change movements (Prisching, 1993/1994). Ontological stability was prioritized (Balabkins, 1993/1994) and legislation intended to ease the life and hardships faced by the working population was one method of undercutting the promises of idealistic social prophets (Balabkins, 1993/1994).

After facing accusations of anarchist and socialist sympathies at various points in his career, Ely was much more circumspect as he aged on this topic. World War I provided an opportunity for him to demonstrate his adherence to social norms, especially the deployment of appropriate sentiment in public. Ely threw himself into this role with considerable energy, railing against the country that provided him with an axiology and ethics that made him such a force for social good.

Kinley's criticism was detailed and presented as his opinion as the Vice-President of the University of Illinois. The report he authored, entitled "The Aims and Claims of Germany", was positioned as a manuscript produced to explicate "the relations of the farmer to the war and . . . a program of production to be recommended to the state". Realistically, the report did none of these things. It emphasized that Kinley (1918a) continued to be active in relation to state-level organizations and was often quite philosophical regarding the nature of German society, the ideological foundations of the country, and the commitment to efficiency that pervaded its industry. Kinley, like his GHSE colleagues, was still in awe of the economic might of the nation.

The relativism that we expect in GHSE writings is present. In this case, he relativizes the notion of efficiency. This is something we registered in other chapters, but his comments take the arguments about efficiency much further than we remarked upon previously. Where Frederick Taylor, Arch Shaw, and Louis Brandeis, for example, generally viewed efficiency in positive terms, the GHSE paid considerable attention to the dark side of this concomitant of increasingly large corporations. In Kinley's paper, he links the micro-level activities of firms with the cultural, philosophical, and ideological underpinnings of Germanic society, and their alleged desire for global supremacy. In some respects, he is replicating the warning strategy that Ely claimed to perform in relation to anarchism and socialism in the 1880s, albeit focusing his attention on a currently pressing concern. As he explains:

> The doctrine of efficiency has been much preached of late years, and [the] German example in this respect has been held up for the world to follow. We must remember, however, that efficiency, after all, is a relative matter. Efficiency is desirable only if its purpose is approvable. Efficiency, or perfection in the performance of a given act, is worthwhile only if the act is worthwhile. To make a thief efficient is not a good thing. To be an efficient liar, or robber, or murderer is not a good thing. Now it is true that in industry and trade, in

> the art of war and the machinery of education, as well as in other lines, the German people in the past two generations have attained, in some respects, a greater perfection or efficiency than most of the rest of the world. They have done so, however, because they have been bending all their energies for a definite specific purpose: preparation for war.
>
> (Kinley, 1918a, p. 7)

The period between the 1870s and 1900 are depicted as a golden period for the country. Yet, this was also apparently a period of indoctrination that traveling students experienced (see also Kinley, 1925, p. 236). However, we need to be cautious in agreeing with Kinley. He is suggesting that some individuals who were taught on the continent were uncritically imbibing German values and superiority. This is inconsistent with Ely's social objectivity or Schmoller's "multi-dimensional method" (Balabkins, 1993/1994). Kinley appears to be making a standard elitist attribution move, where only a select number of the anointed can avoid the psychological manipulations of propaganda, norms, or accepted wisdom.

Whatever the reason, the intellectual faculties of "some" of his peers are completely underrated, with their credulousness overwhelming their critical sensibilities. For his argument to hold water, he could only really be referring to those who were dipping into GHSE content superficially. This may have been true in certain cases. In Chapter 2 we noted that it was fashionable for students to educationally tour the continent, attending various institutions to expose themselves to the leading minds. Equally, there were those who were more seriously committed to their education and presumably better able to distinguish valid from questionable arguments. Kinley is hedging his interpretation in such loose terms that it is difficult to determine who are his targets.

What he is effectively claiming is that students and the professoriate-in-training were exposed to critical reading and analytic skills by the GHSE and subsequently avoided turning them upon their educational experience, none of which appears reasonable.

> In industry and trade, in literature and education, in military growth and civil administration she [Germany] assumed to take the place of leadership and was acknowledged as leader in these matters . . . by thousands of our own people who, too busy to look below the surface, or too shallow in their appreciation of German political philosophy and its goal, preached and taught for years the doctrines of German superiority. American students and American university professors went for higher education to Germany, and without realizing the trend of the philosophical ideas which underlay the education they received, came back in scores and hundreds to spread the story of German efficiency and intellectual progress. Some of them were slavish followers of the doctrines of their teachers, and have been unable to rid themselves of the imperialistic point of view acquired at these German seats of learning. They have unconsciously spread doctrines that are pernicious in a democracy.
>
> (Kinley, 1918a, p. 6)

He is vociferously critical of the country for its desire to extend its territory and influence throughout the world. He takes this argument to the extreme; one of the aims of Germany was world domination. Embedded within this narrative, economic power would be compounded courtesy of the efficiency of the industrial complex. The kinds of cutthroat competition that caused havoc in America were nothing compared to the systematic destruction of industrial competitors that Germany had in mind. Kinley cites numerous examples to support his proposition – all of which are intended to undermine the legitimacy of the nation, its contribution to the world, and interest in the general welfare that was an axiological predicate of GHSE economics. Morality, ethics, international law, national sovereignty, none of these circumscribed the objectives of the country. So that we cannot be accused of overstating the unstinting nature of his argument, an extended quotation is in order.

> She [Germany] has insidiously tried to destroy the industrial and commercial plans of other countries, and undermine their economic and social organization. . . . Not only has the German autocracy thrown the shadow of its sinister designs across the path of the world's progress, but in its immediate methods of carrying out its purposes, it has crucified humanity and has violated every principle of kindliness and righteousness. . . . In their conduct of war they have defied and broken treaties and international law whenever it has suited their purpose. . . . They have violated every moral principle, in the commission of robbery, murder and rape. Neither age, sex nor condition has been a protection against their violence. Old men, women and even babes in arms – it made no difference, all must be trampled in the march of their glorious army.
>
> (Kinley, 1918a, p. 23)

The subjectification of the population of the world is the terminal point. To achieve it, the country will use its power, influence, and trade connections to ensure the continuance of economic growth using available resources to circumscribe the business and industrial activities of their competitors. He draws from Gustav Schmoller, one of the most prominent members of the younger school, to substantiate his narrative which discusses German intent in regulating South America as a stepping stone towards the control of the US mainland. Citing members of the German Historical School in this way can only have helped contribute, whether intentionally or not, to its delegitimization.

Now we know that Schmoller was a vocal nationalist. Even so, Senn (1993/1994, p. 302) warns us that his political position has been frequently misrepresented. We need to keep this in mind. According to Kinley, Schmoller is said to have asserted, "We must desire that at any cost a German country containing some 20 or 30 million Germans may grow up in the coming century in Brazil. . . . Unless our connection with Brazil is always secured by ships of war, and unless Germany is able to exercise pressure there our development is threatened" (Schmoller in Kinley, 1918a, p. 29). The citations which follow Schmoller are steadily more redolent of imperialistic intent (i.e. enhancing Germany's power through economic control maintained by military muscle). South American countries and their defenses need to be overawed. Insurrection prevented. Additional weaker countries are going to be trampled without mercy, with ideological support provided by the penmanship of highly biased authors.

As historical documents, his 1918a and 1918b papers illuminate the difficulties some academics faced, especially when their background was linked with Germany. Kinley is careful to say that he did not view himself as anti-German – a move that Ely had replicated. In focusing upon the country and its leadership, we are not being provided with a critique of the average individual struggling to negotiate his/her everyday life. To be sure, even stating this without some equivocation is difficult. The 1918a paper is more sympathetic to the individual German; the 1918b manuscript much less so, with comments like the following being typical. "We must face the fact that after this war Germany will hate the world and that her people will be an obstacle to every attempt at world progress" (Kinley, 1918b, p. 9). Within these papers, we gain an insight into Kinley's projection of a view of human nature onto the German people. Put simply, he presents the country as subscribing to Social Darwinism.[1] In making his case, he is voiding a commitment to social objectivity, using literature selectively and sometimes – but not always – vaguely.

Kinley asserts that the German axiology hinges on a "fundamental and unchallengeable premise that what the Germans want is right . . . that no such word as 'wrong' can be recognized in their vocabulary" (Kinley, 1918a, p. 17). His argument becomes progressively stronger as he gets into his stride. It leaves little ground for difference in perspective among swathes of intellectuals.

He succumbs to the problem of induction. He indicates that he has read "a great deal" of published German work but cannot claim to have consumed it all. His strong statements are thus vulnerable to falsification. But given the cultural climate, we can speculate that counterpoints would be unlikely to cause Kinley or his audience much concern.

> Being very scientific, by a perversion of reasoning, they [the Germans] argue that what they call the biological law of life, the right of the fittest to survive, confers upon the strong the right to extirpate the weak. They do not ask who is the fittest to survive. They beg the question by taking it for granted that the only being fit to survive is the one endowed with brute strength. They then confuse the exertion of brute force with moral right. In short, in this matter they have followed the custom which runs through all German political and philosophical as well as psychological arguments. They first have made up their minds what they want to establish, and then interpret the data which they have in hand in such a way as to sustain their point. I have read a great deal of German political and economic literature in the past fifteen years, and have been impressed every time with this fact. They prove what they want to prove, and show either a real indifference to the facts, or a complete failure to realize that they are not on their side.
>
> (Kinley, 1918a, p. 17)

Kinley's reasoning becomes as perverse as that he is critiquing. He ties himself in knots. The foregoing extended quotation is immediately followed by this.

> No better citizens of our own country have come from any part of the world than those of German stock. It would have been a great thing for German moral and educational influence to spread over the civilized world through the impress of her character and training of her sons and daughters. But this was not enough to satisfy the autocratic government of the Empire. Wherever a German goes he must remain a German, and retain his connections to his home government.
>
> (Kinley, 1918a, pp. 17–18)

So, on the one hand, literature produced within the borders of this country is somehow problematic, yet, on the other, the educational system and its products – the sons and daughters of the nation – are desirable. This makes little sense without mental gymnastics. What really jars is that despite the criticism he levels at Germany, Kinley states that there are often justifiable reasons for engaging in war, helping protect other countries and their freedom being the most significant. Certainly, protecting the United States is a major factor. It is the affront to its Exceptionalism that seems to sting Kinley and he invokes it as a moral imperative to action.

> But there are more important reasons for our intervention [above and beyond humanitarian motives]. Our pride and national dignity have been insulted by the system of propaganda which has undertaken to corrupt and undermine our public opinion, to falsify and to destroy our political and moral ideals, to interfere with our industry and trade by the destruction, at the risk of life, of industrial and other establishments. As a far-seeing people we are called on to interpose ourselves to prevent the growth of an autocratic government to a point of strength where at its leisure and pleasure it can defy the Monroe doctrine which we have regarded as one of the greatest safeguards of liberty in the western hemisphere. But even more specifically: We were insultingly told that we must not sell munitions of war. Apparently it was the high prerogative of the German nation to do this to any belligerent, but we might not do it if it injured or even displeased the German autocracy.
>
> (Kinley, 1918a, p. 33)

Kinley's position in the end, in spite of the occasional glimmers of tolerance with respect to everyday Germans caught up in political dynamics which they cannot control, is unswerving. Germany must be defeated and he underlines this emphatically.

> The system of government for which militaristic, autocratic Germany stands cannot exist side by side with democracy. One must be crushed if the other is to survive. Let us not deceive ourselves on this matter. If the Allies permit the survival of an autocracy powerful enough to begin another war, it will destroy

> civilization. Never can the world be safe for democracy. Therefore, there can be no peace in this conflict by compromise or negotiation or discussion. One system of political and economic organization or the other must go down in complete defeat. We must so punish this autocracy and crush its spirit that at least for generations to come it will not rear its head again.
>
> (Kinley, 1918b, p. 9)

These levels of patriotic sentiment placed the GHSE outside the bounds of legitimate discourse. The strength of the vitriol espoused by Kinley would indicate that this is a reasonable assumption until proven otherwise.

Complexity and marketing history: the dark side

Within this book we have been attentive to the impact of the wider cultural environment on marketing thought and practice. The environment in which our pioneers lived and worked shaped and continues to shape the way we reflect upon our subject. Looking at the GHSE and its influence on marketing, it is tempting to stress its positive contribution. We can point to the activist element in its writings, the commitment to distributive justice, and the focus on the amelioration of social problems. They wanted to use their empirical research and theory production to help foster a progressive educational climate. This would directly impact upon the next generation of students. They were trained to be attentive to the social world, engaging in the "look and see" method, to determine where and how they could make a difference. This could mean helping educate farmers, engaging with unions, or legislators.

While the progressive, ethically inflected economics and marketing practice had many beneficial ramifications, it also contained assumptions that were capable of being manipulated to justify a series of morally and ethically bankrupt positions. The organic and dynamic concept of society implied that the social world could be shaped and planned. Within the orbit of the GHSE this entailed the production of knowledge that contributed to informed decision- and policy-making.

One of the dangers inherent in this worldview is that individual members were part of a preexisting society, with the latter's interests constraining the activities of the former (Leonard, 2016). Their rights as individuals could be restricted. This may take more positive-looking forms: controls over employment, government legislation to protect consumers, and so forth.

But there was a potential dark side to the organic metaphor. Some progressive academics and legislators were influenced by racist, xenophobic, and eugenic views which led them to suggest the delimitation of individual rights in much more questionable ways. Immigration laws and controls sought to contain certain populations; this was extended with eugenic assertions about the value of "social selection", that is, the preferential breeding and support for more desirable groups in society (Leonard, 2016). References to "race suicide" were not uncommon and calls were made for supposedly endangered groups (read, specific members of the white population) to support their race through appropriate breeding programs.

As was discussed in Chapter 3, Ely and writers associated with progressivist causes and institutional economics did possess a view of human nature that stressed that people were not equal (e.g. Commons, 1964). In some respects, this was reflective of empirical realism and advances in psychological research. It might be treated as a breath of fresh air, providing a counterpoint to the unrealistic caricature of economic man. However, we are on a slippery slope. As indicated above, the GHSE viewed society in holistic terms; it was ontologically prior to the individual. One of the implications of this viewpoint was that when interpreted in a certain light, it could excuse differential treatment of various groups for the good of the wider community.

Correspondingly, stressing difference had the potential to lead to draconian policies. The American Economic Association – initially a bastion of progressivist values – was headed by a variety of figures who were vocal about the need to ensure the vitality of capitalism via the control of undesirable populations (i.e. the "unfit" and the unemployable were candidates for sterilization and social isolation) (Leonard, 2005). Progressivism was consequently a split discourse in the sense that some groups were viewed as more deserving of social support than others. Where Kinley seemed to perceive all groups as possible candidates for social mobility, Ely and Commons were less sure (cf. Commons, 1964). They had a somewhat negative view of immigrants and referenced long-standing stratification (Leonard, 2016, p. 8). As Ely grew older, his conservative stance developed into a form of elitism. Leonard leaves us in no doubt in this regard.

> It was high time, Ely said, to abandon the outmoded eighteenth-century doctrine that all men were equal as a false and pernicious doctrine. The wiser and stronger were obligated to lead the feebler members of the community. . . . Ely granted that public education could uplift ordinary people. At the same time, he doubted that all Americans were educable. Even after instruction, some remained unworthy of the ballot. How many? Governing New York City would be easier, Ely once ventured, "if thirteen per centum of the poorest and most dependent voters were disenfranchised." Ely's elitism did not soften. It hardened. The "human rubbish heap," he wrote in 1922, was far larger than a "submerged tenth." The intelligence testers had scientifically demonstrated that 22 percent of US Army recruits were inferior.
>
> (Leonard, 2016, p. 53)

Profoundly dubious claims were made that intelligence varied by skin color, the lighter, the better, apparently (Leonard, 2016, p. 73). When Bateman (2003) finds the progressives silent on some race issues – and laments this feature of their work – Leonard uncovered almost the reverse where eugenics was concerned. In a dispiriting series of statements, we are told:

> Ely lauded the Army testing, because it enabled the state to scientifically inventory the fitness of the human stock. We census our farm animals and test our soils, Ely observed. Surely it was no less important to take stock of our

> human resources, ascertain where defects exist, and apply suitable remedies. Ely allowed that eugenic science was still in its infancy, but, he claimed, 'we have got far enough to recognize that there are certain human beings who are absolutely unfit, and should be prevented from a continuation of their kind.' Four years after the war, Ely was still beating the drum. Economic progress, he said, unavoidably left behind large numbers of "absolutely unfit" people incapable of meeting the demands of modern life. The absolutely unfit would plague society until society controlled their breeding. For Ely, the price of progress was eugenics.
>
> (Leonard, 2016, p. 74)

Despite the fact that there was a presence of these kinds of racist ideas in the economics literature from the 1880s through to 1920, there were declines after this historical point (Cherry, 1976). Eugenics as a focus experienced declines in the 1930s – although the actual practices continued late into the twentieth century in various "civilized" countries (Leonard, 2005). What we need to appreciate is that racist views were widespread. They were found among those labeled as progressive, socialist, feminist, and conservative alike (e.g. Leonard, 2016, pp. 38, 114, 179–180). Commensurately, "[h]undreds, perhaps thousands of Progressive Era scholars and scientists called themselves eugenicists" (Leonard, 2016, p. 99). These figures indicate that racism, race selection, immigration controls, and so forth were not universally supported practices and there were famous exemplars who railed against racial hierarchies. Even so, one of the central progressives in our account, Richard Ely, advocated "social selection", the removal of the unfit from society, and there are various ways in which these ideas could have permeated marketing and consumption research. At the present time, we have negligible amounts of literature that explore these issues. Much more is required.

Firstly, in reflections on marketing research, forms of market segmentation, and customer divestment. All were generating discussion in the early twentieth century and – as Ward (2009; 2010) documented – often hinged on racially charged and socially judgmental valuations of individual worth. There was also substantial debate about the consumption habits of certain races, the eugenic implications of providing goods and services that might prolong health and life, thereby enabling dysgenic effects, that is, perpetuating undesirable groups and their habits in future generations (e.g. Leonard, 2016, p. 121). A perennial worry at this point was the reduction in the quality of life experienced by the white races, which were – it was claimed – unable to subsist at the meagre level of other groups (the Chinese were mentioned frequently). This was accompanied by entreaties bemoaning the low birth rates of the "white" (Anglo Saxon or Nordic) community, which would inexorably lead to "race suicide" (e.g. Leonard, 2016, p. 134, 149). Exploring this material will entail a multiple disciplinary approach, engaging with marketing, sociology, psychology, and anthropological studies to flesh out the polyhedron-like complexity of these disputes.

Racist views were expressed in the marketing literature (Tadajewski, 2012). At present, however, there has been little attention given to the importation and application of eugenic ideas in the necessary detail. Given Leonard's (2016) claim that these views were widespread and that they did garner support among the progressives in our narrative, it seems likely that there is a genealogical thread awaiting exposure, explication, and critique (after all, Kinley does touch upon related themes). As Cherry (1976, p. 148) points out,

> Many . . . leading economists, such as Richard T. Ely, John R. Commons, and Thomas N. Carver, were vocal in their racial beliefs before the turn of the century. For example, Ely [1891, p. 402] felt that the 'most general statement possible is that the causes of poverty are hereditary and environmental, producing weak physical, mental and moral constitutions.' He explicitly rejects economic conditions as a significant cause of poverty, and doesn't even mention the possibility of discrimination.

When undertaking the research for this book, we started with an image of Ely as a progressive. We knew about the activist claims associated with the GHSE. Greater attention to Ely's record has encouraged us to be more cautious about stressing the positivity of the contributions he provided. He did not live in a vacuum and with the growth of research illuminating how racism has impacted upon the history of marketing thought (Tadajewski, 2012; Davis, 2017), we knew we had to be alert to the possibility that this could be a feature in our research.

Certainly, it is an area that warrants a great deal more attention from those interested in the history of marketing thought. In Chapter 3 we stressed Ely's caution about discussing socialism, but the conditions of acceptability (Foucault, 2015) for racist views were less stringent. It was easier to be racist than advocate alternative methods of economic organization in the late nineteenth century. In his summary of socialist publications, he writes,

> The socialists are great advocates of the rights of women and endeavor to secure their help in the cause. In this they have met with some little success, and the women seem the most violent. *The colored are also sought, and once one of their candidates for member of Congress was a negro. It is doubtful if many of the colored race are sufficiently intelligent to grasp the aims and principles of socialism, but they are said to show great fondness for organizations for various purposes and to display, in cases, even greater fidelity to the rules of labor-unions than white men.*
>
> (Ely, 1885, p. 58; emphasis added)

Recent analyses have been scathing of Ely and the progressives. We might recall that at Ely's trial various quotations were marshalled from orthodox economics to demonstrate that some of the most central and relatively uncontroversial figures in this tradition appeared in a dim light when their ideas were used selectively. Thies and Daza (2011) do the same type of citational listing to reveal the racism embedded within Ely's work. They do not claim that their analysis is balanced. It is a selection and purposive in nature. There are a number of quotes taken from Ely's publications, and in an abstracted form, taken out of context, they do document the presence of eugenic ideas, aspects of racist projection, multiple instances of stereotyping, xenophobia directed against Germans, and critiques of "negroes" that present them as akin to "grownup children" (Thies and Daza, 2011, p. 151).

Bateman (2003) joins the emerging chorus questioning the purity of the progressive movement, directing his attention to various people including Ely. We are not excusing any arguments that were racist or xenophobic, but we do want to respectfully suggest that scholars are more careful than Bateman, who comments that despite their subscription to the look-and-see methodology, GHSE pioneers were remarkably blind to the racism that surrounded them. His comments are worth repeating.

> We often look back at the young 'ethical economists' who founded the AEA with some fondness because they had so many . . . traits that we would like to claim for ourselves: they were intellectuals who worked hard to influence public policy, and they tried to make the emerging American industrialism more humane for the workers who did not always fare well under the laissez-faire system that was advocated by the older generation of economists. But the stark reality is that they were not interested in helping the freedmen, who were slipping into the world of lynching and Jim Crow that was emerging at the end of the nineteenth century. . . . American economists were not where we wish they had been, calling for the same kind of public scrutiny and fair treatment that they found themselves able to muster in the name of white workers.
>
> (Bateman, 2003, p. 714)

As our foregoing quote from Ely indicates, they were not blind. They were racist in certain respects. The evidence provided by Cherry (1976), Leonard (2016), and Thies and Daza (2011) is disconcerting. Bateman wants to look back at the historical record and find something that he desires. It is easy with hindsight to say that people living in a specific context should have acted differently. We must read what they were doing against the currents of the time and attempt to understand why they did what they did. It is probably unreasonable to attribute our own values to them and critique them for failing to live up to our standards.

In doing so, he is arguing that all scholars, at all times, must register social problems that surround them. We have much sympathy for this point and do agree that there is a great need for activism, but this is a high benchmark for professional responsibility. What the above literature traces, in effect, is the fact that the progressive movement is not homogenous or consistent. Like the GHSE, it was shaped by multiple factors. Some of these are country-specific focuses and cultural-level influences that shaped what was attended to, discussed, and studied. Others are the result of personal interests. The project of unpacking the influence of the progressive movement, the ethical economics of people like Ely, and the axiological values being transmitted through all these different participants in academic life needs much more exploration.

To conclude this section, the connections between marketing and racism remain woefully underexplored. Those relating to eugenic thought and marketing are even less well understood. The fact that there are links between people like Ely who were so important for the first generation of marketing thinkers and these deleterious ideologies and practices requires us to examine the darker side of marketing theory and practice.

Ways forward

Doing this research will be risky and it is not recommended to PhD candidates or researchers trying to hit markers set by the ticking tenure clock. The links are often not direct and will require substantial background knowledge to help orient the researcher to the relevant material.

Eugenic controls were widely supported by people from across the political spectrum, including liberal through to very conservative. John Commons (economist), Richard Ely, Simon Patten (economist), Henry Farnam (economist), Edward Ross (sociologist), and Frank Fetter (economist) all expressed a variety of related concerns mainly cohering around the idea that assistance to the poor was undermining the interests of society by enabling the weak and feeble to survive. Frank Taussig fantasized about murdering criminals and the addicted, but admitted that this was not feasible, so would settle for forced incarceration as a substitute (Leonard, 2005, p. 214). These were not private views, otherwise detached from his pedagogic role. They were central: "Generations of Harvard students, and many others who used Taussig's economics text, were taught that dealing with the unemployable required stern eugenic remedies" (Leonard, 2016, p. 165).

With respect to eugenics, an investigator tackling this topic will need to register the fact that progressivist projects were often intertwined with wider debates about the value of specific populations, classes, races, and intellects. The ambiguity that Leonard (2005) sees running through progressivism about how we can best achieve the social justice and welfare aims that are woven into the GHSE axiology will complicate arguments considerably, requiring us to approach each item of analysis in a prismatic fashion. Each statement has to be interpreted against the cultural context and paradigmatic tradition in which a scholar is embedded, and connected to his overall intellectual development. There are multiple facets which have to be taken into account. In some cases, it will be more apparent that an individual is making a racist or eugenicist argument. He may make a statement about race suicide, for instance. That should alert the reader to a likely interpretation.

Although we have reservations about Friedman's (2015) analysis of Ely's writings, it does provide us with a useful example of the kind of prismatic analysis we have in mind and the caution that we are recommending for historians going forward in relation to the issues of racism or eugenics. Unusually, he distances Ely from eugenics. So, while Ely did edit a book series that published content dealing with this topic (e.g. Leonard, 2005, p. 218), we must be careful about claiming causality between this editorial activity and his own views. The same could apply in other cases.

As we have said repeatedly, the approach taken by the GHSE was historical. They wanted to emphasize how history structures the economic system and organization of society. We are born into a world that preexists us. It is our condition of possibility, the atmosphere that textures our existence. When Ely talks in terms of "peoples of a lower civilization", Friedman suggests that we need to recall that history shapes all of our life-worlds. He argues that different ways of life cannot be modified wholesale by eugenics and this was not what Ely was claiming. Rather, Ely's argument was historicist and he was extending his view of human nature – that people are not equal and that we should not assume so – to other cultures and contexts. In doing so, he is raising the question of how industrial growth and the benefits of economic expansion can be brought to other countries (i.e. a basic "civilizing" discourse).

Education can assist, but we must be careful as any interventions need to take account of the historical and cultural development of a people, and intervention can do more harm than good, especially if this is stimulated at a pace unsuited to the country and population at hand (Friedman, 2015). Researchers can interpret this presentation of Ely's opinion in multiple ways. Through one lens, his expectation that elevating the lifestyles of populations outside of US borders might take time may imply a negative characterization of certain groups. This needs to be determined on a case-by-case analysis. Making a judgment call is rendered much more complex when we take seriously the statements made by Ely or Kinley on the dynamic nature of society (Ely, 1910b), the importance of education being tailored to the populations it serves (i.e. educational relativism) (Kinley, 1906, 1910), and their hope that knowledge and information can help people better negotiate the issues that life throws at them (Ely, 1910b).

Whether the topic was one of different countries or the United States itself, Ely's account was cautious and he supported it via the latest arguments in disciplines like psychology. This needs to be registered when making claims about Ely's perceptions of human inequality. We have said that he held an optimistic view in part – it was an optimism that the world could be better, that the life circumstances experienced by those facing hardship might be ameliorated to some – often very limited – extent. Inequality and realism are fundamental to his worldview and he attempts to offer guidance about how unequal power relations, especially those faced by people at lower socio-economic levels, can be dealt with via unions and concerted class solidarity (e.g. Ely, 1902, p. 76).

History, the material basis of society, and the ongoing existence of a class system in the United States would deny opportunity to some, whilst making the lives of others much easier (Ely, 1902). Ely was not disingenuous on this front. Kinley was often much more optimistic than Ely, particularly when he stressed the role of the teacher in inculcating the view that their students had equal "social and economic opportunity in all lines of life" (Kinley, 1906, p. 396; see also Kinley, 1949, pp. 150–151). Ely's stance is less inflected by a middle-class sensibility that merit overcomes structural preconditions and the affordances of wealth. His concept of the psychology of the individual was equally explicit (e.g. Ely, 1902, p. 64).

This returns us to Bateman's (2003) desire to look back at the history of his discipline (economics) and find progressive thinkers who did act differently. He may never find an academic who is totally pure in his commitments, never espousing a view – of whatever kind – that makes him cringe later in his life. We are all human, we all make mistakes, sometimes serious misjudgments, and we can all be inconsistent in what we say and do (Commons, 1964). There is plenty of evidence to suggest that some people have stood out against the racism and related issues we have discussed so far, and that spirit reminds us that although society forms a condition of possibility for social action, it does not determine it. The organic and dynamic nature of the ontological commitments of the GHSE must alert us to the fact that they believed that social change was possible. We also know that some of them experienced considerable political pressures to act in ways that were consistent with the social conventions of the time.

Sweeping statements about the lack of a concerted effort to undermine racist or xenophobic views therefore need to be treated with caution unless they can be substantiated. What we would suggest is that a more productive way forward is to look for logical ways that socially cognizant, progressive scholars might try to advance their agendas without rupturing the (undesirable and deleterious) political assumption grounds of those who appointed themselves the guardians of the status quo, that is, the business and industrial leaders that occupied positions of power on university boards. Here is where a bridge to marketing can be found. It is in our discipline that progressivist values were advanced. The progressivist threads that we explicated in Chapter 3 in relation to Ely and his role at Wisconsin in training some of the most influential pioneers in our discipline can be linked to the more socially circumscribed marketing management of Chapters 5 and 6. But they are united in the conduit of David Kinley.

Kinley is a complex figure. His views are sometimes progressivist, but he was a vocal critic who was prone to making contentious claims about Germany. In spite of the fact that his progressivism is circumscribed on the basis of current social norms, he is an important figure in that he was trained as an economist, embodied GHSE values, and worked against some of the racism that Bateman (2003) hoped to see ethical economists undermining. Kinley did this in a subtle manner, but one in which he demonstrates how progressive marketing practice could be, especially when directed internationally. First, we need to unpack how racism was treated in the economics literature, and then explain how Kinley's thought moves in similar directions to the environmental argument marshalled in this body of scholarship by the progressives, but in a novel fashion.

In the material that deals with racism (Cherry, 1976; Bateman, 2003), reference is made to the various ways this was understood by economists. It is parsed into literature predominantly taking a eugenic approach (i.e. the "genetic racial position"), which held that recent immigrants from certain countries were undesirable "stock" and should be subject to eugenic controls (e.g. some form of elimination from the population). The "environmental" position on race and topics like immigration was still negative, stressing the social shaping of populations in directions that would detrimentally affect American workers. This literature could be distasteful. But what is important for this analysis is that Kinley does not fit into either category. He twists what looks like an environmental position in a positive way, invoking GHSE assumptions, including social, cultural, and economic relativity, combined with the set of ideas associated with the marketing concept, when looking at US trade with South America. Kinley is, we submit, the anti-racist, anti-xenophobe that Bateman (2003) was looking for without success.[2]

Marketing and the deflation of prejudice

We treat Kinley's reflections on developing trade relations with South America as an exemplar that indicates that further research will – we expect – complicate our understanding of progressivism, the GHSE, issues of race and racism in ways that cannot be neglected. If these ideas are found in Kinley, we would encourage other academics interested in exploring the multi-faceted nature of progressivism to engage with figures who operate on the borderlines between economics and marketing in future.

Importantly, our close reading of Kinley will illustrate how marketing was a vehicle whose conceptual apparatus and argumentation was used to deflate the prejudice that historians of economic thought are linking to the progressives. Kinley's argument unites the German inflection of his orientation, progressive values, while doing so to advance the business and industrial interests of companies in the United States and the country as a whole (cf. Kinley, 1949, pp. 69–70). The GHSE, institutionalism, managerialism, and progressivism are merged. This was somewhat unusual at the time. The business literature, advertising trade cards, and public pronouncements all exhibited varying degrees of racism; whiteness was elevated to a pantheon of perfection, often being connected to narratives of progress, economic growth and rising standards of living (Domosh, 2006; Ramamurthy, 2003). Foreigners were the "targets" of American companies. They were not really considered serious business partners (cf. Kinley, 1949, pp. 67–68). Kinley's writing avoids most of these crass stereotypes and "civilizing" discourses.

He describes the nature of trade with South America historically, explains how business conferences have been undertaken with a view to improving relations between the countries for trade and political reasons. The attention from US producers being directed towards South America is obviously not altruistic. Kinley registers this and points out that manufacturers need to find export markets for their items. Efficient factory management, combined with the saturation of domestic markets, along with the desire for greater profit, all made international markets more desirable. In this he is at one with Simon Litman. What was essential, however, was that trade was established and conducted efficiently and effectively. Kinley diagnoses various reasons why there had been problems in the past and sketches ways to overcome whatever impasses exist to hamper trade relations.

In his analysis, we see familiar GHSE assumptions being invoked. Locational relativism is a feature. He reminds his readers that while he is talking about South America, it should not be assumed that these countries are homogenous. As he puts it,

> We must remember that it is dangerous to write of South America as a whole, for South America is a continent, whose climate varies from tropical to nearly antarctic. Moreover, it comprises eighteen or twenty countries, whose people are, to be sure, mostly of Spanish origin, yet differ considerably in economic and political conditions, with centuries of different relationships to the natives of the country, and with interests varying in some cases as widely as those of any two European countries.
>
> (Kinley, 1911, p. 55)

His argument does not spare criticism of the United States. It is relatively simple to determine why international public perception of the country is negative. He attributes this to the treatment other nations have received at the hands of America in the past, whether this was meted out by government, industrialists, or as a function of the negligent practices of travelers: "prejudice has been created against us on account of the character and conduct of some of our own representatives in the past, but also by a class of fellow citizens who, although small in numbers, have frequently drifted to those countries" (Kinley, 1911, p. 60).

His statements support our proposition that Kinley can be considered in his 1911 and 1918a papers a manifestation of non-racist, non-xenophobic views (the fact that this is not true in the case of Germany merely emphasizes the point about the heterogeneity and inconsistency of progressivist discourse). It is far removed from the language that Thies and Daza (2011) pull from Ely's work. We will use Kinley's own words extensively in what follows.

> Of some consequence . . . is the feeling of prejudice that has existed between the peoples of South America and ourselves. They have felt, not altogether without justification, that our attitude was domineering, that we were lacking in culture, and that our personal and national ideals were so far different from their own that they and we could not get on well together. On the other hand, too many of us have been inclined to think of the people of South America as uncivilized, barbarous or even savage; and in so far as they were of European descent, to look upon them as degenerate scions of a race of cruel conquerors, who exploited the country. At the same time, many of our people have thought that the people of South American countries lack virility, resourcefulness, and the energy which we have been so long worshipping. Both views are wrong. Yet the accusation that we are domineering is not without foundation.
>
> (Kinley, 1911, p. 59)

The public interpretation of American interests in the Southern hemisphere is somewhat mistaken, Kinley alleges. He is referring to the Monroe Doctrine as a source of confusion about how the United States perceives its role in that part of the world.

> From an attempt to protect the weak and struggling states of the southern continent against the encroachments of Europe, we have passed, in the minds of some, even of our own citizens, to an attitude of attempting to influence, if

> not control, their actions. Many of the people in South America therefore distrusted our purpose, and feared our power. . . . [T]heir distrust and fear is not altogether without foundation.
>
> (Kinley, 1918a, p. 60)

His 1918a paper is an attempt to play a small role in revising public interpretations of US intentions in this part of the world. Equally, it is an advisory document that encourages business people to change their approach to potential clients (e.g. business partners) and the ultimate customer in these markets. He is encouraging them to adopt the marketing concept. His remarks add a further dimension to the way this concept has been understood. In the work of many contemporary academics, it is treated as a synonym for achieving shareholder value (Tadajewski and Jones, 2012). For practitioners like Percival White (1927), a figure whose ideas we explored in some depth in Chapter 6, he associated the marketing concept with ethics. Business people were told to think carefully about what they produced and whether it was truly needed in the market.

Kinley's comments can be taken as an extension of White's in terms of having an ethical concern with fostering positive social relationships between peoples, deflating tensions and prejudice, to achieve country, company, and individual gains. It is an instrumental ethics, but an ethics that aims to contribute to positive human interaction nonetheless. He stresses the necessity of understanding the culture and customs, extant business practices, engaging productively with local business people, employing "natives" to help navigate the nuances of the new market, and seeking advice about practices that might seem unfamiliar to American manufacturers and tradespeople.

He sounds a note of caution about involvement in any activities that can be interpreted as exploitative such as transfers of natural resources and wealth out of the country adopted as a trading partner (see also Kinley, 1918b, p. 11). This is likely to be profitable in the short term but to harm company interests in the medium and long term, skewing the ability of other, more responsible organizations to enter the market in future. Mutual benefit, he submits, is the order of the day. Infrastructure projects that improve trade links, transportation, distribution, and so forth are valuable methods of creating "confidence and good will" between the US and South America (Kinley, 1918a, p. 67). Many companies, he appreciates, are not able to engage in such large capital expenditures and will have to pursue strategies consistent with their resources and capabilities.

It is essential, he writes, that those wanting to transact business in foreign countries speak the language of their interlocutors. Not doing so reflects badly on the individual concerned and the home country more broadly. It signifies a complete failure to understand basic principles of marketing.

> The character of our business agents and their methods of selling goods have not always been happy from the point of view of the South American business man. Frequently the representatives of American business firms have not been able to converse with their prospective customers in the language of the latter.

> A knowledge of the vernacular is essential for one who is trying to introduce business. Of course, it is possible to talk through an interpreter, but one can hardly push business very extensively through an interpreter. Moreover, our representatives have been grossly ignorant, when compared with their German and even their English fellows, not only of the language but of the customs and needs of the countries.
>
> (Kinley, 1918a, p. 63)

Market awareness and customer focus are crucial factors which must inform international marketing practice, he avers. American business people must not view these locations as "dumping grounds" for stock that cannot be sold in another fashion. Treating them in such an inconsiderate way sends negative messages about how the market and its people are viewed and fails to develop commercial relations. Trade needs to be continuous, confidence developed, with trust as the aim. These factors will help generate the requisite financial flows. Currently, forms of engagement were lamentable, and he outlines the inadequacies of some US business people.

> As a rule they have been unable to quote prices or measures or weights in the standards known to the prospective purchaser. Our people have been generally satisfied with sending bulky catalogs and price lists printed in English, describing their goods in yards, pounds and dollars, when the native was looking for meters, kilograms and pesos. Our business representatives have not studied the markets of the South American countries. They have not known what kinds of goods the people want, nor in what sizes, shapes or patterns. . . . [I]t has certainly been true in large measure of our own, that they have assumed the attitude of 'take it or leave it', when dealing with their South American customers.
>
> (Kinley, 1918a, pp. 63–64)

Running throughout this discussion is the issue of overcoming prejudice and taking a realistic look at the marketplace and its participants and reorienting practice if success is desired. Registering the reality of the market rather than being committed to perverted judgments due to the misleading prism of prejudice is his call to arms; a dose of realism can be highly profitable. As he tells his audience,

> Our unwillingness to extend credit . . . is due largely to our ignorance of the South American people and South American trade customs. In some quarters there seems to be a prejudice against the honesty of the South American merchants. This prejudice is mainly due to ignorance. It is at least doubtful whether there are any more failures to meet obligations among the merchants of Argentina, Chile, Brazil, and elsewhere, in proportion to business done, than in our own country or in Europe. To a considerable extent the prejudice has arisen from ill-considered extension of credit under conditions where the risk was large and full inquiry had not been made.
>
> (Kinley, 1918a, p. 63)

To get closer to their customer, to ensure an appropriate flow of goods along with the service necessary to maintain them, Kinley proposes that the commission house is one vehicle that will enable multiple US firms, none of which could fund operations in international locations on their own, to participate in the global marketplace. Once again, he stresses that these houses will help firms "be sure that orders would be promptly filled with goods made to suit the needs . . . of the country" (Kinley, 1918a, p. 67). He suggests that "[t]hese agencies, or commission houses, should employ natives as largely as possible, and should insist that their superior officers shall also speak the language of the country. In this way only can existing . . . needs become known and properly met, and new wants stimulated and developed"[3] (Kinley, 1918a, pp. 67–68).

The moral of Kinley's story is that all parties to a transaction, especially those working from different cultural and economic backgrounds, will have prejudices of various kinds. These need to be dispelled if productive trade relations are sought, along with the positive concomitants that accompany them, such as infrastructure development and improved quality of life. Marketing intelligence gathering and producing and distributing goods and services in ways congruent with the needs of the target market were the means of enabling mutually satisfying exchanges that would persist in the long term. Kinley, consequently, is an economist trained in the GHSE tradition whose knowledge of marketing and distribution was drawn upon to help deflate prejudice rather than reaffirm it.

If Bateman (2003) had looked in the direction of a pioneering contributor to marketing, the dismay he felt at ethical economists not living up to the high standards he retrospectively was setting them might have been tempered. We speculate that further engagement with marketing thinkers operating in this period and writing about related subjects affords opportunities to understand how ethically oriented scholars strove to enact their axiological and political values at the same time as they avoided arousing the ire of powerful groups.

Discussion and conclusion

The impact of the GHSE has been outlined in this book. Initially our attention focused on questioning the historical accuracy of Bartels' seminal account, which failed to register the importance of the German Historical School. His extremely forthright comment to a then doctoral candidate in the mid-1980s – Brian Jones – that there was no influence to be discerned between these academics and the rise of marketing (Bartels, 1985) was too tempting to be ignored. He said it too quickly, too abruptly, and it did not square with the emerging anecdotal evidence that was being unearthed. This started our study of the GHSE, which has continued in fits and starts over the past 30 years. We knew there was more to this narrative than had previously been excavated and have continued to plumb the depths of this strand of research ever since.

Where other academics have devoted their focus to the epistemological and methodological features of this discourse (Jones and Monieson, 1990; Jones and Tadajewski, 2015), we have studied the entire set of paradigmatic assumptions underwriting this school of thought. Beyond this, we unpacked the political value system that motivated the social activism that generated the commitment of the academics working at the University of Wisconsin. As was made apparent, there were distinct differences in terms of their research focus, axiology, and politics. This was true within Wisconsin (e.g. Ely, H.C. Taylor), it was even more discernible at more managerial schools like Birmingham (e.g. William Ashley) and Harvard (e.g. Edwin Gay, Arch Shaw). Nonetheless, these universities shared a bedrock in the GHSE. The point of difference, if we are permitted to operate at a general level for a moment, is that they had a diverse mixture of stakeholders who had differing expectations about what a university – and business – education entailed.

For Jones and Monieson (1990), there was little overlap between these perspectives beyond a methodological orientation towards historically focused research and an epistemological predilection for induction. In this text, we added a considerable level of complexity to this account – firstly, by revealing an important condition of possibility for the marketing discipline, Richard Ely. More than this, we explored how his career nearly came to a juddering halt. He was the subject of multiple academic "trials", all of which could have derailed his prospects and contributions, thereby changing the course of our discipline forever. When we began to tackle these issues, a quotation from Wittgenstein kept coming to mind: "One of the most important methods is to imagine a historical development of our ideas from what has actually occurred" (Wittgenstein, 1998, p. 45e). This reverberated throughout our minds as we wrote Chapter 3. What would have happened if Ely had suffered irreversible harm to his career? Fortunately, we will never know. David Kinley helped support him through his tribulations.

Continuing the theme of emphasizing links that marketing historians had ignored, we realized that underwriting the entire development of marketing theory, thought, and practice was a concern with socialism. Academics and practitioners were interested in it, concerned by it, and reacted to it. This has been a feature of our discipline since its origins. It influenced Ely in the late nineteenth century, shaped the trajectory in the 1950s, 1960s, and 1970s, (Tadajewski, 2006a, 2010b) and has recently reappeared in modified form in contemporary literature (Cova *et al.*, 2013).

Towards the end of the book we took a slightly unusual route. Rather than end with a summary of the trajectory that we had covered, we deepened our contribution. We pointed out that historians of economic thought were looking at their progressive ancestors and bemoaning what they saw (Bateman, 2003). They were not as progressive as they hoped. What we did find was that Bateman (2003) missed an important and we believe quite logical move. If you were a progressive working in a university where business leaders held considerable sway, then you would try to perform your value system in an unobtrusive fashion. We think that David Kinley did so. Now, we are not saying he was perfect, or that he was progressivism personified. His comments about Germany revealed explicitly that progressivism was a split discourse. It was contradictory and inconsistent, and one individual could manifest multiple stances, some far less salubrious than others. This is something that needs to be registered about this vein of thought.

Progressivism was the production of human beings. It will reflect their contradictions and inconsistencies. It will reflect the best of intentions and some of the most hateful statements ever to be uttered in academic and public discourse. As scholars, we cannot shy away from these features. We must confront them.

Although we acknowledge that Kinley was inconsistent in his position, we made the case that he united the progressivism of the GHSE with the emerging marketing management approach (e.g. White, 1927). He did this – we believe – to avoid the scrutiny of powerful gatekeepers. Put differently, invoking the marketing concept to deflate prejudice and advance business interests was about as politically unproblematic as was possible at the time. Our close reading of his scholarship demonstrates that he negotiated this fine line with self-possession. He articulates a new interpretation of the marketing concept, making it part of a political project intended to improve human relations.

But, let us end on a slightly speculative note. Our point in doing so is to encourage others to further explore what we have started to flesh out. The end of a book is not really the end-point. It is a prod to further research. Historical research in marketing is a never-ending project. There is always something new to discover – some novel way of thinking about our subject. We have some idea about why the GHSE was gradually elided from the history of marketing thought.

Our narrative runs as follows. A business agenda rather than the interest group pluralism of the GHSE took hold (White, 1927) and accelerated in the immediate aftermath of the Second World War, assisted by the financial support of large philanthropic foundations (Tadajewski, 2006a). The desire of the big three philanthropic groups – Ford, Carnegie, and Rockefeller – to contribute to the US economy as a way of demonstrating their own ideological congruency with the social climate should ring bells for attentive readers of Chapter 3. Ely's increased caution after his academic trials was refracted at the organizational level by these foundations, which found themselves under scrutiny in the McCarthy and Cold War era. They engaged in a related strategy to Ely. Perform a commitment to currently circulating social mores, especially the need to avoid looking like supporting any subversive research and the "social sciences" did appear seditious. The business disciplines, by contrast, spoke to conservatism, with helping grow the economy; a contribution to the Cold War that buttressed the legitimacy and credibility of all concerned.

As part of their attempt to legitimate their activities, the Ford and Carnegie philanthropies, most notably, investigated current practices in business schools, their educational provision, and their commitment to scientific and objective research (i.e. ostensibly non-political research). They eventually delivered reports which condemned the nature of their pedagogy; the quality of the research (it was too descriptive); and the teaching staff, which were critiqued for lacking appropriate qualifications (i.e. the PhD degree). Philanthropic funding was used to support a variety of stimulus packages, all of which promoted and embedded the managerial approach within the firmament. Social objectivity pretty much vanished in this climate. Deviation from American values was suspect, and not condemning socialism was likely to attract attention. The institutional economics training that many of the second generation of marketing scholars were applying in their descriptions of marketing and channel management was devalued in the face of the continued growth of logical empiricism (Tadajewski and Jones, 2012), refinements of survey research (Bottom, 2006), and uptake of quantitative methodologies (Cochoy, 1998; Tadajewski, 2006a), itself supported by the application of computer technology to marketing research. The status quo had taken hold and remains tenacious in its grip even today.

This point about the rise of the computer is worthy of further discussion. It contains a potential reason why the original literature of the GHSE was so firmly excised from our collective consciousness over the course of the twentieth century. Whereas in the late nineteenth and early twentieth centuries, students heading to the continent were conversant in German, this skill became less important as marketing education became more widespread in the United States.[4] Both economics and marketing are communicated mainly through "the English language" (Balabkins, 1993/1994, p. 28). One of the implications of this is that those writers whose publications have not been widely translated, most notably Schmoller, have been neglected. This is even more notable in the period after World War II (Senn, 1993/1994). Undergraduates no longer needed to travel to the continent for study. They were positively discouraged from doing so. There was no motivation for them to read original German source material. The cutting edge had shifted. It was America, not Germany, shaping the frontiers of economics and marketing.

Compounding this were the requirements and reward structure of the PhD degree itself. In the post Ford and Carnegie era, postgraduates looked to the future, not the past. And the future was the computer. With the rise of computing technology and the programming languages that accompanied it, learning a foreign language as part of the PhD process was sidelined in preference for the ability to manipulate advanced mathematics and program in Fortran (cf. Senn, 1993/1994, p. 314).

So, in summary, the GHSE might not have been mentioned by marketing historians in their reflections in the 1930s and 1940s. There were many reasons for this and we have identified as many as possible. The point is – we believe – it never actually disappeared (Morgan and Rutherford, 1998; Rutherford, 2010). It was partially subsumed (some references to institutional perspectives appear in the 1950s, related work appears periodically, and there has been a resurgence of interest recently in history and the construction of institutional legitimacy in a variant of consumer research). The politics might have been the aspect most quickly jettisoned (they were eventually reincorporated by macromarketing and critical marketing studies). But the use of the "scientific method", the combination of induction and deduction, empirical data collection, the refinement or rejection of hypotheses, and the use of statistics and large samples have long characterized our scholarly landscape and continues to do so today.

The point of difference is that we do not call it – as Kinley did – a politically motivated form of research. All research is political. It usually contributes to the affirmation, refinement, or reflection of the status quo. It makes claims about the good life. That is politics. Marketing has always been political. What has happened is that certain interest groups have more sway than they should have in terms of our knowledge production. The GHSE would be the first to suggest we revisit and rebalance our affiliations. Perhaps, after all, there are important lessons to learn from our ancestors.

Notes

1 We assume that this is a reflection of the impact of William Graham Sumner on Kinley. In his autobiography, Kinley (1949, p. 22) stresses the influence of Sumner on his development, positioning him as a "counterbalance" to Ely's view of the economic world.

2 Kinley's autobiography provides telling hints that he would exhibit anti-racist values. He appears to have been pro-abolitionist and joined a church that supported these values in his youth (1949, p. 18).

3 No doubt, there is room for a critically oriented discourse analyst to offer valuable insight into the language being deployed in this quotation.

4 We would be remiss not to signal an element of serendipity here. German was often read and understood by many American college students in the very early twentieth century. This was not the case in the United Kingdom. This makes William Ashley even more of an anomaly than he already appears. In reference to Ashley, P.C. Newman opines, "he was one of the comparatively few English economists of his generation who was able to read German readily" (Newman in Senn, 1993/1994, p. 286).

References

Abend, G. (2013), "The Origins of Business Ethics in American Universities, 1902–1936", *Business Ethics Quarterly*, Vol.23 No.2, pp. 171–205.

Abraham, W. and Weingast, H. (1942), *The Economics of Gustav Schmoller: Grundriss der Allegemeinen Volkswirtschaftlehre*, Brooklyn College, New York.

Adamson, J. (1901), "Birmingham University and Commerce", unpublished MS, UC 8/iv/5/3, Cadbury Research Library Archives, University of Birmingham, Birmingham, UK.

Agnew, H.E. (1941), "The History of the American Marketing Association", *Journal of Marketing*, Vol.5 No.4, pp. 374–379.

Alderson, W. (1951), "Progress in the Theory of Marketing", in Wales, H.G. (Ed.), *Changing Perspectives in Marketing*, University of Illinois Press, Urbana-Champaign, IL, pp. 77–90.

Arndt, J. (1981), "The Political Economy of Marketing Systems: Reviving the Institutional Approach", *Journal of Macromarketing*, Vol.1 No.2, pp. 36–47.

Ashley, A. (1932), *William James Ashley: A Life*, P.S. King & Son Ltd., London.

Ashley, C.A. (1938), "Sir William Ashley and the Rise of Schools of Commerce", *The Commerce Journal*, March, pp. 40–50.

Ashley, W.J. (1888), *An Introduction to English Economic History and Theory, Part I, The Middle Ages*, Longmans, Green & Co., London.

Ashley, W.J. (1895), "Roscher's Program of 1843", *Quarterly Journal of Economics*, Vol.9, pp. 99–105.

Ashley, W.J. (1900), *Surveys Historic and Economic*, Longmans, Green & Co., London.

Ashley, W.J. (1901), *The Times*, August 1, quoted in Kadish, A. (1991), "The Foundation of Birmingham's Faculty of Commerce as a Statement on the Nature of Economics", *The Manchester School*, Vol.59 No.2, pp. 160–172.

Ashley, W.J. (1902), "The Faculty of Commerce in the University of Birmingham: Its Purpose and Programme", unpublished MS, *William James Ashley Papers*, UC-8/iv/5, Cadbury Research Library Archives, University of Birmingham, Birmingham, UK.

Ashley, W.J. (1902–12; 1917–18), "Minute Books of Sir William Ashley's Commerce Seminar", *William James Ashley Papers*, UA35/19/iii/6–10, Cadbury Research Library Archives, University of Birmingham, Birmingham, UK.

Ashley, W.J. (1903a), "German Educational Experiments", *The Times*, April 2, p. 12.

Ashley, W.J. (1903b), "The Universities and Commercial Education", *The North American Review*, Vol.176 No.554, pp. 31–38.

Ashley, W.J. (1903c), "Our Education: What It Is and What It Ought to Be", *World's Work*, Vol.1, pp. 267–272.

Ashley, W.J. (1906), "A Science of Commerce and Some Prolegomena", *Science Progress in the Twentieth Century*, Vol.1, July. Available: www.biodiversitylibrary.org/item/18563 [accessed 15/05/2013].

Ashley, W.J. (Ed.). (1907), *British Industries: A Series of General Reviews for Business Men and Students*, Longmans, Green & Co., London.

Ashley, W.J. (1907–12; 1913–20), "Letter Books of the Dean of the Faculty of Commerce, 1907–12 and 1913–20", *William James Ashley Papers*, UC 3/vii/4–5, Cadbury Research Library Archives, University of Birmingham, Birmingham, UK.

Ashley, W.J. (1908), "The Enlargement of Economics", *Economic Journal*, Vol.18 No.70, pp. 181–204.

Ashley, W.J. (1926a), *Commercial Education*, Williams & Norgate Ltd., London.

Ashley, W.J. (1926b), *Business Economics*, Longmans, Green, & Co., London.

Austin, Mr. (1903), "Organization of Retail Trade", in Ashley, W.J. (1902–12; 1917–18), "Minute Books of Sir William Ashley's Commerce Seminar", *William James Ashley Papers*, UA35/19/iii/6–10, Cadbury Research Library Archives, University of Birmingham, Birmingham, UK.

Backhaus, J.G. (1993/1994), "Gustav Schmoller and the Problems of Today", *History of Economic Ideas*, Vol.1/2 No.3/1, pp. 3–25.

Bakan, J. (2005), *The Corporation: The Pathological Pursuit of Profit and Power*, Constable, London.

Baker, M.J. (2013), "Michael J. Baker: Reflections on a Career in Marketing", *Journal of Historical Research in Marketing*, Vol.5 No.2, pp. 223–230.

Balabkins, N.W. (1993/1994), "Gustav Schmoller and the Emergence of Welfare Capitalism", *History of Economic Ideas*, Vol.1/2 No.3/1, pp. 27–42.

Bartels, R. (1941), "Marketing Literature – Development and Appraisal", unpublished PhD dissertation, Ohio State University, Columbus, OH.

Bartels, R. (1951), "Influences on the Development of Marketing Thought, 1900–1923", *Journal of Marketing*, Vol.16 No.1, pp. 1–17.

Bartels, R. (1962), *The Development of Marketing Thought*, Irwin Press, Homewood, IL.

Bartels, R. (1976), *The History of Marketing Thought*, Grid, Columbus, OH.

Bartels, R. (1985), "Bartels to D.G. Brian Jones, August 19", unpublished correspondence.

Bartels, R. (1988), *The History of Marketing Thought*, Publishing Horizons, Columbus, OH.

Barzun, J. and Graff, H. (2004), *The Modern Researcher*, Wadsworth/Thomson Learning, Belmont, CA.

Bateman, B.W. (1998), "Clearing the Ground: The Demise of the Social Gospel Movement and the Rise of Neoclassicalism in American Economics", *History of Political Economy*, Vol.30 Supplement, pp. 29–52.

Bateman, B.W. (2003), "Race, Intellectual History, and American Economics: A Prolegomenon to the Past", *History of Political Economy*, Vol.35 No.4, pp. 713–730.

Bateman, B.W. (2005), "Bringing in the State? The Life and Times of Laissez-faire in the Nineteenth Century United States", *History of Political Economy*, Vol.37 Supplement, pp. 175–199.

Beard, F.K. (2016), "A History of Advertising and Sales Promotion", in Jones, D.G.B. and Tadajewski, M. (Eds.), *The Routledge Companion to Marketing History*, Routledge, New York, pp. 203–224.

Betz, H.K. (1988), "How Does the Historical School Fit?", *History of Political Economy*, Vol.20 No.3, pp. 409–430.

Bolton, C.J. (1976), "The British Historical School in Political Economy: Its History and Significance", unpublished PhD dissertation, Texas A&M University, College Station, Texas.

Boorstin, D.J. (1974), *The Americans: The Democratic Experience*, Vintage Books, New York.

Bottom, W.P. (2006), "Before the Ford Foundation: Development of the Research Based Model of Business Education". Available: https://apps.olin.wustl.edu/workingpapers/pdf/2006-09-016.pdf [accessed 28/07/2017].

Brooks, R. (1906), "Brooks to H. W. Farnam", unpublished correspondence, Group 203, Series 11, Box 248, "Economic Survey Regarding German Influence on Economics in the United States", *Farnam Family Papers*, Yale University Archives, New Haven, CT.

Brown, G. (1951), "What Economists Should Know About Marketing", *Journal of Marketing*, Vol.16 No.1, pp. 60–66.

Bruce, K. (2007), "Early Labor Economics: Its Debt to the Management Practice of Henry S. Dennison", *Journal of Political Economy*, Vol.39 No.3, pp. 403–433.

Bruce, K. and Nyland, C. (2001), "Scientific Management, Institutionalism, and Business Stabilization: 1903–1923", *Journal of Economic Issues*, Vol.35 No.4, pp. 955–978.

Bryce, J. (1899), "Commercial Education", *The North American Review*, Vol.168 No.511, pp. 694–707.

Bucher, K. (1892), "Die Gewerblichen Betriebsformen im Ihrer Historischen Entwickelung", *Schmoller's Jahrbuch*, Vol.16, p. 1271.

Bussiere, D. (2000), "Evidence of a Marketing Periodic Literature Within the American Economic Association: 1895–1936", *Journal of Macromarketing*, Vol.20 No.2, pp. 137–143.

Butler, R.S. (1910), *Marketing Methods*, University of Wisconsin Press, Madison, WI.

Butler, R.S. (1917), *Marketing Methods*, Alexander Hamilton Institute, New York.

Caldwell, B. (2001), "There Really Was a German Historical School of Economics: A Comment on Heath Pearson", *History of Political Economy*, Vol.31 No.3, pp. 649–654.

Carnegie Institution of Washington. (1907), *Annual Report*, Carnegie Institution of Washington, Washington.

Cassels, J.M. (1936), "The Significance of Early Economic Thought on Marketing", *Journal of Marketing*, Vol.1 October, pp. 129–133.

Chandler, A. (1977), *The Visible Hand: The Managerial Revolution in American Business*, Belknap Press, Cambridge, MA.

Chandler, A. (1986), quoted in Kantrow, A.M. (Ed.), "Why History Matters to Managers", *Harvard Business Review*, January–February, pp. 81–88.

Cherington, P.T. (1913), *Advertising as a Business Force*, Doubleday Page & Co., New York.

Cherry, R. (1976), "Racial Thought and the Early Economics Profession", *Review of Social Economy*, Vol.34 No.2, pp. 147–162.

Clark, J.B., McCrea, R.C., Seager, H.R., Rosewater, V., and Kinley, D. (1906), "The Present State of the Theory of Distribution: Discussion", *Publications of the American Economic Association*, Vol.7 No.1, pp. 46–60.

Coats, A.W. (1985), "The American Economic Association and the Economics Profession", *Journal of Economic Literature*, Vol.23 December, pp. 1697–1727.

Cochoy, F. (1998), "Another Discipline for the Market Economy: Marketing as a Performative Knowledge and Know-how for Capitalism", in Callon, M. (Ed.), *The Laws of the Markets*, Blackwell, Oxford, pp. 194–221.

Cochoy, F. (2014), "The American Marketing Association: A Handrail for Marketers and Marketing History", *Journal of Historical Research in Marketing*, Vol.6 No.4, pp. 538–547.

Cole, A. (1970), "The First Dean: A Wondrous Choice", *Harvard Business School Bulletin*, May–June, pp. 32–34.

Commons, J.R. (1924), *Legal Foundations of Capitalism*, Macmillan Co., New York.

Commons, J.R. (1931), "Institutional Economics", *American Economic Review*, Vol.21 No.4, pp. 648–657.

Commons, J.R. (1934), *Institutional Economics*, Macmillan Co., New York.

Commons, J.R. (1964), *Myself: The Autobiography of John R. Commons*, University of Wisconsin Press, Madison, WI.

Conrad, J. (1868), "Die Statistik der Landwirthschaftlichen Production", *Jahrbucher fur Nationalokonomie und Statistik*, Vol.10, p. 81.

Conrad, J. (1882), "Der Konsum an Nothwendigen Nahrungsmitteln im Berlin vor Hundert Jahren und im der Gegenwart", *Jahrbucher fur Nationalokonomie und Statistik*, Vol.3, p. 509.

Conrad, J. (1910), *Grundiss zum Studiem der Politischen Okonomie*, Erster Teil, Jena.

Converse, P.D. (1933), "The First Decade of Marketing Literature", *NATMA Bulletin*, November Supplement, pp. 1–4.

Converse, P.D. (1944), "P.D. Converse to H.C. Taylor, May 29", unpublished correspondence, *Henry Charles Taylor Papers*, State Historical Society of Wisconsin, Madison, WI.

Converse, P.D. (1945a), "Fred Clark's Bibliography as of the Early 1920s", *Journal of Marketing*, Vol.10 No.3, pp. 54–57.

Converse, P.D. (1945b), "The Development of the Science of Marketing", *Journal of Marketing*, Vol.10 No.3, pp. 14–23.

Converse, P.D. (1952), "Notes on the Origins of the American Marketing Association", *Journal of Marketing*, Vol.17 July, pp. 65–67.

Converse, P.D. (1959), *The Beginning of Marketing Thought in the United States*, Bureau of Business Research, University of Texas, Austin, TX.

Coolsen, F.G. (1960), *Marketing Thought in the United States in the Late Nineteenth Century*, The Texas Tech Press, Lubbock, TX.

Copeland, M. (1920), *Marketing Problems*, A.W. Shaw Co., Chicago, IL.

Copeland, M. (1958), *And Mark an Era: The Story of the Harvard Business School*, Little, Brown & Co., Boston, MA.

Cova, B., Maclaran, P., and Bradshaw, A. (2013), "Rethinking Consumer Culture Theory From the Postmodern to the Communist Horizon", *Marketing Theory*, Vol.13 No.2, pp. 213–225.

Craig, G.A. (1978), *Germany 1866–1945*, Oxford University Press, New York.

Crane, A. and Desmond, J. (2002), "Societal Marketing and Morality", *European Journal of Marketing*, Vol.36 No.5/6, pp. 548–569.

Crawford, E. (1911), "Salutory", *Mill Supplies*, Vol.1 January, pp. 1–2.

Cruikshank, J.L. (1987), *A Delicate Experiment: The Harvard Business School 1908–1945*, Harvard Business School Press, Cambridge, MA.

Cuff, R. (1996), "Edwin F. Gay, Arch W. Shaw, and the Uses of History in Early Graduate Business Education", *Journal of Management History*, Vol.2 No.3, pp. 9–25.

Davis, J.F. (2017), *Pioneering African-American Women in the Advertising Business: Biographies of MAD black WOMEN*, Routledge, London.

Dean, C.C. (1997), "Primer of Scientific Management By Frank B. Gilbreth: A Response to Publication of Taylor's Principles in *The American Magazine*", *Journal of Management History*, Vol.3 No.1, pp. 31–41.

Dean, J. (1951), *Managerial Economics*, Prentice Hall, Englewood Cliffs, NJ.

Dillard, D. (1967), *Economic Development of the North Atlantic Community*, Prentice Hall, Englewood Cliffs, NJ.

Dixon, D.F. (1978), "The Origins of Macromarketing Thought", in Fisk, G. and Nason, R.W. (Eds.), *Macromarketing: New Steps on the Learning Curve*, University of Colorado, Boulder, CO, pp. 9–28.

Dixon, D.F. (1979), "Prejudice v Marketing? An Examination of Historical Sources", *Akron Business and Economic Review*, Vol.10 Fall, pp. 37–42.

Dixon, D.F. (1980), "Medieval Macromarketing Thought", in Fisk, G. and White, P. (Eds.), *Macromarketing*, University of Colorado, Boulder, CO, pp. 59–69.

Dixon, D.F. (1981), "The Role of Marketing in Early Theories of Economic Development", *Journal of Macromarketing*, Vol.1 No.2, pp. 19–27.

Dixon, D.F. (1999), "Some Late Nineteenth-Century Antecedents of Marketing Theory", *Journal of Macromarketing*, Vol.19 No.2, pp. 115–125.

Dixon, D.F. (2002), "Emerging Macromarketing Concepts From Socrates to Alfred Marshall", *Journal of Business Research*, Vol.55, pp. 87–95.

Domosh, M. (2006), *American Commodities in an Age of Empire*, Routledge, New York.

Dorfman, J. (1955), "The Role of the German Historical School in American Economic Growth", *American Economic Review – Papers and Proceedings*, Vol.45, pp. 17–39.

Dorfman, J. (1969), *Two Essays By Henry Carter*, Augustus M. Kelley, New York.

Dorfman, J., Ayres, C.E., Chamberlain, N.W., Kuznets, S., and Gordon, R.A. (1963), *Institutional Economics: Veblen, Commons and Mitchell Reconsidered*, University of California Press, Los Angeles, CA.

Duddy, E.A. and Revzan, D.A. (1953), *Marketing: An Institutional Approach*, McGraw Hill, New York.

Eldridge, W. (1924), "Eldridge to Litman, April 29", unpublished correspondence on book, *Essentials of International Trade*, John Wiley & Sons. *Simon Litman Papers*, Record series 9/5/29, Box 3, University of Illinois Archives, Urbana-Champaign, IL.

Eliot, C.W. (1907), "Eliot to F.W. Taylor, March 7", unpublished correspondence, *Charles W. Eliot Papers*, Pusey Library Archives, Harvard University, Cambridge, MA.

Ely, R.T. (1884a), "Commerce and Its Historical Development in Modern Times", unpublished lecture notes – October 10, 1884, *Richard T. Ely Papers*, State Historical Society of Wisconsin, Madison, WI.

Ely, R.T. (1884b), "The Past and the Present of Political Economy", *Johns Hopkins University Series in Historical and Political Science*, second series, Vol.3 March, pp. 1–64.

Ely, R.T. (1885), *Recent American Socialism*, Johns Hopkins, Baltimore, MD.

Ely, R.T. (1886a), "The Economic Discussion in Science", in *Science Economic Discussion*, The Science Co., New York.

Ely, R.T. (1886b), "Ethics and Economics", in *Science Economic Discussion*, The Science Co., New York.

Ely, R.T. (1886c), "Socialism in America", *North American Review*, Vol.142 No.355, pp. 519–525.

Ely, R.T. (1886d), *Science Economic Discussion*, The Science Co., New York.

Ely, R.T. (1891), "Ely to E.A. Ross, June 23", unpublished correspondence, *Richard T. Ely Papers*, State Historical Society of Wisconsin, Madison, WI.

Ely, R.T. (1894), "Fundamental Beliefs in My Social Philosophy", *Forum*, October, pp. 173–183.

Ely, R.T. (1898), *The Social Law of Service*, William Briggs, Toronto.

Ely, R.T. (1899), "Examinations in the Distribution of Wealth, February 16", Teaching and Research Files, unpublished manuscript, *Richard T. Ely Papers*, State Historical Society of Wisconsin, Madison, WI.

Ely, R.T. (1902), "Industrial Liberty", *Publications of the American Economic Association*, Vol.3 No.1, pp. 59–79.

Ely, R.T. (1903), "Statement Made by R.T. Ely at a Faculty Meeting Held in Regard to the Proposal to Abolish the Schools of Economics, of Education and Pharmacy, in the College of Letters and Science, November", unpublished manuscript, *Richard T. Ely Papers*, State Historical Society of Wisconsin, Madison, WI.

Ely, R.T. (1906a), "Ely to H.W. Farnam, November 16", unpublished correspondence, *Richard T. Ely Papers*, State Historical Society of Wisconsin, Madison, WI.

Ely, R.T. (1906b), "Ely to H.W. Farnam, December 18", unpublished correspondence, *Richard T. Ely Papers*, State Historical Society of Wisconsin, Madison, WI.

Ely, R.T. (1910a), "George Mygatt Fisk, In Memoriam", *Madison Democrat*, May 17.

Ely, R.T. (1910b), "Suggestions to Teachers of General Economics", *Journal of Political Economy*, Vol.18 No.6, pp. 437–440.

Ely, R.T. (1915), "Ely to Frank Gilbreth, December 20", unpublished correspondence, *Richard T. Ely Papers*, State Historical Society of Wisconsin, Madison, WI.

Ely, R.T. (1916), "Address to the First Wisconsin Commercial and Industrial Congress, February 18", unpublished manuscript, *Richard T. Ely Papers*, State Historical Society of Wisconsin, Madison, WI.

Ely, R.T. (1917), "Study Program for the American Association for Agricultural Legislation: Topics for Theses and Other Publications", unpublished manuscript, *Richard T. Ely Papers*, State Historical Society of Wisconsin, Madison, WI.

Ely, R.T. (1931), "Remarks of Richard T. Ely at the Annual Meeting of the American Economic Association", unpublished manuscript, *Richard T. Ely Papers*, State Historical Society of Wisconsin, Madison, WI.

Ely, R.T. (1936), "The Founding and Early History of the American Economic Association", *Proceedings of the American Economic Association*, Vol.26 December, pp. 141–150.

Ely, R.T. (1938), *Ground Under Our Feet*, Macmillan Co., New York.

Ely, R.T. (n.d.a), "The German Historical School", unpublished manuscript, *Richard T. Ely Papers*, State Historical Society of Wisconsin, Madison, WI.

Ely, R.T. (n.d.b), "The Story of Economics in the United States", unpublished manuscript, *Richard T. Ely Papers*, State Historical Society of Wisconsin, Madison, WI.

Ely, R.T. (n.d.c), "Economics and Social Science in Relation to Business Education", unpublished manuscript, *Richard T. Ely Papers*, State Historical Society of Wisconsin, Madison, WI.

Engwall, L. and Zamagni, V. (1998), "Introduction", in Engwall, L. and Zamagni, V. (Eds.), *Management Education in Historical Perspective*, Manchester University Press, Manchester, pp. 1–15.

Erdman, H.E. (1921), *The Marketing of Whole Milk*, Macmillan, New York.

Farnam, H.W. (1908), "Deutsch-amerikanische Beziehungen in der Volkswirtschaftslehre", in Schmoller, G. (Ed.), *Die Entwickling der Deutschen Volkswirtschaftslehre im Neunzehnten Jahrundert*, Stephen Geibel & Co., Leipzig.

Fauri, F. (1998), "British and Italian Management Education Before the Second World War: A Comparative Analysis", in Engwall, L. and Zamagni, V. (Eds.), *Management Education in Historical Perspective*, Manchester University Press, Manchester, pp. 34–45.

Fisk, G.M. (1906), "Fisk to H.W. Farnam", unpublished correspondence, Group 203, Series 11, Box 248, "Economic Survey Regarding German Influence on Economics in the United States", *Farnam Family Papers*, Yale University Archives, New Haven, CT.

Foucault, M. (1977/1991), *Discipline and Punish: The Birth of the Prison*, Penguin Publishing, London.

Foucault, M. (2015), *The Punitive Society: Lectures at the College de France, 1972–1973*, Palgrave Macmillan, London.

Fourcade-Gourinchas, M. (2001), "Politics, Institutional Structures, and the Rise of Economics: A Comparative Study", *Theory and Society*, Vol.30 No.3, pp. 397–447.

Fourcade-Gourinchas, M. and Khurana, R. (2013), "From Social Control to Financial Economics: The Linked Ecologies of Economics and Business in Twentieth Century America", *Theory and Society*, Vol.42 No.2, pp. 121–159.

Friedman, G. (2015), "The Rot at the Heart of American Progressivism: Imperialism, Racism and Fear of Democracy in Richard T. Ely's Progressivism". Available: www.umass.edu/economics/sites/default/files/Friedman.pdf [accessed 28/07/2017].

Friedman, W.A. (2004), *Birth of a Salesman: The Transformation of Selling in America*, Harvard University Press, Cambridge, MA.

Fullerton, R.A. (1988), "'How Modern Is Modern Marketing' Marketing's Evolution and the Myth of the 'Production Era'", *Journal of Marketing*, Vol.52 January, pp. 108–125.

Fullerton, R.A. (2011), "Historical Methodology: The Perspective of a Professionally Trained Historian Turned Marketer", *Journal of Historical Research in Marketing*, Vol.3 No.4, pp. 436–448.

Fullerton, R.A. (2016), *The Foundations of Marketing Practice*, Routledge, New York.

Funkhouser, G.R. (1984), "Technological Antecedents of the Modern Marketing Mix", *Journal of Macromarketing*, Vol.4 No.1, pp. 17–28.

Gay, E.F. (1906), "Gay to H.W. Farnam", unpublished correspondence, Group 203, Series 11, Box 248, "Economic Survey Regarding German Influence on Economics in the United States", *Farnam Family Papers*, Yale University Archives, New Haven, CT.

Gay, E.F. (1907–08), "Diaries", unpublished manuscript, *Edwin Francis Gay Collection*, Huntington Library, San Marino, CA.

Gay, E.F. (1907–1914), "Journal", unpublished manuscript, *Edwin Francis Gay Collection*, Huntington Library, San Marino, CA.

Gay, E.F. (1908), "The New Graduate School of Business Administration", *The Harvard Illustrated Magazine*, Vol.9 No.7, pp. 159–161.

Gay, E.F. (1909a), "Gay to F.W. Taylor, October 11", unpublished correspondence, *E.F. Gay Papers*, Baker Library Archives, Cambridge, MA.

Gay, E.F. (1909b), "Gay to Arch W. Shaw, November 1", unpublished correspondence, *E.F. Gay Papers*, Baker Library Archives, Cambridge, MA.

Gay, E.F. (1912a), "The Scientific Study of Retailing", *Hardware Dealer's Magazine*, December, pp. 1215–1217.

Gay, E.F. (1912b), "The History of Modern Commerce as a Field of Investigation – Address to the Historical Association, December 30", *E.F. Gay Papers*, Baker Library Archives, Cambridge, MA.

Gay, E.F. (1914), "Gay to F.W. Taylor, February 13", unpublished correspondence, *E.F. Gay Papers*, Baker Library Archives, Cambridge, MA.

Gay, E.F. (1923), "The Rhythm of History", *Harvard Graduate Magazine*, Vol.32, pp. 1–17.

Gay, E.F. (1926), "The Founding of the Harvard Business School", *Harvard Business Review*, Vol.5, pp. 397–400.

Gay, E.F. (1941), "The Tasks of Economic History", *Journal of Economic History*, Vol.1 December, pp. 9–16.

Gay, E.F. (n.d.a), "Journal", unpublished manuscript, *Edwin Francis Gay Collection*, Huntington Library, San Marino, CA.

Gay, E.F. (n.d.b), "The Point of View of the Economic Historian, Social Ethics Seminary", unpublished manuscript, *Edwin Francis Gay Collection*, Huntington Library, San Marino, CA.

Gilbert, J. and Baker, E. (1997), "Wisconsin Economists and New Deal Agricultural Policy: The Legacy of Progressive Professors", *The Wisconsin Magazine of History*, Vol.80 No.4, pp. 280–312.

Goodwin, C.D. (1998), "The Patrons of Economics in a Time of Transformation", *History of Political Economy*, Vol.30 Supplement, pp. 53–81.

Grisso, K.M. (1980), "David Kinley, 1861–1944: The Career of the Fifth President of the University of Illinois", PhD dissertation, University of Illinois, Urbana-Champaign, IL.

Hagemann, H. (1995), "Roscher and the Theory of Crisis", *Journal of Economic Studies*, Vol.22 No.3/4/5, pp. 171–186.

Hagerty, J.E. (1906), "Hagerty to H.W. Farnam", unpublished correspondence, Group 203, Series 11, Box 248, "Economic Survey Regarding German Influence on Economics in the United States", *Farnam Family Papers*, Yale University Archives, New Haven, CT.

Hagerty, J.E. (1913), *Mercantile Credit*, H. Holt & Company, New York.

Hagerty, J.E. (1936), "Experiences of Our Early Marketing Teachers", *Journal of Marketing*, Vol.1 No.3, pp. 20–27.

Hammond, D.J. (1991), "Alfred Marshall's Methodology", *Methodus*, Vol.3 June, pp. 95–101.

Hammond, M.B. (1897), "The Cotton Industry: An Essay in Economic History", *Publications of the American Economic Association*, December, Vol.12 No.1, pp. 3–371.

Harvard Annual Reports. (1906–1909), Harvard University, Cambridge, MA.

Harvard Business School. (1910–1921), "Graduate School of Business Administration: Topics Considered in Courses, 1910–1921", unpublished manuscript, Baker Library Archives, Harvard University, Cambridge, MA.

Hatfield, H.R. (Ed.). (1904), *Lectures on Commerce*, University of Chicago Press, Chicago, IL.

Heaton, H.A. (1927), "Obituary – Sir William Ashley", *The Economic Journal*, Vol.37 No.148, pp. 683–684.

Heaton, H.A. (1949), "The Making of An Economic Historian", *Journal of Economic History*, Supplement 9, Vol. 9, pp. 1–18.

Heaton, H.A. (1952), *A Scholar in Action: Edwin Francis Gay*, Harvard University Press, Cambridge, MA.

Herbst, J. (1965), *The German Historical School in American Scholarship: A Study in the Transfer of Culture*, Cornell University Press, Ithaca, NY.

Herzberg, D.L. (2001), "Thinking Through War: The Social Thought of Richard T. Ely, John R. Commons, and Edward A. Ross During the First World War", *Journal of the History of the Behavioural Sciences*, Vol.37 No.2, pp. 123–141.

Hibbard, B. (1921), *Marketing Agricultural Products*, D. Appleton & Co., New York.

Hildebrand, B. (1848), *Die National Okonomie der Gegenwart und Zukunst*, J. Rutten, Frankfurt.

Hildebrand, B. (1863), "Die Gegenwartige Aufgabe der Wissenschaft der Nationalokonomie", *Jahrbucher fur Nationalokonomie und Statistik*, Vol.1, p. 145.

Hildebrand, B. (1866), "Zur Geschichte der Deutschen Wollenindustrie", *Jahrbucher fur Nationalokonomie und Statistik*, Vol.6, p. 186, and Vol.7, p. 81.

Hodgson, G.M. (2005), "Alfred Marshall Versus the Historical School", *Journal of Economic Studies*, Vol.32 No.4, pp. 331–348.

Hoeveler, J.D. Jr. (1976), "The University and the Social Gospel: The Intellectual Origins of the 'Wisconsin Idea'", *The Wisconsin Magazine of History*, Vol.59 No.4, pp. 282–298.

Hollander, S.C. (1980), "Some Notes on the Difficulty of Identifying the Marketing Thought Contributions of the Early Institutionalists", in Lamb, C.W. and Dunne, P.M. (Eds.), *Theoretical Developments in Marketing*, American Marketing Association, Chicago, IL, pp. 45–46.

Hollander, S.C. (1986), "The Marketing Concept: A Deja Vu", in Fisk, G. (Ed.), *Marketing Management as a Social Process*, Praeger, New York, pp. 3–29.
Hoyt, C.W. (1913), *Scientific Sales Management: A Practical Application of the Principles of Scientific Management to Selling*, George B. Woolson & Co, New Haven, CT.
Huegy, H.W. (1958), "Paul Delaney Converse", *Journal of Marketing*, Vol.23 No.2, pp. 188–190.
Hunt, S.D. (1976), "The Nature and Scope of Marketing", *Journal of Marketing*, Vol.40 No.3, pp. 17–28.
Hutt, W.H. (1974), *A Rehabilitation of Say's Law*, Ohio University Press, Athens, OH.
Jacques, R. (1996), *Manufacturing the Employee: Management Knowledge From the 19th to 21st Centuries*, Sage Publications, London.
James, E.J. (1893), *Education for Businessmen in Europe*, American Bankers' Association, New York.
James, E.J. (1906), "James to Farnam", unpublished correspondence, Group 203, Series 11, Box 248, "Economic Survey Regarding German Influence on Economics in the United States", *Farnam Family Papers*, Yale University Archives, New Haven, CT.
James, W. (1909), *Meaning of Truth*, Longmans, Green & Co., New York.
Jeans, J.S. (1902), "The British Iron and Steel Industries: Their Conditions and Outlook", lecture delivered 1902, published in Ashley, W.J. (Ed.). (1907), *British Industries: A Series of General Reviews for Business Men and Students*, Longmans, Green & Co., London, pp. 2–38.
Jones, D.G.B. (1997), "The Machine Metaphor in Arch W. Shaw's (1915) Some Problems in Market Distribution", *Journal of Macromarketing*, Vol.17 No.1, pp. 151–158.
Jones, D.G.B. (2012), *Pioneers in Marketing*, Routledge, New York.
Jones, D.G.B. and Monieson, D.D. (1990), "Early Development of the Philosophy of Marketing Thought", *Journal of Marketing*, Vol.54 January, pp. 102–113.
Jones, D.G.B. and Richardson, A.J. (2007), "The Myth of the Marketing Revolution", *Journal of Macromarketing*, Vol.27 No.1, pp. 15–24.
Jones, D.G.B. and Shaw, E.H. (2002), "A History of Marketing Thought", in Weitz, B. and Wensley, R. (Eds.), *Handbook of Marketing*, Sage Publications, London, pp. 39–65.
Jones, D.G.B. and Shaw, E.H. (2006), "Historical Research in the *Journal of Macromarketing*, 1981–2005", *Journal of Macromarketing*, Vol.26 No.2, pp. 178–192.
Jones, D.G.B, Shaw, E.H., and Goldring, D. (2009), "Stanley C. Hollander and the Conferences on Historical Analysis & Research in Marketing", *Journal of Historical Research in Marketing*, Vol.1 No.1, pp. 55-73.
Jones, D.G.B. and Tadajewski, M. (2015), "Origins of Marketing Thought in Britain", *European Journal of Marketing*, Vol.49 No.7/8, pp. 1016–1039.
Jones, D.G.B. and Tadajewski, M. (2016), "A History of Historical Research in Marketing", in Baker, M.J. and Saren, M. (Eds.), *Marketing Theory*, Sage Publications, London, pp. 60–89.
Jones, E.D. (1894), "E.D. Jones to R.T. Ely, January 23", unpublished correspondence, *Richard T. Ely Papers*, State Historical Society of Wisconsin, Madison, WI.
Jones, E.D. (1903a), "Higher Commercial Education and the Business Community", *Publications of the Michigan Political Science Association*, Vol.5, pp. 80–94.
Jones, E.D. (1903b), "Jones to R.T. Ely, March 18", unpublished correspondence, *Richard T. Ely Papers*, State Historical Society of Wisconsin, Madison, WI.
Jones, E.D. (1904), "Education and Industry", *The Popular Science Monthly*, March, pp. 431–444.

Jones, E.D. (1905), "The Manufacturer and the Domestic Market", *Annals of the American Association of Political and Social Science*, Vol.25 January, pp. 1–20.

Jones, E.D. (1907), "Jones to H.C. Taylor, March 16", unpublished correspondence, *Henry Charles Taylor Papers*, State Historical Society of Wisconsin, Madison, WI.

Jones, E.D. (1910), "The Causes of the Increased Cost of Agricultural Staples and the Influence of This Upon the Recent Evolution of Other Objects of Expenditure", *Michigan Academy of Science Twelfth Report*, October, pp. 137–142.

Jones, E.D. (1911a), "The Larger Aspects of Private Business", *Mill Supplies*, Vol.1 January, p. 3.

Jones, E.D. (1911b), "What Goods Are Worthy of Manufacture?", *Mill Supplies*, Vol.1 February, pp. 57–58.

Jones, E.D. (1911c), "Standardization: Its Effect on Quality", *Mill Supplies*, Vol.1 March, pp. 99–100.

Jones, E.D. (1911d), "Cost Accounting and Efficiency", *Mill Supplies*, Vol.1 April, pp. 149–152.

Jones, E.D. (1911e), "Buyers' Specifications: Scientific Purchasing", *Mill Supplies*, Vol.1 May, pp. 209–210.

Jones, E.D. (1911f), "Quantity Prices Versus Classified Lists", *Mill Supplies*, Vol.1 June, pp. 245–246.

Jones, E.D. (1911g), "The Cancellation of Orders", *Mill Supplies*, Vol.1 July, pp. 291–292.

Jones, E.D. (1911h), "The Restriction of Prices", *Mill Supplies*, Vol.1 August, pp. 339–340.

Jones, E.D. (1911i), "Advertising and Trade Brands", *Mill Supplies*, Vol.1 August, pp. 391–392.

Jones, E.D. (1911j), "Our System of Weights and Measures Indefensible", *Mill Supplies*, Vol.1 October, pp. 430–432.

Jones, E.D. (1911k), "Functions of a System of Grades", *Mill Supplies*, Vol.1 December, pp. 529–530.

Jones, E.D. (1912a), "Some Problems of Price", *Mill Supplies*, Vol.2 January, pp. 9–10.

Jones, E.D. (1912b), "List Prices and Discounts", *Mill Supplies*, Vol.2 February, pp. 59–62.

Jones, E.D. (1912c), "The Perfect Market Outlined", *Mill Supplies*, Vol.2 March, pp. 115–121.

Jones, E.D. (1912d), "Cost of Living and Marketing of Farm Products", *Mill Supplies*, Vol.2 May, pp. 283–285.

Jones, E.D. (1912e), "Cost of Living and the Retail Trade", *Mill Supplies*, Vol.2 August, pp. 406–408.

Jones, E.D. (1912f), "Principles of Modern Retail Merchandising", *Mill Supplies*, Vol.2 September, pp. 461–462.

Jones, E.D. (1912g), "Functions of the Merchant", *Mill Supplies*, Vol.2 November, pp. 575–577.

Jones, E.D. (1913a), "Some Propositions Concerning University Instruction in Business Administration", *Journal of Political Economy*, Vol.21 No.3, pp. 185–195.

Jones, E.D. (1913b), "Functions of Trade Marks", *Mill Supplies*, Vol.3 February, pp. 69–70.

Jones, E.D. (1913c), "The Purchasing Department", *Mill Supplies*, Vol.3 March, pp. 130–132.

Jones, E.D. (1913d), "History of American Machine-Tool Manufacture", *Mill Supplies*, Vol.3 November, pp. 623–628.

Jones, E.D. (1913e), "History of American Machine-Tool Manufacture, Part II", *Mill Supplies*, Vol.3 December, pp. 684–686.

Jones, E.D. (1913f), *Business Administration – The Scientific Principles of a New Profession*, Engineering Magazine Co., New York.
Jones, E.D. (1914a), "Evolution of Accuracy in Manufacture", *Mill Supplies*, Vol.4 January, pp. 23–24.
Jones, E.D. (1914b), *The Business Administrator, His Models in War, Statecraft and Science*, Engineering Magazine Co., New York.
Jones, E.D. (1916), *The Administration of Industrial Enterprises*, Longmans, Green & Co., New York.
Jones, E.D. (1918), "Jones to R.T. Ely, February 3", unpublished correspondence, *Richard T. Ely Papers*, State Historical Society of Wisconsin, Madison, WI.
Jones, E.D. (1920), *Industrial Leadership and Executive Ability*, Engineering Magazine Co., New York.
Jones, F.M. (1971), "The Foundation of Marketing Thought", unpublished working paper – October 28, University of Illinois, Urbana-Champaign, IL.
Kadish, A. (1991), "The Foundation of Birmingham's Faculty of Commerce as a Statement on the Nature of Economics", *The Manchester School*, Vol.59 No.2, pp. 160–172.
Kangas, J.E. (1966), "The Influence of Economic Theory on Marketing Thought", unpublished PhD dissertation, University of Cincinnati, Cincinnati, OH.
Keith, R. (1960), "The Marketing Revolution", *Journal of Marketing*, Vol.24 No.3, pp. 35–38.
Khurana, R. (2007), *From Higher Aims to Higher Hands*, Princeton University Press, Princeton, NJ.
Kinley, D. (1895), "Credit Instruments in Retail Trade", *Publications of the American Economic Association*, Vol.10 No.3, pp. 72–78.
Kinley, D. (1899), "Farm and Home Proprietorship and Real Estate Mortgage Indebtedness", *Publications of the American Economic Association*, [No Volume Given] No.2, pp. 219–245.
Kinley, D. (1906), "Democracy in Education", *The Elementary School Teacher*, Vol.6 No.8, pp. 377–397.
Kinley, D. (1908), "D. Kinley to S. Litman, May 14", unpublished correspondence, *Simon Litman Papers*, Record series 9/5/29, Box 4, Appointments, University of Illinois Archives, Urbana-Champaign, IL.
Kinley, D. (1910), "The General Course a Citizenship Course", *Journal of Political Economy*, Vol.18 No.6, pp. 440–443.
Kinley, D. (1911), "The Promotion of Trade With South America", *American Economic Review*, Vol.1 No.1, pp. 50–71.
Kinley, D. (1914), "The Service of Statistics to Economics", *Publications of the American Statistical Association*, Vol.14 No.105, pp. 11–20.
Kinley, D. (1918a), "The Aims and Claims of Germany", unpublished manuscript, University of Illinois, College of Agriculture, Urbana-Champaign, IL.
Kinley, D. (1918b), "The Great Condition", *University of Illinois Bulletin*, Vol.15 No.48, pp. 3–12.
Kinley, D. (1925), "The Curriculum and Some of Its Consequences", *Bulletin of the American Association of University Professors*, Vol.11 No.5, pp. 231–236.
Kinley, D. (1949), *The Autobiography of David Kinley*, University of Illinois Press, Urbana-Champaign, IL.
Kinley, D., Lindsay, S.M., Roberts, G., Marburg, T., Weber, A.F., Folwell, W.W., Commons, J.R., and Devine, E.T. (1902), "The Workman's Position in the Light of Economic

Progress: Discussion", *Publications of the American Economic Association*, Vol.3 No.1, pp. 213–234.

Kitchen, M. (1978), *The Political Economy of Germany, 1815–1914*, McGill-Queen's Press, Montreal.

Knies, K. (1853), *Die Politische Okonomie vom Standpunkte der Geschichtlichen Methode*, C.A. Schwetschke und Sohn, Braunschweig.

Knittel, A. (1895), "Zur Geschichte des Deutschen Genossenschaftswesens", *Schmoller's Jahrbuch*, Vol.19, p. 1380.

Koot, G.M. (1980), "English Historical Economics and the Emergence of Economic History in England", *History of Political Economy*, Vol.12 No.2, pp. 174–205.

Koot, G.M. (1987), *English Historical Economics, 1870–1926*, Cambridge University Press, Cambridge, MA.

Kuhn, T.S. (1962), *The Structure of Scientific Revolutions*, University of Chicago Press, Chicago, IL.

Lazer, W. (1979), "Some Observations on the Development of Marketing Thought", in Ferrell, O.C., Brown, S.W., and Lamb, C.W. (Eds.), *Conceptual and Theoretical Developments in Marketing*, American Marketing Association, Chicago, IL, pp. 652–664.

Leonard, T.C. (2005), "Retrospectives: Eugenics and Economics in the Progressive Era", *Journal of Economic Perspectives*, Vol.19 No.4, pp. 207–224.

Leonard, T.C. (2016), *Illiberal Reformers: Race, Eugenics & American Economics in the Progressive Era*, Princeton University Press, Princeton, NJ.

Lindsey, B. (2002), *Against the Dead Hand – The Uncertain Struggle for Global Capitalism*, John Wiley & Sons, New York.

Litman, S. (ca. 1902–08), "Mechanism and Technique of Commerce", unpublished MS, *Simon Litman Papers*, Record series 9/5/29, Box 3, University of Illinois Archives, Urbana-Champaign, IL.

Litman, S. (1910), *Trade and Commerce*, LaSalle Extension University, Chicago, IL.

Litman, S. (1919), "Effects of War on Foreign Trade", *Historical Outlook*, Vol.10 February, pp. 74–76.

Litman, S. (1920), *Prices and Price Control in Great Britain and the United States During the World War*, Oxford University Press (American Branch), New York.

Litman, S. (1921), "Foreign Trade of the United States Since Armistice", *Annals of the American Academy of Political and Social Science*, Vol.94 March, pp. 1–7.

Litman, S. (1926), "Effects of World War on Trade", *Annals of the American Academy of Political and Social Science*, Vol.127 September, pp. 23–29.

Litman, S. (1923/1927), *Essentials of International Trade*, John Wiley & Sons, New York.

Litman, S. (1924–32), "Correspondence on book, *Essentials of International Trade*, John Wiley & Sons, Inc.", *Simon Litman Papers*, Record series 9/5/29, Box 3, University of Illinois Archives, Urbana-Champaign, IL.

Litman, S. (1945), "David Kinley 1861–1944", *American Economic Review*, Vol.35 No.5, pp. 1041–1044.

Litman, S. (1950), "The Beginnings of Teaching Marketing in American Universities", *Journal of Marketing*, Vol.15 No.4, pp. 220–223.

Litman, S. (1957), *Ray Frank Litman: A Memoir*, American Jewish Historical Society, New York.

Litman, S. (1963), "Looking Back: An Autobiographical Sketch", unpublished MS, *Simon Litman Papers*, Record series 9/5/29, Box 1, University of Illinois Archives, Urbana-Champaign, IL.

Litterer, J.A. (1961), "Systematic Management: The Search for Order and Integration", *The Business History Review*, Vol.35 No.4, pp. 461–476.
Locke, R.R. (1984), *The End of Practical Man: Entrepreneurship and Higher Education in Germany, France, and Great Britain, 1880–1940*, JAI Press, Greenwich, CT.
Locke, R.R. (1985), "Business Education in Germany: Past Systems and Current Practice", *Business History Review*, Vol.59 No.2, pp. 232–253.
Macklin, T. (1921), *Efficient Marketing for Agriculture*, Macmillan & Co., New York.
Maclaran, P., Saren, M., Stern, B., and Tadajewski, M. (2009), "Introduction", in Maclaran, P., Saren, M., Stern, B., and Tadajewski, M. (Eds.), *The SAGE Handbook of Marketing Theory*, Sage, London, pp. 1–24.
Maddison, A. (2007), *Contours of the World Economy, 1–2030 AD: Essays in Macro-economic History*, Oxford University Press, Oxford.
Marshall, A. (1919), *Industry and Trade*, second edition, Macmillan & Co., London.
Marshall, A. (1956), quoted in Pigou, A.C. (Ed.), *Memorials of Alfred Marshall*, Kelley & Millman, New York, p. 165.
Martin, S.O. (1916), "The Bureau of Business Research", *Harvard Alumni Bulletin*, pp. 266–269.
Maynard, H.H. (1941), "Marketing Courses Prior to 1910", *Journal of Marketing*, Vol.5 April, pp. 382–384.
Maynard, H.H. (1942), "Early Teachers of Marketing", *Journal of Marketing*, Vol.7 No.2, pp. 158–159.
Mehren, G.L. (1960), "Henry E. Erdman", *Journal of Marketing*, Vol.24 No.4, pp. 77–79.
Menger, C. (1883), *Untersuchungen uber die Methode der Sozialwissenschaften und der Politischen Oekonomie insbesondere*, Verlag von Duncker Humblot, Leipzig.
Meyer, B.E. (1906), "Meyer to Henry W. Farnam", unpublished correspondence, Group 203, Series 11, Box 248, "Economic Survey Regarding German Influence on Economics in the United States", *Farnam Family Papers*, Yale University Archives, New Haven, CT.
Meyer, H.D. (1998), "The German Handelshochschulen, 1898–1933: A New Departure in Management Education and Why It Failed", in Engwall, L. and Zamagni, V. (Eds.), *Management Education in Historical Perspective*, Manchester University Press, Manchester, pp. 19–32.
Milonakis, D. and Fine, B. (2009), *From Political Economy to Economics*, Routledge, London.
Mitchell, W.C. (1913), *Business Cycles*, University of California Press, Berkeley, CA.
Mitchell, W.C. (1918), "Bentham's Felicific Calculus", *Political Science Quarterly*, Vol.33 June, pp. 161–183.
Mitchell, W.C. (1969), *Types of Economic Theory: From Mercantalism to Institutionalism*, volume 1, Augustus Kelley Publishers, New York.
Morgan, M.S. and Rutherford, M. (1998), "American Economics: The Character of the Transformation", *History of Political Economy*, Vol.30 Supplement, pp. 1–26.
Morison, S.E. (1930), *The Development of Harvard University*, Harvard University Press, Cambridge, MA.
Myles, J.C. (1956), "German Historicism and American Economics – A Study of the Influence of the German Historical School on American Economic Thought", unpublished PhD dissertation, Princeton University, Princeton, NJ.
Neal, T. (1902), "A Commercial Faculty – Its Limitations and Possibilities", unpublished lecture, UA21, Birmingham: Cadbury Research Library Archives, University of Birmingham, Birmingham, UK.
Nishizawa, T. (2002), *Marshall, Ashley on Education of Businessmen and 'Science of Business'? Marshall's School of Economics in the Making*, Hitotsubashi University Center for Historical Social Science, Tokyo.

Norwood, J.S. (1961), "An 18th Century Plan for Business Education", *Journal of Marketing*, Vol.25 No.6, pp. 52–55.

Nyland, C. (1996), "Taylorism, John R. Commons, and the Hoxie Report", *Journal of Economic Issues*, Vol.30 No.4, pp. 985–1016.

Nyland, C., Bruce, K., and Burns, P. (2014), "Taylorism, the International Labour Organization, and the Genesis and Diffusion of Codetermination", *Organization Studies*, Vol.35 No.8, pp. 1149–1169.

Nystrom, P. (1915a), *The Economics of Retailing*, Ronald Press, New York.

Nystrom, P. (1915b), "Nystrom to Richard T. Ely", unpublished correspondence, *Ely Papers*, State Historical Society of Wisconsin, Madison, WI.

Oppenheim, H. (1871), *Der Kathedersozialismus*, R. Oppenheim, Berlin.

Pearson, H. (1999), "Was There Really a German Historical School of Economics", *History of Political Economy*, Vol.31 No.3, pp. 547–562.

Petty, R. (2016), "A History of Brand Identity Protection and Brand Marketing", in Jones, D.G.B. and Tadajewski, M. (Eds.), *The Routledge Companion to Marketing History*, Routledge, New York, pp. 97–114.

Postlethwayt, M. (1774), *The Universal Dictionary of Trade and Commerce*, two volumes, reprinted (1971), Augustus M. Kelly Publishers, New York.

Prisching, M. (1993/1994), "Schmoller's Theory of Society", *History of Economic Ideas*, Vol.1/2 No.3/1, pp. 117–142.

Pulver, G.C. (Ed.). (1984), "Improving Agriculture and Rural Life", in Cannon, M. (Ed.), *Achievements in Agricultural Economics, 1909–1984*, University of Wisconsin, Madison, WI, pp. 3–14.

Rader, B. (1966), *The Academic Mind and Reform: The Influence of Richard T. Ely in American Life*, University of Kentucky Press, Lexington, KY.

Ramamurthy, A. (2003), *Imperial Persuaders: Images of Africa and Asia in British Advertising*, Manchester University Press, Manchester.

Rastall, B. (1909), "Business Sciences", unpublished booklet, University of Wisconsin Extension Division, University of Wisconsin, Madison, WI, p. 7.

Redlich, F. (1957), "Academic Education for Business: Its Development and the Contribution of Ignaz Jastrow (1856–1937)", *Business History Review*, Vol.31 Spring, pp. 35–93.

Richardson, H.G. (1941), "Business Training in Medieval Oxford", *The American History Review*, Vol.46 No.2, pp. 259–280.

Ringer, F.K. (1969), *The Decline of the German Mandarins*, Harvard University Press, Cambridge, MA.

Rolnick, S.R. (1955), "An Exceptional Decision: The Trial of Professor Richard T. Ely by the Board of Regents of the University of Wisconsin, 1894", *Journal of the Arkansas Academy of Science*, Vol.8 No.22, pp. 198–203.

Roosevelt, T. (1912), "Introduction", in McCarthy, C. (Ed.), *The Wisconsin Idea*, Macmillan & Co., New York, p. vii.

Roscher, W. (1843), *Grundriss zu Vorlesungen uber die Staatswirthschaft – Nach Geschichtlicher Methode*, Dieterische Buchhandlung, Gottingen.

Roscher, W. (1878), *Principles of Political Economy*, translated by Lalor, J.J., Callaghan & Co., Chicago, IL.

Ross, D. (1977–1978), "Socialism and American Liberalism: Academic Social Thought in the 1880s", *Perspectives in American History*, Vol.1, pp. 7–79.

Rutherford, M. (1994), "Predatory Practices or Reasonable Values? American Institutionalists on the Nature of Market Transactions", *History of Political Economy*, Vol.26 Supplement, pp. 253–275.

Rutherford, M. (1997), "American Institutionalism and the History of Economics", *Journal of the History of Economic Thought*, Vol.19 Fall, pp. 178–195.

Rutherford, M. (2006), "Wisconsin Institutionalism: John R. Commons and His Students", *Labor History*, Vol.47 No.2, pp. 161–188.

Rutherford, M. (2010), "Science and Social Control: The Institutionalist Movement in American Economics, 1918–1947", *Erasmus Journal for Philosophy and Economics*, Vol.3 No.2, pp. 47–71.

Salley, C.D. (1993/1994), "Gustav Schmoller, William Dilthey, and the German Rejection of Positivism", *History of Economic Ideas*, Vol.1/2 No.3/1, pp. 81–91.

Sanderson, M. (1972), *The Universities and British Industry, 1850–1970*, Routledge, London.

Savitt, R. (1980), "Historical Research in Marketing", *Journal of Marketing*, Vol.44 No.4, pp. 52–58.

Schachter, H.L. (2016), "Frederick Winslow Taylor, Henry Hallowell Farquhar, and the Dilemma of Relating Management Education to Organizational Practice", *Journal of Management History*, Vol.22 No.2, pp. 199–213.

Schanz, G. (1877), "Zur Geschichte der Deutchen Gesellenverbande", *Schmoller's Jahrbuch*, Vol.1, p. 242.

Scheel, H. (1882), "Die Deutsche Handelsstatistik", *Schmoller's Jahrbuch*, Vol.6, pp. 23–55.

Scheel, H. (1887), "Die Landwirthschaftlichen Betriebe im Deutschen Reich", *Schmoller's Jahrbuch*, Vol.11, pp. 1011–1025.

Schlabach, T.F. (1963–1964), "An Aristocrat on Trial: The Case of Richard T. Ely", *The Wisconsin Magazine of History*, Vol.47 No.2, pp. 146–159.

Schmid, J. (1896), "Die Entwicklung der Osterreich Gewerbegenossenschaften", *Schmoller's Jahrbuch*, Vol.20, p. 335.

Schmoller, G. (1883), "Zur Methodologie der Staats un Sozialwissenschaften", *Schmoller's Jahrbuch*, Vol.7, pp. 975–994.

Schmoller, G. (1890–1893), "Die Geschichtliche Entwickelung der Anternehmung", *Schmoller's Jahrbuch*, 13 parts.

Schneider, D. (1993/1994), "Schmoller and the Theory of the Corporation and of Corporate Control", *History of Economic Ideas*, Vol.1/2 No.3/1, pp. 357–377.

Schone, M. (1899), "Die Moderne Entwickelung des Schumachergewerbes", *Schmoller's Jahrbuch*, Vol.23, p. 696.

Scott, W.D. (1903), *The Theory of Advertising*, Small, Maynard & Co., Boston, MA.

Scott, W.R. (1928), "Memoir: Sir William Ashley", *The Economic History Review*, Vol.1 No.2, pp. 319–321.

Scovill, H.T. (1952), "1902–1952, 50 Years of Education for Business at The University of Illinois", unpublished pamphlet, *Commerce and Business Administration, Dean's Office Announcements*, Series 9/1/0/1, Box 1, University of Illinois Archives, Urbana-Champaign, IL.

Scully, J.I. (1996), "Machines Made of Words: The Influence of Engineering Metaphor on Marketing Thought and Practice", *Journal of Macromarketing*, Vol.16 No.2, pp. 70–83.

Seager, H.R. (1893), "Economics at Berlin and Vienna", *Journal of Political Economy*, Vol.1, pp. 236–252.

Senn, P.R. (1993/1994), "Gustav Von Schmoller in English: How Has He Fared?", *History of Economic Ideas*, Vol.1/2 No.3/1, pp. 267–329.

Senn, P.R. (2005), "The German Historical Schools in the History of Economic Thought", *Journal of Economic Studies*, Vol.32 No.3, pp. 185–255.

Shaw, A.W. (1911), "'Scientific Management' in Business", *The American Review of Reviews*, Vol.43 February, pp. 327–332.

Shaw, A.W. (1912), "Some Problems in Market Distribution", *Quarterly Journal of Economics*, Vol.26 No.4, pp. 703–765.

Shaw, A.W. (1915), *Some Problems in Market Distribution*, Harvard University Press, Cambridge, MA.

Shaw, A.W. (1944), "Shaw to Edwin Francis Gay, May 11", unpublished correspondence, *Edwin Francis Gay Papers*, Baker Library Archives, Harvard University, Cambridge, MA.

Shaw, A.W. (1950), "Acceptance Speech at the 1950 Converse Award", unpublished MS, *Edwin Francis Gay Collection*, Huntington Library, San Marino, CA.

Shaw, E.H. (1995), "The First Dialogue on Macromarketing", *Journal of Macromarketing*, Vol.15 No.1, pp. 7–20.

Shaw, E.H. (2016), "Ancient and Medieval Marketing", chapter two in Jones, D.G.B. and Tadajewski, M. (Eds.), *The Routledge Companion to Marketing History*, Routledge, New York, pp. 23–40.

Shaw, E.H. and Jones, D.G.B. (2005), "A History of Schools of Marketing Thought", *Marketing Theory*, Vol.5 No.3, pp. 239–281.

Shaw, E.H. and Tamilia, R. (2001), "Robert Bartels and the History of Marketing Thought", *Journal of Macromarketing*, Vol.21 No.2, pp. 156–163.

Sheehan, J.J. (1966), *The Career of Lujo Brentano*, University of Chicago Press, Chicago, IL.

Sheldon, S. (1889), "Why Our Science Students go to Germany", *Atlantic Monthly*, Vol.63 No.378, pp. 463–466.

Simha, A. and Lemak, D.J. (2010), "The Value of Original Source Readings in Management Education: The Case of Frederick Winslow Taylor", *Journal of Management History*, Vol.16 No.2, pp. 233–252.

Smith, B. (1974; 1990), *Education for Management: Its Conception and Implementation in the Faculty of Commerce at Birmingham, University of Birmingham*, University of Birmingham, Birmingham, UK.

Smith, J.G. (1928), "Education for Business in Great Britain", in Marshall, L.C. (Ed.), *The Collegiate School of Business, Its Status at the Close of the First Quarter of the Twentieth Century*, University of Chicago Press, Chicago, IL, pp. 362–418.

Sparling, S.E. (1906), *Introduction to Business Organization*, Macmillan Publishing, New York.

Spender, J.-C. (2005), "Speaking About Management Education: Some History of the Search for Academic Legitimacy and the Ownership and Control of Management Knowledge", *Management Decision*, Vol.43 No.10, pp. 1282–1292.

Stolper, G. (1967), *The German Economy, 1870 to the Present*, translated by Stolper, T., Harcourt Brace Inc., New York.

Strasser, S. (1989), *Satisfaction Guaranteed: The Making of the American Mass Market*, Pantheon Books, New York.

Streissler, E. and Milford, K. (1993/1994), "Theoretical and Methodological Positions of German Economics in the Middle of the Nineteenth Century", *History of Economic Ideas*, Vol.1/2 No.3/1, pp. 43–79.

Tadajewski, M. (2006a), "The Ordering of Marketing Theory: The Influence of McCarthyism and the Cold War", *Marketing Theory*, Vol.6 No.2, pp. 163–200.

Tadajewski, M. (2006b), "Remembering Motivation Research: Toward an Alternative Genealogy of Interpretive Consumer Research", *Marketing Theory*, Vol.6 No.2, pp. 429–466.

Tadajewski, M. (2008), "Relationship Marketing at Wanamaker's in the Nineteenth and Early Twentieth Centuries", *Journal of Macromarketing*, Vol.28 No.2, pp. 169–182.

Tadajewski, M. (2009), "Competition, Cooperation and Open Price Associations: Relationship Marketing and Arthur Jerome Eddy (1859–1920)", *Journal of Historical Research in Marketing*, Vol.1 No.1, pp. 122–143.

Tadajewski, M. (2010a), "Critical Marketing Studies: Logical Empiricism, Critical Performativity and Marketing Practice", *Marketing Theory*, Vol.10 No.2, pp. 210–222.

Tadajewski, M. (2010b), "Reading 'The Marketing Revolution' Through the Prism of the FBI", *Journal of Marketing Management*, Vol.26 No.1–2, pp. 90–107.

Tadajewski, M. (2011), "Correspondence Sales Education in the Early Twentieth Century: The Case of the Sheldon School (1902–39)", *Business History*, Vol.53 No.7, pp. 1130–1151.

Tadajewski, M. (2012), "Character Analysis in Marketing Theory and Practice", *Marketing Theory*, Vol.12 No.4, pp. 485–508.

Tadajewski, M. (2015a), "'The Complete English Tradesman' – Business Relations, Trust, and Honesty or Let's Rethink the History of Relationship Marketing", *Journal of Historical Research in Marketing*, Vol.7 No.3, pp. 407–422.

Tadajewski, M. (2015b), "Charting Relationship Marketing Practice: It Really Didn't Emerge in the 1970s", *Journal of Historical Research in Marketing*, Vol.7 No.4, pp. 486–508.

Tadajewski, M. (2016), "The Alternative 'Marketing Revolution': Infra-power, the Compromising Consumer and Goodwill Creation", *Journal of Historical Research in Marketing*, Vol. 8 No. 2, pp. 308–334.

Tadajewski, M. (2017), "The Rotary Club and the Promotion of the Social Responsibilities of Business in the Early 20th Century", *Business and Society*, Vol.56 No.7, pp. 975–1003.

Tadajewski, M. and Jones, D.G.B. (2012), "Scientific Marketing Management and the Emergence of the Ethical Marketing Concept", *Journal of Marketing Management*, Vol.28 No.1–2, pp. 37–61.

Tadajewski, M. and Jones, D.G.B. (2014), "Historical Research in Marketing Theory and Practice: A Review Essay", *Journal of Marketing Management*, Vol.30 No.11–12, pp. 1239–1291.

Tadajewski, M. and Jones, D.G.B. (2016), "Hyper-power, the Marketing Concept and Consumer as 'Boss'", *Marketing Theory*, Vol.16 No.4, pp. 513–531.

Tadajewski, M. and Saren, M. (2009), "Rethinking the Emergence of Relationship Marketing", *Journal of Macromarketing*, Vol.29 No.2, pp. 193–206.

Tasaki, S. (1905), "Commerce III (3) and Commerce III (4) Course Notes", unpublished document, US64/2001/18, Cadbury Research Library Archives, University of Birmingham, Birmingham, UK.

Taussig, F.W. (1906), "Taussig to Henry Farnam", unpublished correspondence, Group 203, Series 11, Box 248, "Economic Survey Regarding German Influence on Economics in the United States", *Farnam Family Papers*, Yale University Archives, New Haven, CT.

Taussig, F.W. (1907), "Taussig to Edwin Francis Gay", unpublished correspondence, *Charles W. Eliot Papers*, Pusey Library Archives, Harvard University, Cambridge, MA.

Taylor, C.C. (1953), *The Farmer Movement, 1620–1920*, American Book Co., New York.

Taylor, F.W. (1903), "Shop Management", *Transactions of the American Society of Mechanical Engineers*, Vol.24, pp. 1337–1480.

Taylor, F.W. (1906), "Address at the Opening of the Engineering Building of the University of Pennsylvania, October 19", unpublished manuscript, *Charles W. Eliot Papers*, Harvard University Archives, Cambridge, MA.

Taylor, F.W. (1907), *On the Art of Cutting Metals*, American Society of Mechanical Engineers, New York.

Taylor, F.W. (1909), "Taylor to Edwin Francis Gay, April 19", unpublished correspondence, *Frederick W. Taylor Papers*, Stevens Institute of Technology, Hoboken, NJ.

Taylor, F.W. (1911/1998), *The Principles of Scientific Management*, Dover, New York.

Taylor, H.C. (1905), *An Introduction to the Study of Agricultural Economics*, Macmillan, New York.

Taylor, H.C. (1906), "Taylor to Henry Farnam", unpublished correspondence, Group 203, Series 11, Box 248, "Economic Survey Regarding German Influence on Economics in the United States", *Farnam Family Papers*, Yale University Archives, New Haven, CT.

Taylor, H.C. (1908), "H.C. Taylor to B.H. Hibbard, March 18", unpublished correspondence, *Henry Charles Taylor Papers*, State Historical Society of Wisconsin, Madison, WI.

Taylor, H.C. (1913), "Taylor to Russell, January 18", unpublished correspondence, *Henry Charles Taylor Papers*, State Historical Society of Wisconsin, Madison, WI.

Taylor, H.C. (1917), "American Association of Agricultural Legislation", unpublished manuscript, *Henry Charles Taylor Papers*, State Historical Society of Wisconsin, Madison, WI.

Taylor, H.C. (1922), *What's Back of Marketing?* American Institute of Agriculture, Chicago, IL.

Taylor, H.C. (1924), "Courses in Marketing", *Journal of Farm Economics*, Vol.6 January, pp. 20–27.

Taylor, H.C. (1939), "Statement With Regard to the Development of Agricultural History in the U.S. Department of Agriculture, May 23", unpublished manuscript, *Henry Charles Taylor Papers*, State Historical Society of Wisconsin, Madison, WI.

Taylor, H.C. (1940), "Early History of Agricultural Economics", *Journal of Farm Economics*, Vol.22 February, pp. 84–97.

Taylor, H.C. (1941), "The Development of Research and Education in Agricultural Cooperation and Marketing at the University of Wisconsin, 1910–1920", unpublished manuscript, *Henry Charles Taylor Papers*, State Historical Society of Wisconsin, Madison, WI.

Taylor, H.C. (1944), "H.C. Taylor to Paul D. Converse, June 1", unpublished correspondence, *Henry Charles Taylor Papers*, State Historical Society of Wisconsin, Madison, WI.

Taylor, H.C. (1960), "Plus Ultra", unpublished autobiography, *Henry Charles Taylor Papers*, State Historical Society of Wisconsin, Madison, WI.

Taylor, H.C. (1992), *A Farm Economist in Washington, 1919–1925*, Department of Agricultural Economics, University of Wisconsin–Madison, Madison, WI.

Taylor, H.C., Schoenfeld, W.A., and Wehrwein, G.S. (1913), "The Marketing of Wisconsin Cheese", Bulletin 231, April, University of Wisconsin Agricultural Experiment Station, Madison, WI.

Taylor, H.C. and Taylor, A.D. (1952), *The Story of Agricultural Economics in the United States 1840–1932*, Greenwood Press, Westport, CT.

Thakara, A.M. (1913), "German Educational Courses in Cooperation and Marketing", unpublished report, *Benjamin Hibbard Papers*, University of Wisconsin Library Archives, Madison, WI.

Thies, C.F. and Daza, R. (2011), "Richard T. Ely: The Confederate Flag of the AEA?", *Economic Journal Watch*, Vol.8 No.2, pp. 147–156.

Thompson, J.W. (1942), *A History of Historical Writing*, volume II, Macmillan Co., New York.

Thwing, C.F. (1928), *The American and the German University*, Macmillan Co., New York.

Tribe, K. (1993), "Political Economy in the Northern Civic Universities", in Kadish, A. and Tribe, K. (Eds.), *The Market for Political Economy*, Taylor & Francis, London, pp. 184–226.

Tribe, K. (2002), "Historical Schools of Economics: German and English", *Keele Economics Research Papers*. Available: www.keele.ac.uk/depts/ec/web/wpapers/kerp0202.pdf, pp. 1–20.

Tribe, K. (2003), "The Faculty of Commerce and Manchester Economics, 1903–44", *The Manchester School*, Vol.71 No.6, pp. 680–710.

Twede, D. (2016), "History of Packaging", in Jones, D.G.B. and Tadajewski, M. (Eds.), *The Routledge Companion to Marketing History*, Routledge, New York, pp. 115–130.

Tyler, H.W. and Cheyney, E.P. (1938), "Academic Freedom", *The Annals of the American Academy of Political and Social Science*, Vol.200 No.1, pp. 102–118.

University of Birmingham. (1902–1910), "Exam Papers and Syllabi, 1902–10", UC sections 5–6, Cadbury Research Library Archives, University of Birmingham, Birmingham, UK.

University of Birmingham. (1903–04), "Calendars", Cadbury Research Library Archives, University of Birmingham, Birmingham, UK.

University of California. (1902–03; 1903–04), *Bulletin*, University of California Press, Berkeley, CA.

University of Illinois. (1908–09 through 1920–21), *Bulletin*, University of Illinois, Urbana-Champaign, IL.

University of Michigan. (1901; 1903/1904), *University of Michigan Catalogue*, University of Michigan, Ann Arbor, MI.

University of Wisconsin. (1892/1893; 1900/1901; 1904/1905), *University of Wisconsin Catalogue*, University of Wisconsin, Madison, WI.

University of Wisconsin. (1907), "Extension Division – Courses in Political Economy, October", *University of Wisconsin Catalogue*, University of Wisconsin, Madison, WI.

University of Wisconsin. (1909/1910), "Extension Division Bulletin", *University of Wisconsin Catalogue*, University of Wisconsin, Madison, WI.

University of Wisconsin. (1913), "Bulletin 231", *Agricultural Experiment Station Bulletins*, University of Wisconsin, Madison, WI.

University of Wisconsin. (1916), "Report of the Committee – First Wisconsin Commercial and Industrial Congress, February 29", unpublished manuscript, *School of Economics*, University of Wisconsin Archives, Madison, WI.

Usher, A.P. (1938), "William James Ashley, a Pioneer in Higher Education", *The Canadian Journal of Economics and Political Science*, Vol.4 No.2, pp. 151–163.

Usui, K. (2008), *The Development of Marketing Management*, Ashgate, Hampshire, UK.

Vargo, S. and Lusch, R. (2004), "Evolving to a New Dominant Logic for Marketing", *Journal of Marketing*, Vol.68 No.1, pp. 1–17.

Veblen, T. (1898), "Why Is Economics Not an Evolutionary Science?", *Quarterly Journal of Economics*, Vol.12 No.4, pp. 373–397.

Veblen, T. (1899a), *The Theory of the Leisure Class: An Economic Study of the Evolution of Institutions*, Macmillan Co., New York.

Veblen, T. (1899b), "The Preconceptions of Economic Science", *Quarterly Journal of Economics*, Vol.13 January, pp. 121–150; Vol.13 July, pp. 396–426; Vol.14 No.2, pp. 240–269.

Vincent, E.W. and Hinton, P. (1947), *The University of Birmingham, Its History and Significance*, Cornish Brothers, Birmingham, UK.

Wagner-Tsukamoto, S. (2007), "An Institutional Economic Reconstruction of Scientific Management: On the Lost Theoretical Logic of Taylorism", *Academy of Management Review*, Vol.32 No.1, pp. 105–117.

Ward, D.B. (2009), "Capitalism, Early Market Research, and the Creation of the American Consumer", *Journal of Historical Research in Marketing*, Vol.1 No.2, pp. 200–223.

Ward, D.B. (2010), *A New Brand of Business: Charles Coolidge Parlin, Curtis Publishing Company, and the Origins of Market Research*, Temple University Press, Philadelphia, PA.

Weber, M. (1975), *Roscher and Knies: The Logical Problems of Historical Economics*, translated by Oakes, G., Free Press, New York.

Weld, L.D.H. (1915), *Studies in the Marketing of Farm Products*, University of Minnesota, Minneapolis, MN.

Weld, L.D.H. (1941), "Early Experiences in Teaching Courses in Marketing", *Journal of Marketing*, Vol.5 No.4, pp. 380–381.

Wensley, R.J. (2017), "Research in the Gap Between the Obvious and the Improbable", *Journal of Historical Research in Marketing*, Vol.9 No.3, pp. 302–318.

White, P. (1927), *Scientific Marketing Management: Its Principles and Methods*, Harper & Brothers, New York.

Wilkie, W.W. and Moore, E.S. (1999), "Marketing's Contributions to Society", *Journal of Marketing*, Vol.63 Special Issue, pp. 198–218.

Wills, G. (1976), "Special Issue: Business School Graffiti", *European Journal of Marketing*, Vol.12 No.1, pp. 1–135.

Witkowski, T. (2010), "The Marketing Discipline Comes of Age, 1934–1936", *Journal of Historical Research in Marketing*, Vol.2 No.4, pp. 370–396.

Witkowski, T. (2012), "Marketing Education and Acculturation in the Early Twentieth Century: Evidence From Polish Language Texts on Selling and Salesmanship", *Journal of Historical Research in Marketing*, Vol.4 No.1, pp. 97–128.

Wittgenstein, L. (1998), *Culture and Value*, revised edition, Blackwell, London.

Wright, J. (1980), "The Biographical Approach to the Study of Marketing Thought", in Lamb, C.W. and Dunne, P.M. (Eds.), *Theoretical Developments in Marketing*, American Marketing Association, Chicago, IL, pp. 43–44.

Wright, J. and Dimsdale, P.B. (Eds.). (1974), *Pioneers in Marketing*, Georgia State University, Atlanta, GA.

Index

Italic page numbers indicate figure; bold indicate tables.